Palgrave Studies in the History of Finance

The study of the history of financial institutions, markets, instruments and concepts is vital if we are to understand the role played by finance today. At the same time, the methodologies developed by finance academics can provide a new perspective for historical studies. Palgrave Studies in the History of Finance is a multi-disciplinary effort to emphasise the role played by finance in the past, and what lessons historical experiences have for us. It presents original research, in both authored monographs and edited collections, from historians, finance academics and economists, as well as financial practitioners.

Kent McKeever

The Role of Tontines, 1750–1800

Studies in the Financial History of Georgian Britain

palgrave
macmillan

Kent McKeever
New York, NY, USA

ISSN 2662-5164 ISSN 2662-5172 (electronic)
Palgrave Studies in the History of Finance
ISBN 978-3-032-12848-5 ISBN 978-3-032-12849-2 (eBook)
https://doi.org/10.1007/978-3-032-12849-2

Cover credit: 'Richmond Bridge' by William Alfred Delamotte

This Palgrave Macmillan imprint is published by the registered company Springer Nature Switzerland AG
The registered company address is: Gewerbestrasse 11, 6330 Cham, Switzerland

Preface

This book is focused on the description, use, and impact of tontines, an intriguing but now neglected kind of investment scheme. The key characteristics of a tontine were ownership participation limited by the life of a shareholder or nominee, an increase in dividends paid to a shrinking pool of shareholders through time, and the chance of a large payout as the tontine expired.

The project started as an investigation of the 1785 Covent Garden Theatre Life Tontine. In my 2009 article I had assumed it was a means of financing the building of the theatre, but slowly realized it existed far too late for that to be true. As I learned more about it and the environment in which it was created, I was lured into trying to understand the flourishing of tontines generally in the latter part of the eighteenth century. I slowly came to appreciate that they were a standard part of the financial landscape but had been ignored in most economic histories of the period. I also came to realize they were not the sinister scheme they are now commonly seen to be, but only a variant investment option in a world where everyday risk was at a higher level than we live with today.

The text provides an understanding of the tontine as a *sui generis* thing during a particular time in history, and I attempt to capture that moment primarily via native and contemporary reports. Perhaps in the way original instrument performances try to better express the music of Handel and Mozart, if you will forgive the metaphor.

It does not have a thesis connecting it to the history of corporations, or the evolution of insurance, or the conceptualization of mutual funds, or stating the case for the revival of the tontine in some modern form. Nor is there deep economic analysis. Others work along those lines. I optimistically feel this text can contribute to their knowledge and ideas. My task is simply an attempt to present tontines at the point when they were common, to celebrate their usefulness and impact, and appreciate their variations.

Market Context

However, to understand the context of tontines in Georgian England, a short introduction to the financial market in London at the time is necessary.

A first step is to understand how the word 'annuity' was used during this period. It overlaps with the modern use of the term but had other meanings which have become obsolete. At that time, 'annuity' was a broad term encompassing any legal instrument that had the effect of distributing a set amount of money on a regular, usually annual, basis. A pension might be referred to as a government annuity. A person could arrange, for an agreed sum of money, for a second person to make regular payments to them. That would be a private annuity. An annuity could be for the life of the recipient and would be called a 'life annuity.' Or it could be for a set number of years and be called a 'term annuity.'

The government sold annuities based on anticipated tax revenues. The shorthand of the period conceived these as shares with a value of £100 and were generally referred to by the amount of interest each share paid. The most common were the Three Percent Consolidated Annuities originally issued in 1751 and continued into the Victorian era. They were colloquially known as the 'Consols.' The transactions in this annuity were crucial in the development of the stock market. The word 'stock' was used as a generic term covering not only the shares in companies, but the government annuities as well.

The second thread that shaped the financial markets in London after the Glorious Revolution of 1688 was the slow stabilization of the way the government borrowed money to meet the anticipated expenditures of its annual budget. Through trial-and-error there emerged what ultimately became known as the Stock Exchange. It developed as a substantially informal, free-standing institution within a matrix of the Royal Exchange, the Office of the Exchequer, the Bank of England, and the merchants and merchant companies of the time.

The British Government's Annual Loans

By the latter half of the eighteenth century, the institutions that ultimately evolved into the modern stock exchange did not deal exclusively in stocks. In fact, the majority of the transactions were in the 'Annuities,' the financial instruments that represented the national debt of the United Kingdom. The traded Annuities were essentially a promise by the Government to pay a set interest on a loan of a set amount. At the retail level, it was understood that a loan share was expressed in a value of £100 and the annual interest was arranged in varied pools paying three percent, three and a half percent, four percent, and five percent. By the 1750s, the administration of the annuity process was executed primarily by the Bank of England and secondarily by the East India Company and the South Sea Company.

Except for the Long and Short Annuities, these stocks had no termination date. The government could redeem them, but rarely did. The effect was that the national debt grew, especially during the Seven Years' War and the American Revolution, much to the distress of some of the (tiny) electorate. But it meant there was constant growth in the instruments that could be traded on the exchange. The prices went up-and-down, descending to roughly half par value in the midst of the Wars with France from 1792 through 1815. However, no matter what an investor paid for the annuity, the government paid the interest on the issued (or 'par') value. At the lowest point of the market, an annuity with a par value of £100, which paid three percent (£3) a year, could be bought for £50, thus paying a real return of six percent.

These annuities were, by far, the major portion of what was traded on the stock exchange, far outweighing the actual stocks traded. However, while the market consisted of trade in the annuities and trading in the stocks of the three major companies, the Bank of England, the East India Company, and the South Sea Company, all kinds of share-based entrepreneurial endeavors existed in a less formal market which financed canals, mines, turnpikes, and trade generally. Commercial organizations were usually developed as partnerships. Private banks, for example, were limited by law to partnerships of no more than six partners.

A much fuller description of the development of the London financial market of this period can be found in my recently published short text *Portrait of the Georgian Stock Market.*

Tontines were developed mid-eighteenth century to finance local projects but became more diverse in the latter part of the century. They were a regular portion of the less formal securities market outlined above. This text focuses on tontines and how they functioned within the commerce of the time.

Notes on Orthography

'Percent' had not yet reached the status of a word. It was still an abbreviation for 'per centum,' Latin for 'per hundred,' and usually presented as 'per Cent.' I will convert all the uses to the modern 'percent.'

Spelling was not entirely settled at this time. If an archaic spelling is included in a quotation, it will be kept unless it is misleading.

The formal name for Siprut's Tontine was 'The Society for Annuities Encreasing to the Survivor' spelling 'increasing' as 'encreasing.' Later texts sometimes used the modern 'increasing.' I will use the original spelling in writing the name of the Society. Some writers used 'increasing,' and if that is in a quoted text, that will be preserved.

Notes on Money

The printing conventions of the time meant the indication of a number being a sum of money did not include the use of the '£' symbol, which was used mostly in manuscript. One hundred and five pounds would be printed as 105l. with a lower case 'l.' at the end of the number representing the pounds. Similarly, 's.' for shillings and 'd.' for pence. In transcriptions from printed texts, I have generally converted this format to the traditional '£x/x/x' (pounds/shillings/pence) format to make it less confusing.

The primary means of payment for larger transactions was the bill of exchange. It was used roughly the way we would use a check, although the merchant or bank agreeing to give cash on such a bill would usually take a fee, known as a discount. For long distance transactions, an issuer might send two or three bills of exchange to cover the same debt by different means to cover the possibility of one being lost in transit. The text would say first, second, third, etc. Once one was presented for payment, the others became null.

Confusingly 'bills' were also a generic term for government payment orders. Exchequer bills were used to pay basic everyday government debts. Navy, Victualling, Ordnance, and Transport bills paid for those services as needed by the Navy and Army. A secondary market existed for the period between the government issuing the payment order and actually paying it, which could be several years. This market was part of the stock exchange. In addition, the government would accept unpaid bills in payment for government debt in the interim.

A Context: The Cost of Living and Life in Georgian London Generally

In 1786, John Trusler published *The London adviser and guide: containing every instruction and information useful and necessary to persons living in London, and coming to reside there* [1]... which has a wide range of miscellaneous information on aspects of life in London. This ranges from the weight of a loaf of bread (pages 26–27), the seasonal variations of price of coal (32 to 50 shillings a chaldron), the cost of property and life insurance from the various companies, the cost of a sedan chair (one shilling for the first mile), a list of the newspapers, noting which are 'opposition' papers (pages 124–126), stamp duties (pages 139-143), etc. Starting on page 167 and continuing through page 180 is "An estimate of the expences attending a family..." which is quite detailed and provides an excellent snapshot of the circumstances of a middle-class family.

Using the conservative measure of the Retail Price Index, £100 in 1720, the year of the South Sea Bubble, was worth roughly £110 in 1765, the point just before the tontines take off. At that point, the rate of inflation increases, so that by the end of the Napoleonic Wars in 1815 the pound had essentially halved in value.

[1] London: printed for the author, No. 14, Red Lion-Street, Clerkenwell, 1786.

The price of gold, used for the Guinea coins, remained remarkably stable, hovering around £4.25 an ounce from 1720 through 1765. By 1815, it had increased by only fifteen percent, to just short of five pounds.

New York, USA

Kent McKeever

Contents

About the Author

Kent McKeever was the Director of the Library of the Columbia University Law School from 1994 through 2019. His published works have focused on the history of the financial institutions known as Tontines including *A Short History of Tontines*, 15 Fordham J. Corp. & Fin. L. 491 (2009), *The Evolution of the Tontine in North America, and Tontines in Portugal—Nicholas Bourey's Paleo-tontine in 1641*, and two chapters in Hellwege, Phillip, Ed., *The Past, Present, and Future of Tontines*, Berlin, Duncker & Humblot, 2018. This text, as well as *A Portrait of the Georgian Stock Market*, were completed shortly before his death in February 2025.

List of Figures

CHAPTER 1

Introduction

The tontine was a form of joint-stock financial venture through which investors owned a share for the term of their own lives or the lives of a nominee. The participants received dividends that increased proportionately as their fellow participants or nominees died off. The tontine agreement or 'settlement' document typically included a provision that the longest-lived participants were to divide the capital funds or share outright ownership of underlying property once a triggering provision was reached. Because of this age/mortality issue, investors typically nominated young people as the life on which the tontine share would be based. The nominee would often be a participant's child or some other young relative and would often inherit the share on the original purchaser's death.

A comparison to a standard company model may be useful. If a project, say a bridge, was to be financed through a joint-stock process, one option would be a straightforward company. In that case, the shares were perpetual, and the shareholder could pass them to heirs or legatees when the shareholder died. A company of one hundred shares stayed at one hundred shares for the life of the company, which could be infinite. The dividends were paid to all the shareholders.

If a tontine scheme were chosen, the shares were extinguished after a designated period. That period was either the life of the shareholder, or, more commonly, the life of a nominee named by the shareholder at the beginning of the project. The nominee was almost invariably a child or

K. McKeever, *The Role of Tontines, 1750–1800*, Palgrave Studies in the History of Finance, https://doi.org/10.1007/978-3-032-12849-2_1

someone younger than the subscriber, so the share would be productive for as long as possible. As the shareholders or their nominees died, the interest that had been assigned to them would revert to the pool of the other participants, thus the dividends to the remaining participants would increase as time went on.

The crude attraction of the tontine was the 'pot of gold' tease inherent in the form. It added the possibility of both increasing interest during the life of the nominee and the possible, albeit low probability, chance of a large payout to the longest lived. It competed in the market with bonds and shares that also paid interest, but without any enhancing elements.

Background

The tontine developed in the mid-seventeenth century in continental Europe, most seriously in France, as a tool for government revenue. Like the near simultaneous working out of the principles of calculus by Newton and Leibniz, tontine-like proposals developed independently in several locations. Other continental governments, national, regional, and municipal, soon adopted various forms of revenue-oriented tontines.

By the 1670s, entrepreneurs, usually notaries, in the Netherlands, created private financial tontines involving joint ownership of shares in the Dutch East India Company, facilitating broader participation than the high price of the shares would have allowed. Private tontines also developed and flourished in the latter part of the eighteenth century in the British Isles. They slowly disappeared in the nineteenth century with the growth of alternatives for investing, including friendly societies, savings banks, the development of the modern form of corporations, and the spreading availability of reliable life insurance, once confined to the rich, to a wider portion of the middle classes. Since then, tontines have developed a slightly sinister reputation related to the notion of participants directly benefiting from their fellow shareholders' deaths.

The purpose of this book is to reintroduce the concept of the tontine, now mostly forgotten, and to establish a sense of its fully legitimate role in eighteenth-century Great Britain, both as in the tontine's impact on the Georgian physical environment and as a financial tool. Tom Paine even used the idea of a national, lifelong tontine to frame out his idea of a kind of proto-social security system one hundred years before Germany implemented the first one. This text is not intended as a theoretical disquisition, but simply to correct the neglect of tontines and describe their everyday use during the eighteenth century.

David Green has surveyed the breadth of tontine projects in a recent essay *Tontines, annuities and civic improvements in Georgian Britain.*[1] He presents a thesis that tontine-financed buildings were an important element in the development of towns and cities and provided significant venues for social engagement in Georgian England. This text details a few examples and outlines a number of variations throughout the British Isles.

What Makes a Tontine a Tontine

The main element of the corporate endeavor that moves a shareholding enterprise into the category of a tontine is the mode of distributing the income or profits of the enterprise. The subscribers own their shares for the term of a life, either their own or a nominee's, and the shareholder's interest ceases with the end of that life. If all goes well, the flow of income to the surviving shareholders slowly increases as the other shareholders and nominees die off. Tontine ownership is usually structured so that the final shareholder takes full possession of the underlying property of the endeavor, or a final small group of shareholders divide the capital of the endeavor at a set point.

There are corollaries to this principle. It means the endeavor has a life—it is not perpetual, as is the standard company or corporation. The principle can be applied to any sort of group endeavor, so that some tontines are linked to finite physical projects and others exist only as a financial or investment arrangement. In both cases, the tontine ends with the last surviving lives. The substitution of a wife or young heir's life as a nominee in place of the actual subscriber's own life means a tontine can be a form of insurance for a surviving spouse or an intergenerational money transfer for a child. In the latter case, the young nominee had to be alive at the point of the creation of the tontine, so the benefit could only exist for one generation.

The legal form of the underlying project could vary considerably. A construction tontine might involve a statutorily created commission or simply an agreement, typically as a form of deed of trust, among

[1] 46 *Urban History* 649–694 (2019)

co-investors. The tontine would be the result of a clause in the 'constitutional' document of the scheme, or in the indenture representing the subscriber's share. The purely financial tontines tended to be within a trust framework. Toward the end of the wave of tontines, in the mid-nineteenth century, there was one company created in which one class of its shares was standard stockholders' shares and another class was created within a tontine framework.

The notion of a private tontine is connected to a diverse array of enterprises. They first appeared and flourished in England as the financial side of medium-sized construction projects. A small group were basically investment schemes with high share prices. A much larger group were small-sum, short-term investment schemes, but they mostly failed to show a profit. Some tontines were a means for cash-poor landed gentry to obtain immediate capital based on the income of their estates. Capitalizing on the fashion for private tontines, some municipalities used tontine schemes for revenue purposes and civic improvement projects.

The net effect of the breadth of the use of tontine financing is that while there were all sorts of tontines, no single later institutional form can be conclusively traced to a tontine origin.

An Example

In the Georgian era, among the sixty to seventy construction projects funded by tontines, perhaps the most visible was the Glasgow Tontine Building and Coffee Room. The venue was the center of Glasgow's commercial life. References to it always started with the word 'tontine' followed by coffeehouse, library, reading room, exchange, hotel, or tavern. It served all those functions. It started in 1781 with a pool of local investors buying 107 shares of £50 each, for a total of £5,350. The project involved improving and enlarging an existing building. The first dividends were paid in 1793 at slightly more than six percent. In 1819, it was paying £20 a year. The last surviving shareholder was a Mrs. Cecelia Douglas, originally a nominee of two different subscribers, neither of whom was her parent. As the final survivor, she owned shares numbered 70 and 92 and took over sole ownership of the property in 1861. She died in July 1862 and in 1864 her trustees sold the property for £7,000.

The Environment

During the latter part of the eighteenth century, tontines were simply another variation in the many ways the upper-middle-class could invest. The mortality risk, which seems so off-putting today, was just another factor in a financial economy in which risk was a large part of the picture. The reliability of the Government Annuities, known as Consols and other national debt-related securities, came with a relatively low interest rate. Tontines teased a slightly higher initial interest rate bolstered by the potential increase over time and the possibility of being one of the 'winners' of the final distribution.

A significant branch of the scholarship in the history and economics of eighteenth century Britain has focused on the development of corporate structures as both business ventures and financial tools and the evolution of many of the individual commodity-trading businesses into merchant houses whose day-to-day transactions increasingly took on banking functions.

The big mercantile trading companies were a class unto themselves, led by the East India Company. As the century progressed, the securities related to the three big joint-stock companies, the East India Company, the Bank of England, and the South Sea Company, formed the core of the of the nascent stock market. However, a large portion of that exchange was focused on trading in Government debt in the form of 'annuities' issued primarily via the Bank of England and to a lesser extent by the East India Company and the South Sea Company. The primary annuities all through this period were the Bank of England's Three Percent 'Consols,' or consolidated annuities, mentioned constantly in the newspapers and other literature of the period.

Alongside this 'open' market was a less visible trade in securities related to other group ventures, such as the smaller international trading companies, canal companies, turnpike trusts, insurance companies, and mines. These were also traded by the stockbrokers of the period, but in a much more informal and unrecorded market, privately or through auctions. Many of these auctions were distress sales, involving either bankruptcy or the disposal of an estate. The most visible record of this activity is the regular newspaper and broadside advertisements for auctions of stock or other financial instruments.

Tontines were not widely used for canals, turnpikes, and mines. Turnpike trusts were created via statutes and the financing involved bonds, so the role of a shareholder as such did not exist. However, the administration of the trusts was closely related to the small companies of the period. Canals also involved statutory authorization, but the greater capital needs meant a corporate form and shareholders were part of the process. Mines tended to be partnerships. Tontine options occasionally show up in reports of preliminary discussions of canal projects, but do not seem to have ever been the final choice.

From roughly 1770 on, shares in tontines joined the other securities being traded on the informal market. Tontines were only a small part of this process. While mostly local, there were some with nationwide participation.

Tontines as Small 'Companies'

Traditionally, the 1720 Bubble Act and its limitation on joint-stock companies has been seen as having stymied the development of the modern corporation for the rest of the eighteenth century. During that period, formal incorporation required either a Royal Charter or a Parliamentary Act. In practice, the entrepreneurs who went this route tended to work on getting a Parliamentary Act. The benefits of incorporation were stated succinctly by Robin Pearson:

> A charter granted a body of investors perpetual succession, the right to use a common seal; to raise a stock of transferrable shares that were sometimes tax-free; to borrow and lend money; to purchase land; to levy tolls, mortgage tolls, and grant annuities; to sue and be sued in the corporate name, without all partners having to be named as parties individually, thus allowing debts to be more easily recovered through the courts; and to choose their own governors, directors, and officers and make their own by-laws.[2]

The rigmarole and costs involved in getting charter or Parliamentary act were often beyond the means of the entrepreneurs proposing smaller projects who might have wanted the benefits.

[2] *The Bubble Act and the First Corporate Economy*, a chapter in Paul, H. et al., The Bubble Act, Palgrave/Springer 2023, 13–36. Pearson provides a superb short survey of the various forms of 'unofficial' corporate-like bodies but does not mention Tontines.

However, the traditional notion of corporate stagnation has been challenged. Ron Harris in his 2000 book *Industrializing English Law*[3] shows how various means were taken to create enterprises with substantial shareholder ownership without formal incorporation. The 'deed of settlement' used to create a partnership was stretched to cover organizations which functioned more like corporations than partnerships. 'Tontine' gets only one reference in this book, in a disparaging text on attitudes toward speculation at page 223.

This is echoed by Rob McQueen in the preliminary chapter of his *A Social History of Company Law.*[4] It presents the case that the real effect of the Bubble Act's suppression of non-chartered corporations was the development of a range of informal solutions to the creation and support of shareholder enterprises so that when the Joint Stock Companies Act of 1844 was drafted and passed, it reflected extensive experience with many forms of joint economic enterprise in the eighteenth and early nineteenth centuries. Tontines are not mentioned by McQueen.

The legal form of non-governmental tontines in this period tended to be a variation on the trust/partnership models described by Harris and McQueen. The tontine aspect of an enterprise tended to be confined to its financing. In most cases, the actual execution of the underlying project followed standard forms of similar projects funded in more traditional manners.

The Tontine Era, 1750 to 1825

The 1720 Bubble Act made company creation a function of Parliamentary action and Royal Charter. In effect it made the creation of companies an onerous and expensive process involving petitions and what we would now call extensive lobbying. Canal and turnpike companies, which needed powers of eminent domain, were the result of Parliamentary action. The Bubble Act was repealed in 1825.

To get around these restrictions, entrepreneurs used a number of other forms of shareholder organizations, most notably partnerships, and a wide range of trust-based structures, one form of which was the tontine. Private

[3] Cambridge, New York: Cambridge University Press, 2000.

[4] London, New York: Routledge, 2016.

banks, for example, were partnerships limited by law to six partners. Mines were also usually operated by partnerships.

Although the first tontines appeared toward the end of the reign of George II, they flourished during the long reign of George III, 1760 to 1819. Their importance dwindled with the repeal of the Bubble Act six years later, which had the effect of making the creation of corporations much simpler.

During this period, roughly 65 traceable tontines were proposed to finance construction of some sort, such as a bridge, an assembly hall, or some other large building serving a public purpose. Of these, only twelve of the projects had a Parliamentary act as part of the overall project. The rest were private endeavors generally using a trust structure.

Provision for Old Age

A second stream of economic pressure was the groping for effective means of saving both for old age and as a provision for spouses and descendants. The first life insurance company had appeared in 1706, but the field did not really take off until the 1750s. The policies were aimed at the upper classes. Besides the life annuities provided by the government, there were a range of experiments with commercial annuity schemes, but most failed. Private banking also mostly served richest members of society. Savings banks, serving a lower economic class, did not develop until the early 1800s. Working class Box Clubs and Benefit Societies existed for rudimentary health and funeral expense purposes. The increasing dividends within the tontine structure made them an attractive investment in a world with few reliable competitors. The tontines serving this purpose were either government revenue schemes or private investment/pension schemes.

During the period outlined above, the Parliament issued three tontines, but only the one in 1789 had a substantial pool of subscribers, and even that failed to reach anticipated targets. Another three tontines were created to provide revenue for Ireland. These sold out, with a majority of the shares purchased in England. The City of Dublin issued a tontine as well. At least eight private investment tontine schemes were created before 1792, with the capital consisting of securities purchased on the open market or the income from landed estates. Some failed.

In the 1790s, in particular, there was a fad for 'small-sum, short-term' schemes labeled tontines that had teams between five and seven years, and which took in weekly or monthly payments during that term. Some payments were as low as a shilling. The biggest ones had large numbers of subscribers from across the country. Virtually all of them lost money. Many were swindles, but the honest ones could not cope amid the economic problems of the time.

Tontines were as highly visible as other operations executing similar functions. They were used to finance the construction of two bridges over the Thames in London. They helped build public buildings such as assembly rooms, inns, and coffee houses throughout the country. Other projects included markets, warehouses, hotels, libraries, theatres, local housing, churches, courthouses, and at least one jail. Governments, both national and local, tried tontines as a form of borrowing, with varying degrees of success. Purely financial tontines were developed, functioning like modern mutual funds, serving as both an investment and a pension.

It is likely there were far more tontines than show up in any extant records. There were certainly more proposals published in newspapers than there are records of their success or failures. And, as with any human endeavor, tontines likely served as a framework for swindles, although the evidence may simply be that they were run incompetently.

An Investment or a Gamble?

There is a question as to whether tontines were serious investment tools or simply a form of gambling. Bob Harris in his *Gambling in Britain in the Long Eighteenth Century*[5] provides the classic image:

> Widespread forms of contemporary personal finance, purchasing and borrowing on life annuities and buying shares in commercial tontine schemes, the latter of which emerged in the later eighteenth century, might very plausibly be viewed as gambling. As the cosmopolitan radical Joel Barlow pointed out in the early 1790s: 'A tontine partakes at once of the nature of lotteries and of simple life-annuities, and involves itself in the principal vices of both. Like a lottery it is founded in the spirit of gambling.'

To a certain extent, this putative dichotomy is ridiculous. Tontines flourished in a financial environment in which national lottery tickets were

[5] Cambridge, New York: Cambridge Univ. Press, 2022

bought and sold in the stock market, just like shares in the Bank of England, the East India Company, and the National Debt instruments.[6]

Christiane Eisenberg's essay *Capitalist Horse Sense: Sports Betting and Option Trading during the English Financial Revolution, 1690-1740*[7] outlines the interplay between the evolution of betting on sporting events and the working of the stockjobbing markets of the period. While she does not mention tontines, her text shows the aleatory nature of the tontine investment would not have fazed anyone at the time.

However, in the debate surrounding the issuing and revision of the National Tontine of 1789, the *Public Advertiser* had this line: "The public see Tontine in a very different point of view from every other fund—they consider it as a life annuity." This is clearly an expression of the notion that a tontine was not simply a gamble.

Susannah Ottaway's *The Decline of Life: Old Age in Eighteenth-Century England*[8] reviews many aspects of aging during this period. However, like the company historians, she also neglects the tontine, focusing more on how benefit societies worked. She includes only one reference to a tontine, mentioning the Yorkshire Tontine as a generic example without reporting it was a failure.[9]

To make the issue a little more complicated, some tontines mixed a lottery element into their schemes. Hermann Wagenvoort describes a Dutch one:

> ... in which the names of the insured in one age class were registered in an order determined by chance. In the event of the death of an insured person, the share in the interest from this portion was not, as usual, made available jointly to the other participants in the contract, but to the person whose portion on the list followed or preceded that of the deceased nominee. This person therefore received a double benefit in subsequent

[6] See McKeever, *A Portrait of the Georgian Stock Market*, London: Palgrave Macmillan, 2026

[7] 37 *International Journal of the History of Sport* 323–336m (2022)

[8] Cambridge, New York: Cambridge University Press, 2004.

[9] The last outbreak of the plague in the British Isles was in the 1660s. Did the population grow more relaxed about gamble-able lifespans after no plagues for a generation or two?

> years, while the benefits on the portions of the other participants did not increase but remained the same.[10]

These kinds of variations do not seem to have appeared in any British tontine.

For each of the tontines examined in depth, the names and status of the participants are presented because an awareness of the people involved provides evidence of the social context of the schemes. The classic early tontines involved the upper middle classes. Some tontines were essentially local, others were national. But they were not an outlier investment—they were commonplace. Over time, participation spread. The later small-sum, short-term tontines were clearly designed to reach a much wider pool of investors, and their claims of thousands of subscribers indicated they succeeded at first, although most of them ended up with a financial loss.

Where Tontines Fit In

An example of the commonplace role of tontines can be seen in a post-mortem estate sale advertised in London in December 1784. Within a broader folio of securities, the auction offers shares in two tontines: ten shares in an Irish Government tontine and four shares in the private financial tontine known as the Society for Annuities Encreasing to Survivors. The other securities were shares in a mining company, a municipal commercial wharf in Hull, a municipal paving bond from Southwark, and a share in the newspaper *The Public Ledger.*

The sale was of assets in the estate of John Wilkinson. He was not an unsophisticated investor. He was a 'Sworn Broker,' which meant he was among the elite among the brokers in London. He served as a leading shipbroker in London. As an indication of his importance, he was one of the nine members of the first formal committee of Lloyd's, the maritime insurance organization, as it coalesced into more a structured enterprise in 1772. The sale of the tontines in the advertisement is possible because Mr. Wilkinson's nominees were still alive even though Wilkinson himself had died. Unusually, it seems he did not leave them to his nominees. His daughters, Sibella and Maria, appear on the list of nominees for five shares each in the Third Class of the first Irish Tontine of 1773.

[10] *Tontines, een onderzoek naar de geschiedenis van de lijfrenten…*, Diss. Utrecht, 1961. The translation is a slightly tweaked product of Google Translate.

Auction sales involving tontine shares were not common, but appeared regularly starting in the 1770s.

Another way to assess the role of tontines is to note the investment in them by significant figures. For example, at the age of 54, John Julius Angerstein, Chairman of Lloyd's from 1790-6, bought six shares in the Fifth Class of the National Tontine of 1789. The sum involved, roughly £600 would not have been a significant investment for him. He may simply have been expressing his support for the concept as he was one of the lead subscribers to the Loan of 1789 that included the Tontine. He was often involved in the pre-loan budget negotiations during the governments of Prime Minster William Pitt the Younger.

The financier Peter Thellusson's famous overcontrolling will[11] included legacies to each of his three sons of varying amounts which were intended to give each of them £23,000 when combined with gifts made before his death. The topping-up legacy to his son Charles included shares in the Irish Tontines. Peter Thellusson was instrumental in the brokering of the Irish Tontines in the 1770s, especially to Swiss investors.

Admittedly, tontines tended to be only a small part of the portfolio of a 'Monied Man.' Benjamin Kenton, who died in 1800 left an estate composed almost entirely of securities, valued at £301,971, of which only £400 was in a tontine, specifically the Middlesex Tontine.

Perhaps the extreme is expressed in this short obituary printed in the *Britannic Magazine* in 1798:

> Lately died at Kentish Town, John Little, Esq. aged 84.-The penury of this man's life was a striking instance of the little utility of money in the possession of an avaricious man: just previous to his death, he had denied himself the use of absolute necessaries yet, on his effects being examined, it appeared that he had £25,000 in different tontines, £11,000 in the 4 per cents. and landed property to the amount of £2000 a year; all of which goes to an indigent brother, whom he had discarded years ago for marrying, having himself the utmost antipathy to matrimony, on account of its attendant expences.

Another approach is to look at large block purchases. The following represent purchases of six or more shares of the National Tontine of 1789:

[11] Polden, Patrick, *Peter Thellusson's Will of 1797 and Its Consequences on Chancery Law*, Edwin Mellen Press, 2001

> In the first class, in which the nominees had to be under the age of twenty, there were several such purchases by parents in the names of multiple children. The four children of Col. William Shirreff in Hampshire were nominated in twenty-four shares, six each. Ten shares in the second class were bought for Edmund Kershaw, aged 26, of Stockport, Cheshire.
>
> Twenty (!) shares in the third class were purchased in the name of Giovanna Zanerini, 35, of Minesteed in Hampshire. Zanerini was the maiden name of a ballerina who performed as Mrs. Baccelli and had been the mistress of the Duke of Dorset. He split with her in 1789, just as the Tontine was being issued.
>
> Ten shares of the fourth class were bought by Joseph Sill, 46, an English merchant based in Lisbon. Another ten shares were bought by James Higginson, aged 40, a military officer serving in the West Indies. Seven shares in the fifth class were bought by Joseph Leach, 53, of New Inn, Middlesex. Also, twelve shares were bought by Joseph Salt, 56, of Chelsea in Middlesex.
>
> Six shares in the sixth class were purchased by Joseph Gifford, aged 66, of Taunton in Somersetshire.

A third indication of the relative commonplace role of tontines can be seen in the inclusion of multiple tontine shares in personal financial portfolios. The champion within this group is probably Abraham Prado who had both married money and earned more as the 'Provider General of Bread and Forage to the British Army in Flanders' during the War of the Austrian Succession. He invested in the first private tontine, the Society for Annuities Encreasing for the Survivors, as well as multiple shares of the Richmond Bridge Tontine and the Irish Tontines. The cross ownerships of some of the tontines of the period will be reviewed within each of the chapters discussing specific tontines.

Basics

The online *Oxford English Dictionary* definition of a tontine reads:

> A financial scheme by which the subscribers to a loan or common fund receive each an annuity during his life, which increases as their number is diminished by death, till the last survivor enjoys the whole income; also applied to the share or right of each subscriber.

The OED first use is relatively late:

> 1765 Chron. in Ann. Reg. 71/2 The house of Commons came to a resolution of raising £300,000... by way of tontine, or annuities upon lives, at 3 per cent. with benefit of survivorship.

The word 'tontine' was originally French. It is an eponymous word, derived from the name of Lorenzo Tonti,[12] who proposed a version as a revenue scheme for France in 1652-3. Variations on the idea had appeared in Europe in the first part of the seventeenth century, from Danzig to Lisbon, but Tonti's proposal to the French government was the source of the word.

There is a bit of lexicographical awkwardness in deciding when the word was first used as an English word and not simply using the French word to describe a French thing. All of the French-English Dictionaries in the 1700s through the 1760s use the phrase 'annuities on survivorship' as the translation of the French term. The first bilingual dictionary to give 'tontine' as the translation of the French tontine is *A new dictionary in two parts English and French and French and English Upon a Plan the best calculated to render the Attainment of the French Language more expeditious than any yet extant* in 1763. The word is not in Samuel Johnson's *Dictionary* of 1755 and does not appear in Chambers *Cyclopedia* until the edition of 1786.

'Tontine' certainly appeared in London newspapers before the OED citation from 1765, but usually in describing the French revenue schemes or the occasional deaths of French tontineers who were the final survivors in a tontine and had received large dividends in their last years. The tontine proposals in Denmark (1757) and Austria (1764-5) were also mentioned. The initial tontine-like proposals in England were referred to with variations on the phrase 'life annuities with the benefit of survivorship.'

In the April 16th, 1757, issue of the *London Chronicle* there appears a lengthy review of the history of tontines provoked by the ongoing budget proposals that included the possibility of a tontine. It begins:

[12] The best biographical text is found in Rietsch, Christian, and Georges Gallot Hamonno, *Lorenzo Tonti,* chapter 2 in Hellwege Phillip, *The Past, Present, and Future of Tontines,* Berlin: Duncker & Humblot, 2018

> The Scheme established this Sessions for raising Money by Annuities being borrowed from the French Method of creating Annuities by *Tontine* has occasioned an Inquiry into the Meaning of that Phrase, which is not to be found in some of the best French Dictionaries; and-indeed this is not to be wondered at, since Tontine is no more than a cant Term derived from the Name of an Italian Projector.

The article concludes with this definition:

> The Nature of the Tontine is this: There is an Annuity after a certain Rate of Interest, granted to a Number of People divided into Classes, according to their respective Ages: So that annually the whole Fund of each Class is divided among the Survivors of that Class, till at last it falls to one; and upon the Extinction of that Life, reverts to the Power by which the Tontine was erected, and which becomes thereby Security for the due Payment of the Annuities.

After a few false starts, the first French national tontine was issued in 1689 and was followed intermittently by others through 1759. They varied in design and success rate. The idea was picked up by governments throughout the Continent as detailed in the symposium text *The Past, Present, and Future of Tontines* edited by Phillip Hellwege.[13]

Although written broadly, in the excerpt above, the phrase '... the Power by which the Tontine was erected....' implies a government entity. One of the key developments of the Tontine in Georgian Britain was the growth of *private* tontines.

The term was used earlier, in 1731, in the *Daily Courant* in the text below:

> On Monday next the Lottery of Actions is to be drawn, as usual, at the India House. The same Day will be drawn likewise the Lottery of Augmentation, which is drawn every Year in the manner of a Tontine, with regard to the Annuities payable by that Company.

The context remains unclear. At this point, the word 'actions' was still used as a synonym for 'shares,' akin to the similar French term. Possibilities include the notion that a kind of lottery was used to (1) select

[13] Berlin: Duncker & Humblot, 2018. Declaration of interest – I am the author of two of the chapters.

which purchasers of an oversubscribed issue would get the newly issued shares, or (2) which outstanding annuities would be redeemed. The word 'tontine' may not yet have evolved a set meaning among the English at this point and the intended meaning may be a variant of lottery. The East India Annuities were floating around £94–£96 for the week preceding, so redeeming them at par would have paid roughly five percent above the market value.

French East India Company Example

In the early eighteenth century, the English uses of the words lottery and tontine could be confusing. It was like the result of French schemes such as this one reported in the London *Daily Courant* of May 18th, 1724. It outlines a proposal by the French East India Company that involved a complicated proposal of a lottery, a tontine and what seems to be a stock buy-back:

> The India Company has made a new Lottery, each Ticket to be of 300 Livres ready Money, and two Tenths in Stock with the three Dividends; the first Payment to be made in 100 Livres ready Money and one Tenth in Stock; the 2d, 3d, and 4th Payments are to be of 50 Livres each and the 5th the same, with a Tenth in Stock. This Lottery will be divided into five Classes, and the Company will give Credit for the four last Payments till the 4th Class be drawn. In the first the highest Prize is of 80,000 Livres; in the second of 100,000 Livres; in the third of 150,000; in the fourth of 200,000; and in the fifth of 300,000 Livres. The Benefit Tickets to be paid in ready Money amount to 3,082,750 Livres. There will be 1750 Lots of 150 Livres in Annuities, which will be drawn in the last Class. Moreover, there will be 26,000 Blanks of 55 Livres each, in Annuities, which being in the Method of Tontine, will increase the Stocks of the Survivor in Proportion as the Proprietors die. There will be also some Premiums, and all the Annuities will amount to 1,905,500 Livres. The whole Sum of this Lottery is of 9 Millions ready Money, and 60,000 Tenths in Stock; and in case it be filled up, the Company will gain by it above 3,500,000 Livres.

The article continues stating the new subscriptions initially sold for a twenty percent premium, but fell to ten percent by the evening. The price of the company stock also fell after the first day.

It should be noted that beginning with the lottery incorporated into the English revenue bill of 1694 and repeated in subsequent years, the lottery tickets were in fact also term annuities providing a dividend for a number of years after the date of the lottery. In 1694, the term was sixteen years. In 1710, the equivalent was thirty-two years.[14]

Prehistory: The Earliest Tontine-Like Proposals in England

The first hint of a private English tontine-like scheme was offered to the London Common Council in 1674 called *Proposals for Subscriptions of Money &c....*[15] It was described in a short paragraph by the great Cornelius Walford in the first volume of his *Insurance Cyclopedia.* It advertised shares priced at twenty pounds, but Walford concludes his summary with the statement: "We, however, hear no more of the project."

Another precedent seems to be found in a two-page pamphlet or broadside from 1682:

> A proposal for a yearly increase of wealth, by subscriptions to advance money upon lives: Examined and approved by the city. Which will produce great advantage by survivorship, to such as please to subscribe for one, or more lives of the ages of any, or of all the ten ranks, and for any of the summs of money of each rank, as hereby is exprest.

Ending with:

> The Fund for Security of these Payments shall be settled on Trustees to be nominated by, and chosen out of the Subscribers in each Rank or Class, before their Payment of any Money.
>
> At Mr. Hill's, stationer in Exchange-Alley, Cornhill, subscriptions will be taken for this and the City Bank of Credit.[16]

No other traces exist.

[14] Ashton, John, *A history of English lotteries,* London: Leadenhall Press, 1893

[15] Anonymous; City of London (England). Court of Common Council, digitized in Peo Quest's Early English Books Online.

[16] Also digitized in Peo Quest's Early English Books Online.

Another scheme, called 'Lucky Seventy', was first advertised in *The Tatler* of November 1709 and repeated seven times through January 1710. It does not use the word 'tontine.' The text begins: "The Lucky Seventy: Or, The longest Livers take all. In a proposal for Annuities for Life, with the Benefit of Survivorship...." The basic share was £10, but subscribers could take any number of shares. The place appointed for consulting the articles of agreement and taking subscriptions was the Haberdashers' Hall in Maiden Lane. No name of an organizer is given.

Again, no further trace of this entity has been found. It was mentioned in passing by Walford, who notes he found no further traces of it. Both proposals come after tontine schemes had begun to be implemented on the continent. These vague proposals came at a time when the Dutch were creating similar, more coherent, tontine offerings. The interplay of London merchants with the Amsterdam market at the time was considerable.

Mortuary Tontines

As entrepreneurs struggled to develop life insurance schemes that remained solvent in the early 1700s, one of the competing structures called a 'mortuary tontine' developed. The members contributed a set sum each year, and the accumulation was divided by the heirs or nominees of the members who died that year.

The term was not used at the time. It seems to have first appeared in the history of early life insurance by Edwin Farren in 1844 and was picked up by Walford in the first volume of his *Insurance Cyclopedia* in 1871.

The concept reappears in the later benefit societies some of which included a death benefit, often presented as a means to insure a decent burial. 'Tontine' was adopted as a name for many of these, which flourished in the nineteenth century although they were not really tontines.

Bubbling

The late 1600s was a period when an enormous range of would-be companies were proposed. At the time, the process of getting a new company off the ground was known as 'bubbling.' It was a crude equivalent of the modern 'initial public offering,' or IPO. The meaning of the term changed a bit with the collapse of the 'South Sea Bubble' which had a follow-on effect of eliminating a huge number of entrepreneurial schemes, both legitimate and sketchy. In the long run, it also had the effect of shifting the understanding of the word to mean a market frenzy that would inevitably collapse rather than simply the process for proposing new companies.

The 'Million Act' of 1692-93 was the first attempt by the British Government to use a tontine. It was intended to finance 'a vigorous War against *France*' per the text in the periodic subscriber receipts. It failed as a fund-raising effort, with only about ten percent of the intended funds raised. Slightly more than £108,000 was subscribed via 665 shareholders holding 1,081 shares. There were 1,012 nominees. The necessary funds were ultimately raised via the subsequent sale of more straightforward annuities and a lottery. The Million Act's failure meant the English governments shied away from tontines for the next sixty years.[17]

The Creation and Execution of an English Private Tontine

What follows is generic and not every tontine included every step presented. Note that the tontine aspect of a project had to do with the financing, not the actual business executed by the project. On the whole, the first tontines were projects that could have been financed by standard share structures but were made marginally more attractive by the lure of increased returns as time passed.

Preparatory steps were necessary before any proposal went public. The entrepreneur, often known at the time as the 'projector,' would draft a plan and enlist an endorsing group, at least some of whom were significant public figures such as Members of Parliament and local businessmen. Decisions had to be made as to the legal form. Options included a Parliamentary authorized body or commission, a free-standing trust, or a partnership. The ultimate size of the tontine had to be determined, finite if the underlying project had a set budget, or open ended if the tontine was a financial one.

Whatever form was decided on, a text of what would serve as the constitutional document for the tontine would be created by an attorney hired for the purpose. The official document, often a 'deed of settlement,'

[17] The Million Act is thoroughly described and analyzed in Moshe Milevsky's *King Willian's Tontine*, New York: Cambridge University Press, 2015.

was invariably in the dense legal language of the period, so a shorter and less formal abstract would also be prepared that translated the technical document into more colloquial English. Distributing this would involve a printer. Share indentures or certificates were either printed or written by scriveners. A banker would be designated to manage the money, and a physical space for the management of the operation would be established, perhaps a formally rented office, an office related to the physical aspects of the project, or simply a sub-unit within the bank.

Once the project was ready to proceed, newspaper advertising appeared. This could be quite extensive, as some of the tontines took a while to fill. The advertisements were generally local for physical projects but could be nationwide for financial ones. Advertising was not cheap and was also subject to stamp duty. The initial advertising usually contained an outline of the proposal and a list of the worthies endorsing it. The advertisement would include the offer of the more detailed abstract, as well as a location for subscribing. If installment payments were allowed, the deadlines for each installment would be listed.

As the subscription book started to fill, the advertisements tended to report the state of completeness of the scheme. Tontines tended to have set commencement dates, and it was not impossible for the initial subscribers to receive their first dividends when the subscriptions were still incomplete. Ultimately, a cut-off date for subscription was announced, followed by a date by which the life nominee names had to be submitted. Many tontines had to post 'nudging' advertisements for final payments and naming of nominees. Once the subscription book was full, a list of participants or the nominees was usually printed and distributed to the members.

After the project got off the ground, there was a demand for ongoing reports. These would include the advertising of first dividend availability and the periodic advertising of later dividends. Meetings of managers or trustees might be advertised. There were also reports on the status of the tontine's objectives, such as the construction and operation of a bridge, for example, and the opening of the bridge, assembly hall, or library, etc.

On the whole, the subscribers or shareholders had little say in the management of a tontine. The subscribers were passive investors kept happy by the regular receipt of dividends. The projectors might modify the deed of settlement early in the process in order to encourage sales, but they were not re-negotiated nor changed after the tontine was launched. The deed of settlement might include scheduling meetings to select or elect new trustees, but rarely anything beyond that. There were occasional cases of the shareholders of an aging tontine getting together to cash it out prematurely, but they were rare.

The newspapers would also be the source of ancillary information, such as advertisements for aftermarket transactions, usually auctions of shares.

Finally, after an average of around seventy-five years, there would be the procedures for the closure of the tontine. This might include advertising of impending cessation, tracing any possible stragglers with a claim in the payout and an announcement of property distribution per the original deed. These could be complicated by challenges to the payouts, especially if negative elements arose, such as an outcome worse than simple mattress stuffing, followed by angry public meetings and lawsuits.

Who Actually Benefitted from the Creation of Tontine?

The creators or 'projectors' usually incorporated some sort of fee for themselves. This could be an up-front administrative charge, an ongoing percentage each year, or a percentage of the lump sum on final distribution. It is unclear whether the aristocratic figures and other worthies named in the advertising as supporting the tontines received a fee. Peripherally, newspapers benefitted from the extensive advertising involved and the banks holding the tontine funds enhanced their asset pool.

The administrators usually received fees for their maintenance of records, making payments, etc. This group tended to be the targets of claims of overreaching, particularly in the later small-sum, short-term tontines.

There were also the overt classes of beneficiaries. The shareholder and their nominees, through dividends and the survivorship, increase. If for a construction project, the users of the item created, i.e., the bridge, the assembly hall, the coffee house, etc., were beneficiaries. Landowners who created tontines based on their real property and its income received an immediate lump sum of capital.

Contrary to the popular image, the longest liver rarely walked off with outright ownership of a piece of property. Most tontines were wound up after the pool of tontineers reached a set small number, whereupon the capital was distributed among them, or the object of the tontine was put up for sale and the proceeds split among the final pool. For many construction tontines, the object, such as a bridge, ended up being owned by the local government.

The Shape of This Text

After this brief introduction, a number of the first tontine projects in the west of England will be described. Then four examples will be presented at greater depth. One was created to construct a bridge over the Thames from Richmond to Twickenham, which still stands. The sums raised amounted to £25,000, and the number of shares was 250. This will be followed by a review of the first of the purely financial ones, known as the Society for Annuities Encreasing to Survivors. The sum raised was not confirmable but was likely around £30,000 and the number of participants was at least 300. Then a mature financial one, the Ipswich Universal Tontine, with £68,000 capital, 790 shares, and 511 nominees is described. The fourth is an unusual one created to cover the operating costs of the Covent Garden Theatre consisting of 100 members and earning £25,000 for the impresario.

Subsequent chapters will review a range of tontine variations that developed in Georgian England including the large national one of 1789.

The core tontines were selected in part because the digitized newspapers of the period published enough information on them to get a picture of how they evolved. That initial data has been augmented by material supplied by County, City, and University Archives, and Libraries in the United Kingdom.

A Glimpse of Historical Monetary Comparisons

It is extremely difficult to make direct comparisons between expenses and prices in the eighteenth century and the same items today. That said, using the most conservative variation in the Measuring Worth website,[18] an item priced at £100 in 1785 would cost roughly £15,000 in 2022.

A very thoughtful account is provided by cultural and economic historian Robert D. Hume in *The Value of Money in Eighteenth Century England: Incomes, Prices, Buying Power – and Some Problems in Cultural*

[18] https://www.measuringworth.com/

Economics.[19] It somewhat narrowly surveys salaries, costs, and prices in the arts at the time, but it provides a good snapshot with examples and comparisons to current values.

A broader contemporary sense of the economy of the period can be derived by consulting a pamphlet *The economist. Shewing, in a variety of estimates, from fourscore pounds a year to upwards of 800l. how comfortably and genteely a family may live, with frugality, for little money. Together with the cheapest method of keeping horses and carriages. By a gentleman of experience,* published in the early 1770s that attempted to present budgets for households of different incomes and sizes. It should be seen as describing options for people above the laboring classes. The text starts with a family of six plus one servant with an income of £400, and then presents a set of variations depending on different circumstances. The information is presented at a fairly detailed level. Rather than treating it as a definitive text, however, it is perhaps best used as a rough guide to be scanned for a sense of the economy rather than a means to pin down an exact price for an item.

Exclusions

Certain significant tontines have already attracted sufficient attention and will not be closely examined in this text. The London Freemasons' Tontine of 1775 was the subject of a very detailed analysis in a Master's Thesis from the University of London by Diane Clements in 2018. The Glasgow Tontine Coffee House (1781) was the subject of a fairly detailed examination in 1889 published by the Regality Club.

A history of the Birmingham Library published in 1966 includes a transcription of the 1799 Tontine's deed of settlement and the list of subscribers. The Tontine Hotel, in Peebles, Scotland, was the subject of a self-published monograph in 2012.

In a broader context, Andrew McDiarmid has recently published a somewhat compressed text called *The Tontine, a history*[20] which is loaded with useful information. His essay, entitled *"Hardly a Kent Name Absent: Raising Capital in Scotland via Tontine. 1775–1850"*[21] provides

[19] 77 *Huntington Library Quarterly,* 373 (2015)

[20] London: Routledge, 2025

[21] 43 *Journal of Scottish Historical Studies* 31–53 (2023)

an excellent survey of the various tontine schemes and projects in Scotland including an examination of three failed ones, a truly challenging research project.

Phillip Hellwege's *A History of Tontines in Germany*[22] is a comprehensive review of the concept in German-speaking jurisdictions. It argues quite effectively for the importance of essentially state-issued tontines as significant forerunners of modern life insurance. That is not the case in England, where insurance developed via the large London companies alongside tontines, which tended to be smaller and local. Dr. Hellwege has also edited a symposium covering tontines on the continent generally. On the whole the tontines in the continental context are seen as much more a direct antecedent of modern insurance concepts than developed in the British isles.

Although France is primarily associated with the large government Tontines during the eighteenth century, private tontines were used in the latter part of the eighteenth century in particular to build '*salles de spectacles*', or theatres. Some of these are described in Lauren R. Clay's *Stagestruck: The Business of Theater in Eighteenth-Century France and Its Colonies*.[23] Projects included the cities of d'Angers, Laval, Lille, Louvain, Saumur, etc. The amounts raised by some of the tontines she details, however, seem small compared to equivalent projects in England. For example, the 1776 Tontine that successfully built a theatre in Le Mans consisted of 120 shares of 150 livres, for a total of 18,000 livres, or roughly £800. This is equivalent to the cost of the Assembly Rooms constructed in the town of Beccles, Norfolk, which was supported by a tontine that raised only £625. However, the tontine created by Freemasons to build their hall in London raised £5,000 in 1775.

Nantes, in particular, was the site of several tontines. *L'Hotel garni de France* was funded by a tontine in 1786. It was wound up via an agreement among the last three shareholders in 1874. Another building was constructed in 1793 called Maison Naghel, whose tontine lasted until 1879. A third, known as the Maison Touzeau was started in March 1805. Its winding-up process has not been traced.

A variety of tontine schemes called *contracten van overleving* developed in the Netherlands in the late 1600s and early 1700s continuing

[22] Berlin, Duncker & Humblot, 2018

[23] Ithaca: Cornell University Press, 2013

through the end of the century. A brief description of these can be found in Jonker and Gelderblom's *With a view to hold: The emergence of institutional investors on the Amsterdam securities market during the seventeenth and eighteenth centuries.*[24] They are covered in depth in Hermann Wagenvoort's 1961 Utrecht dissertation, *Tontines, een onderzoek naar de geschiedenis van de lijfrenten....*

Gelderblom and Jonker differentiate between government tontines, which they call 'interest' tontines, and 'capital' tontines, which were privately organized:

> Tontines achieved more prominence as vehicles for private old-age pension and in this form, usually known as capital tontines, they were much closer to institutional investors such as modern life insurance companies and investment trusts. A typical contract would bind together a group of investors subscribing to shares in a block of securities, the interest payments or dividends being shared out amongst the individuals named in the contract until their death. A specified number of last survivors eventually obtained the securities. The first such partnership was probably set up in Amsterdam in 1670, and whereas interest tontines were issued all over the Republic, capital tontines remained by and large an Amsterdam phenomenon. They enjoyed an immediate popularity. Nearly 200 mutual tontine contracts were concluded between 1670 and 1700 and by 1687 printed standard forms had appeared.

They go on to describe derivative structures based on these kinds of organizations. The management of the tontines tended to be by Notaries who would each supervise a number of them. Many were originally based in the stock of the Dutch East India Company, but in 1758, a tontine was advertised in Amsterdam that was based on stock in the Bank of England!

> At the office of the Notary W. J. Vos in Amsterdam.... [a client can be] ...subscribed to Contract of Survival, in the manner of Tontine at the Royal Bank of England, in 100 portions, each of 260 guilders in cash of the establishment in proportion to the years, annually distributed approximately 3 to 6 percent...increased by the distribution of the annuities of the deceased among the living, the capital shared by the 5 longest living.

[24] In Atack, J & L. Neal (Eds.), *The Evolution of Financial Markets and Institutions* (pp. 71–98). Cambridge University Press.

A broader survey of old Dutch Tontines can be found in Boudewijn Sirks' *Tontines in the Dutch Republic and the Early Kingdom (1670–1869)* published as part of Dr. Hellwege's symposium mentioned above.

Tontine is also used in the developing world as another name for a Rotating Savings and Credit Association, 'ROSCA,' especially in Francophone countries. It is a form of microfinance among groups of low-level entrepreneurs. A good recent survey is Zambrano, et al., rotating savings and credit associations: A scoping review, 3 *World Development Sustainability* 100081, (2023) [https://doi.org/10.1016/j.wds.2023.100081]. They bear no relationship to the classic tontine that is the subject of this book.

The tontine slowly disappeared from the British financial environment during the nineteenth century. It is the intention of this text to describe the schemes and the variations that developed to give a sense of both how they worked and how they fit into the markets of the time.

CHAPTER 2

The Early Tontines in the West Country

Subscriber-supported assembly room projects blossomed in the middle 1700s in England. Examples included York, Norwich, Derby, and Newcastle, among others. Assembly rooms were secular, multiple-purpose, spaces configurable for balls, lectures, concerts, and the like, important for the cultural and social life of the upper and middle classes.

The construction of these buildings typically involved shareholding via subscriptions. The one in York is considered the first, constructed in 1730–32, which involved 190 subscribers.[1] The earliest one financed by a tontine was in the West Country, in Bristol. It was the first of several tontine projects proposed and executed in that region. Bristol at that time was the second largest city in England, a very active transatlantic seaport, and an important locus for the early stages of industrialization in South Wales and the surrounding area. In terms of public works, in 1754–56 the City Corporation was focused on building two new bridges at roughly the same time.

[1] https://www.yorkconservationtrust.org/our-buildings/assembly-rooms.

K. McKeever, *The Role of Tontines, 1750–1800*, Palgrave Studies in the History of Finance, https://doi.org/10.1007/978-3-032-12849-2_2

Bristol Assembly Room

The first tontine enabled the construction of the Assembly Room in 1754–5. The 'projectors' were reported to be Cranfield Becher and John Heylym. Becher, a 'merchant' in the language of the time, served as Master of the Society of Merchant Venturers (SMV) in 1756. His business included the trade in enslaved Africans, which was a major part of the shipping based in Bristol. A notorious ledger of one of his ships, the *Jason Gally*, is held in the Bristol Archives.[2] Heylym was a copper mine owner and merchant. The other principal projectors were Morgan Smith, William Barnes the Younger, and John Curtis, all listed as esquire.

It must be acknowledged that a substantial part of the trade-based portion of the economy of the eighteenth century was involved in the slave trade and tontines were no exception. Bristol at that time was the center of that business on the English side. The pool of subscribers to the initial private tontines in Bristol in the 1750s had a high percentage of merchants who were involved in commerce in enslaved persons. The Assembly Room tontine is a classic example of what is now seen as a virtually incomprehensible contradiction between the source of the capital and the high cultural aims of the project. This was not an isolated example. In 1805, one of the last attempts to create a tontine based on the income of an estate involved a plantation in Jamaica. The printed proposal for the tontine was quite blunt about a large portion of the subscription money being laid out for the purchase of enslaved persons.

The Bristol investors were essentially local and were the kind of people one would expect to be involved in a major civic improvement project. Some of them were leaseholders of the land on Prince Street which was transferred to the trust to be used in the project. A record of the underlying transaction is in the Bristol Archives.[3] It shows seventy-two initial subscribers. Additional names are listed in an accompanying Power of Attorney[4] regarding Edward Hillerdon's share naming Thomas Edridge,

[2] *Account book for a slaving voyage of the Jason gally and later household accounts for the Becher family, 1743–1818*, Archive Ref number 45167/1. https://archives.bristol.gov.uk/records/45167/1.

[3] *Indenture of articles of agreement: (1) Becher Heylym, Smith Barnes and Curtis; (2) Subscribers of the Assembly Rooms, 1754 Jun 24–1754 Sep 30. Interests on the Assembly Rooms.* Ref No 01287.

[4] Bristol Archives Ref # 01287–3.

Linen Draper, as his representative. The Power of Attorney incorporates a list of shareholders with seventeen not listed among the original seventy-two, for a total of eighty-nine.

An examination of the share certificate of Joseph Farrell, a 'Virginia merchant',[5] held by the Somerset Archives[6] shows the financing consisted of 120 shares of £30 each. When the nominee pool shrank to three, the shareholders of the surviving nominees were to take the whole property as Tenants in Common. The certificate is a pre-printed form with blanks left to inscribe information about the shareholder and his or her nominee. It is dated June 24th, 1754, and witnessed by Plomer and Lambert,[7] who witnessed the 'Agreement' mentioned above. Farrell did not name a young person as his nominee; he subscribed on his own life.

Fourteen of the subscribers had or will have served as Mayor of Bristol. An overlapping twenty-one served as Sheriff. Eighteen had served as officers of the Society for Merchant Venturers, the elite professional association for shipping merchants. It has been estimated that a quarter of the SMV members were slave traders.[8] Three were Members of Parliament—one was about to be elected as a Member of Parliament for Bristol, in 1756, and another, although local, was elected to Parliament from Cornwall in 1768. Six were officers of local charitable organizations. Only four were women.

The more notable among them included Jarrit Smith, an attorney who had a wide range of interests, including the early development of coal mines and owning shares in various privateers. He was elected to Parliament from Bristol in 1756 through 1768. He served as President of the Colston Society, a socially prominent charity. He married money and died the master of Ashton Court. He was named a Baronet in 1763.

[5] I.e., Tobacco.

[6] Somerset Archives, Ref # DD/GC/71.

[7] John Lambert was an attorney to whom the tragic poet Thomas Chatterton was apprenticed as a scrivener in 1767 at the age of fourteen. He was also involved in the creation of the theatre in 1764 that ultimately received a Royal License in 1778. Its deed of trust and shareholding structure did not involve a tontine.

[8] Böhm, T. and Hillmann, H. *A Closed Elite? Bristol's Society of Merchant Venturers and the Abolition of Slave Trading, Chartering Capitalism: Organizing Markets, States, and Publics* (Political Power and Social Theory, Vol. 29), Emerald Group Publishing Limited, Bingley, 2015, pp. 147–175 at page 158. https://doi.org/10.1108/S0198-871920150000029007.

Another was Samuel Worrall, Gentleman, Town Clerk, Barrister, Banker, founder of the local Exchange Bank, and the long-time Distributor of Stamps for the stamp duty. There were two James Laroches. The elder (1734–c1770) had been at various times Mayor, Sheriff, and Alderman of Bristol and Master and Treasurer of the Society of Merchant Venturers. The younger (1764–1804), a nephew, had also been a Sheriff and Master of the Merchant Venturers. He served in Parliament for Bodmin, Cornwall (which his father, John, had previously held), and was made a Baronet in 1776. Both were heavily involved in the slave trade.

Seventeen of the subscribers are named in David Richardson's compendium *Bristol, Africa and the 18th-century slave trade to America*[9] as merchants or shipowners involved in the slave trade. Roughly half of the subscribers supported privateering voyages, often investing in ownership combinations including other tontineers.[10]

Virtually, all the subscribers were merchants with a few other occupations showing up, most prominently linen drapers. Others included a woolen draper, a surgeon, a doctor of physick, a couple of apothecaries, a druggist, a watchmaker, a dry salter, a sailmaker, an ironmonger, and a sugarbaker. Most of them nominated young relatives as the life on which the tontine share depended. The organization was a trust for the benefit of the shareholders. Unfortunately, there does not seem to be any archival traces or documentation of the progress of the Tontine nor of the final disposition. A later report stated that one of the three finalists was Sir Nathaniel W. Wraxall, Baronet and Member of Parliament, who died in 1831. He was the nominee of his father.

In the *Bristol Journal* of December 20th, 1755, was the following advertisement: "On Wednesday, the 14th January, 1756, will be open'd The New Musick Room, with the oratorio of 'The Messiah'." The venue was primarily for balls and concerts. The motto over the entrance read *'Curas Cithara Tollit.'* This loosely translates as 'Music Dispels Care.'

Walter Ison, in *The Georgian Buildings of Bristol,* concluded from circumstantial evidence that the architect was William Halfpenny. The ground floor had both a coffee room and a tavern. The main hall and

[9] Bristol Record Society, Vol 42, 1991. For a snapshot of the trading business generally, see Brown, Alison and Jonathan Harlow, Eds., *Atlantic Venture Accounts of Eighteenth Century Bristol,* Bristol Record Society, Vol. 74, 2021.

[10] Powell, J. W. D., *Bristol Privateers…*, op. cit.

card rooms were on the next floor up. The assembly room was 84 feet by 34 feet and had both a musicians 'gallery and an organ.' While the primary purpose may have cultural events, it also served as a venue for public meetings, and the City reserved the right to use it six days a year for the Mayor and any royal visits. It became the social center of Bristol, used for concerts, public dinners, lectures, and "during the winter season a ball was held there on each alternate Thursday, conducted by a master-of-ceremonies in strict conformity with the prevailing etiquette of Bath."

The unanswered question, at this point, is where did the tontine idea come from? Lawyers live by precedents, and so far, no model for this form of investment structure has shown up. The word 'tontine' does not appear in any of the documents related to the project. The phrase in Farrell's share is "...with an ultimate limitation of the whole Premises to the Proprietors naming the three last surviving Lives as Tenants in Common," without naming the concept.

One place where tontine financing was used earlier than this for construction projects was in the Netherlands. While the initial continental tontines were promoted by countries and municipalities for revenue purposes, in the latter part of the seventeenth century, Dutch brokers and notaries developed local private versions, the *contracten van overleving*, that were essentially financial tontines investing in Dutch East India Company shares and later in a wider range of securities. These became quite widespread and were occasionally used to fund projects. Although most of the Dutch tontines before the 1750s were either municipal revenue schemes or group purchases of securities, some supported specific projects. One noted example is the 1671 tontine used to fund the *Ronde Lutherse Kerk* in Amsterdam, now an event venue connected to the Marriott Renaissance Hotel.[11] Another was a sea reclamation project ('*polder*') in Enkhuizen/Immerhorn in 1671. The same year the churches of Midwolda and Nieuwolda, near Groningen, created a tontine for a similar project involving canals and dikes worth 36,000 guilders.[12] Tontines were also created by the Lutheran congregations in Rotterdam in 1737 and in Middelburg in 1741.

[11] Wagenvoort, Herman, *Tontines: een onderzoek naar de geschiedenis van de lijfrenten bij wijze van tontine en de contracten van overleeving...* (Thesis) Utrecht: 1961.

[12] Hesse, H., Een lijfrentebreif in 1671 uitgegeven door Midwolda en Nieuwolda, *1931 Groningse Volksalmanak* 105–117.

While the scanty statistics in *The Trade of Bristol in the Eighteenth Century*[13] show that the Netherlands was a comparatively minor part of the overall business of Bristol shippers, there were enough commercial contacts between English traders and the Dutch for Bristal merchants to be aware of these schemes.

If the form was copied from a continental model, would it have used the term 'tontine?' The Dutch texts used the phrase '*contracten van overleving*,' which is reasonably close to a translation of the English phrase 'annuities with survivorship.'

The Idea Spreads

Two years later, in 1757, a tontine was part of the proposal for the annual national government loan. This is roughly the point where the word tontine becomes part of the vocabulary of English. Two and a half million pounds was to be raised via standard annuities and one half million was to be raised by a tontine offering. The reports in the newspapers of the time used both the traditional term of 'annuities with the benefit of survivorship' and, more rarely, 'tontine.' There were few subscribers to the tontine and that portion of the loan was ultimately converted to annuities. More detail can be found in Chapter 7. However, also in 1757, the City of Chester used a tontine to fund civic improvements, including a multi-parish workhouse.

Chester Exchange and House of Industry, 1757

This is another early tontine project from the west of England. It paid for renovations to the city's main market and administrative building, known as the Exchange, and for the construction of a city poorhouse to replace the system of multiple parish poorhouses within the city. Thus, the tontine had a municipal government origin rather than a private one:

[13] Minchinton, Walter E., Bristol Record Society, 1957.

> In 1757, to pay for repairs to the Exchange and building a poor-law workhouse, [Chester] decided to raise £6,000 by issuing annuities under the tontine system. Only £4,000 came in initially, but the city itself subscribed c. £2,000.[14]

The House of Industry, completed in 1759, was located on the River Dee on the outskirts of the Roodee, the ancient racecourse in the center of Chester. The site is now separated from the racetrack area by a railway viaduct. It was built "…for maintaining the in and out poor of the nine parishes within the limits of the city, viz.: St. Oswald's, St. John the Baptist, St. Mary's on the Hill, Holy Trinity, St. Michael's, St. Bridget's, St. Martin's, St. Olave's, and St. Peter's."[15] The parishes had signed a formal union document to enable the creation of a shared poorhouse. It was designed to accommodate four hundred persons, although a later report indicated the average at any time was around one hundred.[16]

The tontine pre-dates the related *Chester (Poor Relief,* etc.*) Act of 1762*, 2 Geo III c 45, by a couple of years. That act created the body known as the Guardians who supervised the poor relief programs, in effect formalizing the powers of the unified institution as a tool to combat vagrancy. It also specified the House of Industry was to be held by the Guardians with rent paid to the city.

The North East Wales Archives[17] hold what amounts to a share certificate in the tontine, although, as is true of the other early schemes, the word tontine is not used. It is a bond dated December 24th, 1757, acknowledging that Richard Richardson, Goldsmith, the Mayor of Chester at the time, was lending the City £150, of which £50 was for an Annuity based on the life of Thomas Richardson, his youngest son.

[14] Lewis, C. P. and A. T. Thacker, Eds., *A History of the County of Chester: Volume 5 Part 1, the City of Chester: General History and Topography,* London, 2003), British History Online http://www.british-history.ac.uk/vch/ches/vol5/pt1[accessed 13 October, 2024].

[15] Bagshaw, Samuel, *History, gazetteer, and directory of the County Palatine of Chester…*, Sheffield: Ridge, 1850.

[16] Lewis, Chris, Building Chester's First Workhouse, 38 *Cheshire History* 50–54 (1998–9).

[17] 'Bond in 100,' 'Reciting an order of the common court held 07 Apr last that 6000 should be raised by their corporation upon their paying annuities of 50…' North East Wales Archives Object Number: D/KK/595.

The details of the arrangement are not specified, however. The document references printed 'proposals or conditions' derived from an order of the 'Assembly or Common Council' on April 7th, 1757, to raise £6000. Richardson senior nominated two other children to the tontine, and it is likely that each child/nominee was named in a parallel document, thus totaling £150.

The underlying conditions are found in a transcription of the Fourth Assembly Books of the City of Chester [ZA/B/4/(168)] digitized on the National Archives website:

> The Committee having met to consider methods for raising money to answer the City's exigencies, it was ordered that £6000 be raised by the Corporation upon their granting annuities for lives and giving security for payment of the same as follows:
>
> While 120 persons live and until reduced to 80, each should receive the rate of 6. 0. 0
> While 80 persons live and until reduced to 60, each should receive the rate of 7. 0. 0
> While 60 persons live and until reduced to 40, each should receive the rate of 9. 0. 0
> While 40 persons live and until reduced to 20, each should receive the rate of 14. 0. 0
> While 20 persons live and until reduced to 10, each should receive the rate of 20. 0. 0
> While 10 persons live and until reduced to 8, each should receive the rate of 35. 0. 0
> While 8 persons live and until reduced to 6, each should receive the rate of 45. 0. 0
> While 6 persons live and until reduced to 4, each should receive the rate of 55. 0. 0
> While 4 persons live and until reduced to 2, each should receive the rate of 100. 0. 0
> While 2 persons live and until reduced to 1, each should receive the rate of 200. 0. 0
> While 1 person lives and until reduced to 0, he should receive the rate of 400. 0. 0

The detailed specificity of the increasing dividends through time was unique. The standard practice was to simply indicate that an increase would take place without providing figures.

The document then lays out nine clauses, called conditions, that provided the formal framework of the proposal. A key clause specified how the continued life of the nominee was to be certified:

> Each party if in Great Britain, was to be produced or certified as being alive on 24th December, the certificate to be sent before 24th January to the Mayor, by the Minister or Churchwarden of the parish of residence. If the person lived overseas the certificate was to be sent under the hand and seal of the Notary Public, signed by the party and an affidavit made by some credible person in England certifying to the annuitant's handwriting.

The Chester Tontine followed the model the Million Act of 1692 (*4 William & Mary C. 3, clauses 12 and 13.*) specifying the use of ministers and churchwardens to verify nominee lives, as did the 1757 failed National Tontine. The Chester Tontine came at the same time as a national tontine was being proposed in Parliament. The local one had no formal classes, but the national proposal had five classes according to the ages of the nominees. (See Chapter 7).

The Tontine was undersubscribed. The step taken to complete the tontine pool was remarkable. The City itself took up forty subscriptions, one-third of the entire offer, and held them in the names of forty young people of the upper classes of the City and vicinity. This ensured that the mathematical calculations underlying the overall scheme were still valid for the eighty primary subscribers. The City's list included the children of once and future mayors and sheriffs, local clergy, merchants, and a judge. They were all male, and a substantial number of them appear on the admissions list of Chester Freemen beginning in the late 1770s. Two listed siblings went on to become Members of Parliament and one other child ultimately became Deputy Lieutenant of Cheshire.

The process anticipated a similar step taken by William Pitt's government when the 1789 National Tontine did not sell out. One of the boys on the City's list, Roger Wilbraham, became a 'wrangler,' i.e., a math scholar, then a tutor at Cambridge. He was later elected to Parliament, serving during the creation of the national tontine and the later amending of it by creating a government-nominated pool of names to flesh out the necessary lives to make the mathematics behind the tontine work. Did he provide the idea to Pitt and his advisors? (See Chapter 8).

On January 31st, 1774, a list of the living Chester annuitants was published in *Adams's Weekly Courant*. It gave the names of twenty-seven individual subscribers with their thirty-nine nominees. It also showed thirty-seven names under the heading of 'Mayor and Citizens of Chester, i.e., the City's list. The same journal published similar lists in 1778 and 1779. The one from January 26th, 1779, showed only the slightest changes: twenty-seven individual subscribers with thirty-eight nominees. The 'Mayor and Citizens of Chester' component had shrunk by one to thirty-six. The residence of some of the nominees had changed.

A similar list, even to the point of graphics, was published in the December 24th, 1813, *Chester Chronicle*. At that point, there were sixteen annuitants, twenty-two lives, and twenty-one in the Mayor and Citizens group. The last published statement of the tontine, from 1834, shows five surviving nominees and two surviving members of the City's list.

The early lists show a majority of the nominees living in Chester or in nearby counties, but there were nominees from Dublin, Cambridgeshire, Birmingham, Oxford, Berkshire, Dorsetshire, Lancashire, London, and one in Amsterdam, a son of a Chester alderman. Two of the local baronets, John Stanley Massey and Pyers Mostyn, were subscribers.

In 1789, two of the Annuities were listed for auction in Chester.[18] They were paying seven percent at that point.

Tontine payments were made until at least 1840.

The Circular Stables in Bristol

In 1761, the Bristol Assembly Room subscriber Morgan Smith, Esq., who was Mayor at the time, was subscriber number one in a subsequent tontine created to build the 'Circular Stables,' a riding school and stables in Stokes Croft on the edge of the city.

While an equestrian center may seem an odd project for a joint venture, the contemporary involvement with horse-related activities was large. Horse riding was a common form of exercise for the people who could afford to own a horse. Individual travel on a horse was regarded as far more pleasant than a trip in a stagecoach. Pleasure excursions in open carriages were a classic see-and-be-seen social activity. Besides stabling the horses, the large circular structure would allow riding under cover. A 'riding master' was encouraged to open a school at the site. It was located on the outskirts of the city.

[18] *Chester Chronicle*, September 4th, 1789.

A contemporary advertisement for a manager provides details: "a regular pile of circular building consisting of fifty-eight stalls, four coach houses, and a good Dwelling House, with a Covered Ride, the Inside of the Circle measuring 331 Feet round, and made commodious for gentlemen exercising in Winter, and bad Weather...."[19] The architect was John Wallis.

The Bristol Archives[20] holds a participant's manuscript Declaration of Interest along with a list of the founding subscribers. While the Declaration is in the traditional long-winded manuscript form of the period, it is, in effect, a shareholder's certificate. The Tontine consisted of ninety-five shares costing £25 each. No interest or dividend rate is given. They were only thirty-eight participants, most holding multiple shares, usually nominating their children as the lives benefiting from the Tontine. The word 'tontine' is not used, with 'survivorship' stated as the principle for extended ownership. The key phrase is "...with an Ultimate Limitation to the Proprietor naming the last and only Surviving Life and his Heirs and Assigns forever...." This is a classic 'winner takes all' clause.

A reference is made to: "an Indenture bearing equal date herewith and made between the said Daniel Smith and John Crofts of the one Part and Morgan Smith Esquire John Noble Thomas Knox and Samuel Sedgley Esquire and others the second parties theretofore carrying into Execution the Scheme for Erecting and Building the Circular Stables and Buildings...." The names listed in the second indenture are the first four names on the Subscribers List. This second indenture is untraced and is likely the foundational document for executing the scheme.

The text in the Bristol Archives was for Edward Harford the Younger. He was a member of an extended family including merchants, tobacco importers, copper manufacturers, and bankers. His nominees were his two sons, Edward Harford the Youngest, age eight, and John Scandret Harford, aged seven. The Tontine organizers were Daniel Smith a Linen Draper, who later served as the project Clerk and Treasurer and John Crofts, Gentleman.

The membership included one Member of Parliament, five men who served as Mayor of Bristol during this period and three more who served as Sheriff. Seven had the honorific 'Esquire' and three were 'Gentlemen.'

[19] *Lloyd's Evening Post,* September 24th, 1760.

[20] Bristol Archives Reference number 19835 (8)K.

Twelve listed their profession as Merchant and six were Linen Drapers. The other businesses represented included Tobacconist, Druggist, Sail-maker, Grocer, and Dry Salter. Five were women. They all seem to be local to Bristol. Most of the lives nominated were the children of the shareholders, although one person nominated King George III.

Six of the thirty-eight Circular Stables shareholders were also subscribers in the Bristol Assembly Room tontine five years earlier. Eighteen appear as share owners in privateers in Powell's *British Privateers...* and an uncertain number seem to have been involved in the slave trade.

The Circular Stables were still around in 1825, although its function at that time was unclear. In 1769, it had been used as a venue for a boxing match,[21] but that probably had mostly to do with the interior space enabling the promoters to set up an appropriate temporary arrangement. An 1825 advertisement indicated the management would consider other uses for the land.[22] It also stated at least fourteen nominees were still alive, although it is hedged by a statement that the figure was uncertain—there might be more. An 1891 source stated that in 1825, fifteen lives of the original ninety-five nominees were still alive.

The site was subject to a small archaeological evaluation by Bristol and Region Archaeological Services in 2006.[23] The summary report reads: "Three trenches were excavated, all of which contained remains of the building, suggesting that existing plans accurately reflect the location of the outer wall of the stables and that the preservation of stone foundations is likely to be good despite fire damage in 1839 and the effects of subsequent development."

The Stables had been reported to have been converted into a circus amphitheater in March 1790, but no contemporary source has been found. The 1794 map of Bristol in Fig 2.1 indicates the location of the Stables. The linking of riding academies and horse-oriented circuses certainly took place elsewhere in England, most notably via Astley's shows in London. An equestrian theatre was built in 1791 on Limekiln-lane, according to George Heath's *New Bristol Guide*, published in 1799. It was described as semi-circular at the eastern end. However, that was in a completely different area of the City.

[21] *Public Advertiser*, June 26th, 1769.

[22] *Bristol Mercury*, January 3rd, 1825.

[23] https://www.bgas.org.uk/tbgas_bg/v125/bg125341.pdf Page 8; See: also https://archaeologydataservice.ac.uk/library/browse/issue.xhtml?recordId=1022354&record Type=GreyLit.

Fig. 2.1 A 1794 map of Bristol from Matthews's *The New History* etc. The Circular Stables are shown by the circular feature in the upper right quadrant. The Assembly Room is between Queens Square and the River Froom in the center of the bottom third of the map. It is labeled with the number 9. Collection of the author

Tangential Questions

While earlier construction projects, such as the Assembly Rooms in York, were developed using a shareholder scheme, it is unclear as to why a tontine structure was chosen for these projects in Bristol and Chester. A possible precedent, a government revenue scheme known as the Million Act of 1693, the only previous tontine in England, included very few nominees from Bristol and the Chester area. Tontine was not yet part of the standard vocabulary in English and was not used by the projectors, although it was used in Bath a decade later. The key phrases used in the Bristol documentation involved variations on the word 'survivors.'

Were there local precedents for this form of investment? Did the merchants have similar contract structures for their ships and/or the cargoes? Another possible precedent is found in Cornelius Walford's 1880 *Insurance Cyclopedia,* Volume Five, which has an unfootnoted anecdote about a salvage agreement in the mid-1600s:

> GAMBLING INS[URANCE] PROJECTS GENERALLY, 1643.
>
> It was prob. about the same date that a Mutual Ins. Co. was formed to aid an adventurer with funds to raise a vessel which, laden with the treasures of the East, had been lost on her passage home; the peculiar feature of the transaction being that if any of the association should die before the object was accomplished, their share was to be transferred to the remaining adventurers. This made the hazard a double one, by the introduction of the tontine principle.

Note this is slightly before Tonti's proposal in France that became the source of the word. A similar ur-tontine was proposed in Portugal in 1641.

These tontines set the model for an extraordinary number of local projects throughout Great Britain. There were three significant branches: local financial investment, significant architectural development, and enhanced social and cultural opportunity for the rising middle classes. A fuller picture is provided in Chapter 11 on the Breadth of Tontines.

The shareholder-financed construction of a theatre in Bristol in 1764 did not use the tontine form, although theatres in other cities were financed by tontines.

Subsequent Tontine Projects in Bristol

There was an extraordinary boom of construction in Bristol right after the end of the American Revolution. It is described in J. R. Ward's essay *Speculative Building at Bristol and Clifton, 1783–1793.*[24] It ended in an economic downturn precipitated in part by the beginning of the wars with France. While Ward's text is informative on the participants and methods involved, it does not mention tontines. However, the boom included a number of tontine projects.

In 1783–5, a tontine supported the completion of what was called St. Stephen's Warehouses, but which were often referred to as the Tontine Warehouses during their long existence. There were 193 shares of £64/5/0 each. A nudging advertisement in *Felix Farley's Bristol Journal*, July 19th, 1783, has a mild threat that if a nominee is not named by a certain date, the subscriber will be inscribed as the life at risk. The Tontine wound down in 1850, but the buildings functioned as warehouses through demolition in 1936.

Tontine-financed projects became a minor trend. On March 6th, 1784, the two adjacent advertisements appeared in *Felix Farley's Bristol Journal.* The first was to announce the availability of land near Park-Row as a leasehold site 'for building on the Tontine Scheme.' The arrangement and plans for the buildings already existed. The particulars of the scheme were available from the landowner and the architect.

The second advertisement was for a similar pre-planned tontine scheme on 'Great-George-Street' that envisioned eight houses. It is unclear how much freedom a lessor would have to develop the property according to his own ideas. A later report indicates this never came to fruition.

Additional residential tontine projects in Bristol at this time included houses in Brunswick Square in 1786, a seemingly dead-on-arrival proposal for sixty houses known as the Queen's Tontine near Ashley Down in 1792, and the Royal York Crescent in Clifden, begun in 1793 but which failed within a year or two without completing any houses when the projector went bankrupt during the general depression of the mid-90s. The project was not completed until 1820. The Crescent is currently a Grade II listed building.

Finally, there are faint traces of a tontine building in the Lewin's Mead section of Bristol. Whatever it was, it was insured in 1793 in the names

[24] 20 *Business History* 3–18, 1978.

of Benjamin Baugh and Thomas Curtis. Baugh was a member of the Corporation of Bristol.

The Brunswick Square Tontine, 1786

The Brunswick Square Tontine was proposed in 1783 and created in 1786. It financed the construction of a row of residences in a fashionable area of the city. One of the subscriber/committee members was the banker, John Scandret Harford, who was a nominee of his father in the Circular Stables Tontine described above. The shares cost 50 Guineas (£52/10/0). A list of the subscribers is held by the Gloucestershire Archives.[25] Virtually, all the nominees were children of the subscribers. Three of the shareholders took five shares, each one in the name of a different child.

In 1858, a newspaper advertisement for a different tontine proposal indicated the Brunswick shares were paying twenty percent interest on the original price. The final distribution of the Tontine was reported in the *Western Daily Press* of December 19th, 1860:

> The number of lives having been reduced to five in October last, a meeting was held, pursuant to the directions contained of the original resolutions of the Tontine, on Thursday, the 13th inst., at which the Right Worshipful the Mayor of Bristol, Odiarne C. Lane, Esq., presided, when a ballot took place to determine the ownership of the houses, the result of which was, that Mrs S. P. Anderson of Henlade, near Taunton, become the owner of the southeast corner house, being the largest and best house of the whole, at present numbered 7; Mr Richard Ash became the owner of No. 8; Miss Frances Wright of No. 9; Mr. R. H. Webb of Nos. 10 and 11.Mrs Anderson, Mr Ash, and Miss Frances Wright held the shares on their own lives, and Mr. Webb on the lives of others.

According to the *Western Daily Press,* December 17th, 1860, Webb had bought his two shares at auction three years earlier for £190.

[25] Gloucestershire Archives Reference # D361/F4.

Small-Sum, Short-Term Tontines Based in Bristol

Bristol also served as the primary location for several of the purely financial small-sum, short-term tontines of the late 1780s and 1790s. They are described in Chapter 8.

Bath, the Would-be Tontines

Saint Margaret's Chapel

In Bath, the architect John Wood the Younger proposed two construction projects in the late 1760s, St. Margaret's Chapel and the new Assembly Rooms near the Circus. The initial advertising for both projects stated the financing was to be executed via a tontine. However, it is clear that the final version of both projects did not involve a tontine.

The new chapel was proposed via an advertisement in the *Bath Chronicle*, for September 22nd, 1768. It indicated: "The Number of Subscribers to be Fifty, at One Hundred Guineas each, to be paid at five equal Payments; every Subscriber, when the Chapel is finished, to nominate a Life for each Share; the Profits of the Chapel to be divided amongst the Subscribers and the Survivors; the Whole to become the sole Property in Fee of the longest Liver." The source for further information was Wood himself, not a broker or agent. The advertisement was repeated several times through November.

The chapel, incorporated into a larger project later known as 'Margaret's-building,' opened in 1773. It seems the proposed tontine was never consummated. A later writer stated: "The building fund was provided by the Rev. Mr. Martyn, Cornelius Norton, and Mr. Linley, organist; Mr. Wm. Linley was the contractor and builder."[26] Sadly, the chapel was destroyed in the Blitz.

In the meantime, Mr. Wood was developing another project with Andrew Sproule. It was a proposal for a somewhat larger tontine-financed building that had a considerable impact.

[26] Wright, G. N., *The Historic Guide to Bath*, Bath: R E Peach, 1864, p 285.

The New (Upper) Assembly Rooms: 1769–71

This is another very early proposal involving tontine funding. This building served as one of the primary venues for concerts, balls, soirees, and gambling all through the Regency period and after. It survives and is currently a National Trust property.

The 1768 construction proposal stated:

> The Number of Shares to be 140 at One Hundred Guineas each: Five Guineas to be paid at the time of Subscribing, into the Bath Bank, which deposit will be returned in case the subscription is not filled on or before the 25th of March next: The remaining Money to be paid by Installments as the Building goes on.
>
> When the Building is completed, the lives are to be nominated by each Subscriber, his or her Executor, one life for each Share. The neat Profit of the Building to be divided annually amongst the several Subscribers, their Executors or Administrators during the life and lives so nominated by him or her. And the whole Building to become the sole Property of [and remain forever so] such Subscriber, his or her Heirs and Assigns, whose Share or Shares shall stand represented by the last surviving Life.[27]

This outlines a classic tontine. However, as executed, there were only sixty-eight subscribers who paid £300 each in a straightforward joint-stock manner, with no nominations, no increase in dividends due to the deaths of fellow shareholders, nor ownership by a final survivor.

Wood and his father were architects based in Bath and produced many of the classical buildings of the period. Sproule, a subscriber, seems to have served more of what would be considered a contractor now. The indenture that created the business indicates Wood and Sproule were the landowners.

The project's extant records are held at the Bath Record Office, including the "Articles of Agreement entered into and agreed upon between all and every the Subscribers of the New Assembly Rooms'; May 1st, 1769, signed on the 4th of May."[28] The Archives also hold a Journal of the initial meetings of the subscribers.

[27] *Bath Chronicle*, December 17th, 1768.

[28] Ref. 0028A/1–3.

The journal describes the creation of two committees, a 'Law' committee and a 'Building' committee. The Law committee focused on the conveyancing of the property and the creation of the organizational structure. The underlying freehold and trust was specified to last 1000 years. The Building committee was concerned with the actual construction and furnishing process.

The drafting lawyer was a Mr. Tyndell, who was instructed to enroll the deed. The project bank was the Bath Bank.

Two of the original subscribers, John Williams and Jonathan Morton Pleydell assigned their shares to John Wadman and John Eyre, Esq., Pleydell who, along with two others, Dr. Harrington and Dr. Brent, were then asked to be the trustees to hold the property for the benefit of the subscribers. Presumably, the assignments were done to avoid a conflict of interest.

Shares started changing hands very quickly. By November 1769, one of the original subscribers, Edward Daniels 'had disposed' of his share and, as he had been a member of the Law committee, he had to be replaced. In March of 1770, two subscribers had missed their payments and were voted to have forfeited their rights, and a third had assigned her share to third person and the new shareholder was approved.

The Articles of Agreement has no reference to nominations of lives, as would be standard in a tontine. It shows seventy-three subscribers confirmed by their signatures. The record list of Original Subscribers as held in the Bath Archives consists of seventy-two entries noting a couple of forfeitures. It is undated but is presumably accurate as to the first purchasers. Later transfers are recorded. The same volume records the proprietors and successors as of February 1780, January 1783, June 1789, Midsummer 1796, Midsummer 1805, and Midsummer 1814. The 1814 list has transfer annotation notes through 1821. In all the later lists, the number of shares is sixty-eight. There is no tontine effect shrinkage even after fifty years.

A kind of 'call' for an additional sum, not to exceed £60 was made on the subscribers to pay for furnishing the Rooms. In April 1771, another committee was created for managing the Rooms. All through this period there were occasional notices of failures to pay subscriptions, including one directed at John Wood, the Architect. He had paid up by the next meeting.

On the whole, however, the Journal does not go into detail as to the accounts of the project.

In May 1770, it was decided to contact a Mr. Wade to see if he would be willing to be the 'Master of Ceremonies' of the new Rooms. This was the title given to the events manager whose function included a fairly public role as an arbiter of fashion. The Master of Ceremonies had an extraordinary social power during this time. In a world of very formal etiquette, he could introduce strangers who had yet to be introduced via families or friends. William Wade had been the Master of Ceremonies at the Old Assembly Rooms. His social standing may be inferred from the fact that his portrait, hung in the Assembly Rooms, was by Gainsborough.

The opening of the New Rooms took place in October 1771. Eventually, it led to what was essentially a social war between the patrons of it and the Old Assembly rooms, fought via meetings, newspaper columns, and pamphlets. The documents of this were reprinted in a 104-page volume entitled *The rival ball rooms, or, a collection of all the pieces published in favour of the new and old assembly-rooms, at Bath, during the disputes about settling the public amusements, in the autumn season, 1774*, Printed by R. Cruttwell, and sold by all the booksellers in Bath.

Aftermarket

On February 23rd, 1835, an auction advertisement for two shares in the Assembly Rooms appeared in the *Times*. The interest per share is still only Five Guineas per £100. No tontine dividend increase is involved.

On April 27th, 1837, another advertisement in the *Bath Chronicle* offered, *inter alia*, "Six SHARES in the UPPER ASSEMBLY ROOMS, held for the remainder of a term of 1000 years, of which upwards of 920 are unexpired." Again, no tontine element is mentioned. This is in contrast to the tontine nature of another lot in the same estate auction for four shares in the 'Tontine Annuity' issuing from the Theatre Royal, Bath.

Another advertisement with similar contrasting lots of the Assembly Room and Theatre Royal shares showed up in 1845. A solo listing for the Assembly Room shares appeared in 1861.

While many sources refer to the Assembly Rooms as having been financed by a tontine, in fact, as actually executed, it was NOT a tontine. Both of John Wood's projects were proposed as tontines but ended up straightforward joint-stock operations in execution. It is possible that the idea of a tontine was a form of teaser, eliciting interest that might not have been forthcoming otherwise. Or the change may have been the result of an insufficient number of subscribers signing up within the tontine framework.

Laura Chapel

Another project in Bath that *did* proceed to completion as a tontine was the Laura Chapel. This is the church attended by Jane Austen. It was the largest Episcopal Chapel in Bath with a capacity of roughly 1,000. It opened in November 1795. An 1864 guide to Bath stated:

> This chapel takes its origination from Laura, Countess of Bath, on whose estate it was erected in the year 1796, on a tontine or survivor-ship scheme, by the Rev. Mr. Leeves; from him it passed to Dr. Randolph, and afterwards to Mr. Grinfield.... .... Laura Chapel is situated in a populous and wealthy locality. It is spacious, enriched by a gallery supported by coupled Corinthian columns, and most conveniently arranged for auditors.[29]

Daniel Cummins, writing about proprietary chapels in Bath,[30] noted:

> For those who could afford the pew rents, the chapel provided 'an elegant and commodious building... rendered comfortable in winter by fires in the recesses' to seat 1,000 people. Laura chapel was said to be very fashionable and 'its returns are very large, from the very high rates at which the pews and sittings are let'. It cannot be forgotten that these chapels were commercial ventures which deliberately targeted the demand for exclusive religious provision in order to make the proprietors financial gains.

A London auction advertisement from the *Morning Post*, of August 13th, 1805 offered 'One Twentieth Share. By way of Tontine in Laura Chapel.' It was paying £6/4/6 annually at that point.

The Lincolnshire Archives[31] hold an exchange of letters whose subject was to pin down the date and place of the burial of a shareholder/annuitant in the Laura Chapel Tontine. While the point was to make sure the dividends to the survivors were correctly allocated, *inter alia*, they

[29] Wright, *Historic Guide to Bath,* op. cit.

[30] Cummins, Daniel, Exclusive oratories and magnificent pagodas, the Anglican proprietary chapels of eighteenth-century Bath, 88 *Historical Research* 254–264 (2012).

[31] Reference numbers Jarvis 5/A/7/76r, Jarvis 5/A/7/76v, Jarvis 5/A/8/12r, Jarvis 5/A/8/12v.

indicate that the annual interest due on Lady Day, 1823, was between eight and nine pounds.

Another auction advertised in the *Morning Post* of May 22nd, 1833, offered three shares paying an interest of 'between £11 and £12 per share.'

The chapel was demolished around 1900 leaving only two doorways standing. They are incorporated into the surrounding building.

A number of later construction projects in Bath were financed via tontines. The construction of a row of houses on Norfolk Crescent, started in 1792, stalled for lack of funds and in 1810 a tontine was created to complete the project. The new Royal Theatre, 1804–5, was the result of a tontine.

> One hundred shares to be created at £200 per share, the share to terminate with a life named and registered at the time of subscribing. Each shareholder to receive three percent per annum, and a right of admission to all performances, transferable once a year. The whole rent-charge of £600 per annum (that is, the three per cent per share, to be paid so long as any one life remained, and to be equally divided among the survivors; but the admission to cease with the life. There was also another class of subscriptions, not carrying free admission, which were £150 per share. The theatre and the whole property connected with it — the patent, wardrobes, scenery and furniture, together with its income—were vested in trustees for the security and interest of the subscribers....
>
> ...The subscriptions were rapidly taken up, and heading the list of subscribers were H.R.H. the Prince of Wales, H.R.H. Princess Charlotte of Wales, and H.R.H. the Duke of York, both the Prince and the Duke of York having manifested considerable interest in the undertaking, which was generally and rightly considered to be of great importance to the city.[32]

As late as 1822, there was a proposal to support the 'valuable and spacious' Masonic Hall in Bath[33] via a tontine whose youngest nominees would have to be at least sixty years old.

In 1789, there were two financial tontines advertised in the Bath Chronicle, both involving Cam and Company (aka Bath Bank) as bankers and both costing £100 a share. One, the Bath Tontine, had three classes

[32] Penley, Benville, *The Bath Stage*, London: Lewis, 1892.

[33] *Bath Chronicle*, September 18th, 1822.

and was roughly similar to the contemporaneous Doncaster Tontine. The other, unnamed, was a variant that involved making no interest payments for the first five years, and then paying dividends from the sixth through the twentieth year, and at the end of twenty years distributing the capital to the remaining subscribers. They remain untraceable.

One of the last gasps of the tontine form was a proposal in 1845 also called the Bath Tontine to create a scheme to hold a group of properties in the Edgar Buildings, one property in Norfolk Crescent, Norfolk House, a Villa, and thirteen cottages and a chapel. The scheme envisioned four hundred shares of £20 each with the whole going to a single survivor at the end of the tontine. Only the proposal shows up in the record.

A Southern Digression, to Weymouth in Dorset

After the New Assembly Rooms in Bath, the projector Andrew Sproule started a new project in Weymouth, a spa town on the south coast in Dorset favored by the Royal family. It is described in:

> The great resort of company to this town for several years past, for the purposes of sea-bathing, encouraged Mr. Sproule of Bath, last year, 1771, to offer proposals for building by subscription, on survivorship, a set of assembly rooms, and an hotel, with the necessary appendages, on a piece of ground adjoining to the town, granted to him by John Tucker, Esq. for the term of 40 years, provided the said grantee, Mr. Tucker, live so long; with a reversionary term of 110 years, granted by the corporation of Weymouth, to commence from the end of the former term. The building to be completed in a plain, workman-like manner, within a year and half from the beginning, for a sum not exceeding £6000. to be raised by subscription, and divided into 60 shares of £100 each, dependant on the life of the subscriber, or his nominee. The whole building, when all the shares are reduced to one, to become the sole and absolute property of the party whose share shall be dependant on such surviving life, his executor and administrator, for the remainder of the aforesaid terms.[34]

The building was known originally as Stacie's Hotel, or Stacey's Hotel, and was renamed the Royal Hotel in the early 1800s. It was seasonal, opening in June each year. The original building survived through 1891.

[34] Hutchin, John, *The history and antiquities of the county of Dorset…*, 1774.

Weymouth was a popular seaside summer resort patronized by George III and his family starting in the 1780s.

An auction advertisement in the *Exeter and Plymouth Gazette*[35] included this lot: "And a certain interest, under a Tontine Deed, to a valuable Leasehold Property, comprising the Royal Hotel, Weymouth, producing nearly £300 per annum, and held under the Corporation of Weymouth, for an unexpired term of 41 years." In the advertising language of the period, the £300 was the total to be shared by the tontineers, not £300 per share.

An administrative document held by the Dorset History Centre[36] shows the status of the Tontine in 1842. There were eleven nominees still alive at that point. Two were nominees of Andrew Sproule, the developer.

Expansion

The idea of construction-oriented tontines expanded from the West Country to the rest of England in the mid-1770s. The Richmond Bridge Project and the Freemasons' Hall were early projects in London. The Freemasons' Hall is thoroughly described in Diane Clements' MRes Thesis from the University of London entitled *Invested in identity: the Freemasons' Tontine of 1775* (2018). The Richmond Bridge scheme might be regarded as the first one in London to reach a pool of investors who were not already known to each other. It is the subject of the next chapter.

[35] June 10th, 1837.

[36] Dorset History Centre Ref. # D 49 5 (4).

CHAPTER 3

The Richmond Bridge Tontine

Richmond in the latter part of the eighteenth century was a suburban /rural borough upriver of London on the Surrey side. Areas directly to the north were royal properties, including a summer palace, Richmond Lodge, an observatory, and the Great Park, used for riding and hunting. While the core was a village, the nearby Royal and aristocratic country residences meant that it was something of a summer resort as well. 1765 saw the opening of the Royal Theatre off the village green for summer performances with London performers. There were also some grand houses, including a retreat for David Garrick the actor and similar mansions including the country residence of the Duke of Buccleuch and 'The Ivy' owned by the Hobart family, whose head was the Earl of Buckinghamshire. On the other side of the river was Twickenham and slightly further east the market town of Uxbridge.

In the early 1770s, proposals to build a bridge to replace the ferry across the Thames from Richmond to Twickenham began to coalesce.[1] The ferry concessionaire proposed a substantially wooden bridge which was disliked by members of the community. A local organizing meeting was held in November of 1772.[2] The movement was boosted by reports in February 1773 that the King was interested in the scheme, to the

[1] *Public Advertiser*, February 28th, 1772.
[2] *Daily Advertiser*, November 20th, 1772.

K. McKeever, *The Role of Tontines, 1750–1800*, Palgrave Studies in the History of Finance, https://doi.org/10.1007/978-3-032-12849-2_3

point of specifying which street should be the connection to the proposed bridge.[3] The choice of the appropriate street was contentious, as it dictated where the bridge would meet the land on the Twickenham shore. That land was owned by the Duchess of Newcastle and managed by her co-trustees, including Lord Frederick Cavendish and they wanted to avoid laying a new road across the property.

A petition to construct a bridge was submitted to Parliament in early February 1773.[4]

It was reviewed via the standard committee process supervised by Sir Francis Vincent, MP for Surrey.[5] A Richmond merchant, William Stallard, testified as to the awkwardness of the approach to the ferry, and how low water made the ferry unusable, necessitating rerouting wagons substantial distances. The ferry concessionaire was heard in his plea to be compensated if the bridge plan went forward.[6] A local 'nimby' objection to the new bridge blocking an established footpath was also raised at the time.[7]

In 1774, a private bill[8] was enacted, similar to the contemporary Turnpike creation acts, authorizing the construction of the bridge supervised by a commission. The Commission consisted of over eighty people, but its awkward size was tempered by having small quorum requirements to act—five members to take a decision, eleven to authorize any borrowing, and nine to supervise investment of accumulated funds. Thus, everyone who claimed an interest had a voice, but only those who were really dedicated to the project would bother with full participation. The size is not unusual. For comparison purposes, in 1772, the Commission to implement "An Act for paving, lighting, cleansing, watering and watching the streets…within…the Parish of St. Pancras," in Middlesex consisted of seventy-five trustees.[9]

While the Act did outline the toll charges, it did not specify a means of financing the project. The initial post-act meeting of the Commissioners on August 5th, 1773, agreed on the rough design of the bridge after the

[3] *Public Advertiser,* March 23rd, 1773.

[4] *Daily Advertiser*, February 3rd, 1773.

[5] *Journal of the House of Commons*, March 2nd, 1773, page 162.

[6] *London Chronicle,* May 22nd, 1773.

[7] *Public Advertiser*, April 27th, 1773.

[8] 13 George III, Chapter 83 (1773).

[9] 12 George III, Chapter 69 (1772).

noted architect, James Paine,[10] had presented a number of alternatives distinguished primarily by the number of arches in the span. The initial discussions also proposed loans modeled on the system used for turnpikes[11]; bonds paying interest derived from the income of the bridge's tolls.[12] These presumably would have had an interest rate slightly higher than the standard Three Percent Government Annuities, but the idea was not followed up. There were reports of substantial offers in this process from David Garrick and an unnamed 'widow in Isleworth,'[13] but the potential subscriptions only amounted to half the projected cost. The failure of the initial proposal may have been due to the scheme being developed in the shadow of the major credit scare of 1772.

In any case, a decision was taken to create a tontine share structure, the first for a project in London. A copy of the Tontine Proposal is held at the Museum of Richmond in London, who have made an image of it available on the web.[14] The shares were to pay an interest rate of four percent, but the payment would increase as the fellow shareholders died. There was no absolute ownership or 'pot of gold' at the end. The bridge would be transferred to municipal ownership with the death of the last shareholder. One of the attractions of this form of financing was that the capital raised did not have to be returned to the shareholders at some point, as was the case with the standard municipal bonding process. The interest was paid from the income of the bridge tolls.

Two hundred shares of £100 each were sold for a total of £20,000. The statute had authorized a sum of £25,000 as a maximum. The initial brokers were Robert Withy of Baker's Coffee House and Francis Watkins. The offering was sold out by May 1774 without significant newspaper advertising. The shares were transferable, and one was offered for resale

[10] Paine's Dictionary of National Biography entry: https://www.oxforddnb.com/search?q=james+paine&searchBtn=Search&isQuickSearch=true.

[11] A good summary of that process can be found in Bogart, Dan, *The Turnpike Roads of England and Wales,* https://www.campop.geog.cam.ac.uk/research/projects/transport/onlineatlas/britishturnpiketrusts.pdf, Section Three: Turnpike Acts.

[12] *London Gazette*, August 7–10, 1773.

[13] *Daily Advertiser*, August 30th, 1773.

[14] The museum is in the process of digitizing its collections. In the meantime the image can be found at https://commons.wikimedia.org/wiki/File:Richmond_Bridge_tontine_proposals,_1774,_Museum_of_Richmond,_London.jpg.

almost immediately, in June of 1774. Auction advertisements show a small aftermarket existed for the shares throughout the existence of the tontine.

As was typical for securities in that era, payment was made in installments, in this case spread out over a couple of years. The initial payment was £10/0/0, and an irregular schedule of payments concluded with the last £12/10/0 due in September 1776. Advertisements as to payment deadlines were published as each date approached. Nominees had to be named when the payment accumulation reached fifty percent.

The bridge was designed, and the construction was supervised, by James Paine, one of the most important architects of the period and an official in the Royal Office of Works, assisted by a colleague, Kenton Couse. The primary contractor was a London builder, Thomas Kerr or Carr. The first stone was laid in August 1774 by Sir Henry Hobart who had been very active in its promotion and construction.[15] The thirteen-year-old Prince of Wales was scheduled to do the honors, but he did not, perhaps an early hint at his lifelong fecklessness. Hobart later served in Parliament from 1786 to 1799. He was the third son of the Earl of Buckinghamshire, and his mother, nee Elizabeth Bristow, had an estate in Richmond.

The project was managed from the Richmond side of the bridge. The Clerk of the Commissioners, Clement Smith, a solicitor, was also the vestry clerk of Richmond town and parish. The bankers were Coutts. The original ferryman was compensated, and Sir Henry Hobart was granted the ferry concession to hold in trust for the Commission. They ran a temporary ferry during the construction process. The grant of that concession included free passage for the Royal family over the bridge. In 1776, it was realized additional capital was needed, so a second tontine offering was made of an additional fifty shares at £100 each for a total of 250 shares.[16]

Richmond Bridge was completed in 1777, with the King first crossing it in January, before it was opened. Carriages were permitted by March 1777. It was immediately appreciated for its simple and graceful beauty.

[15] *London Chronicle*, August 25th, 1774.

[16] A preliminary notice for the second tranche was incorporated into an advertisement for the demolition of two houses to be eliminated in widening the road approaching the bridge. *Daily Advertiser*, October 1776.

One contemporary report stated it was 'one of the most beautiful ornaments of the river and the country adjacent'.[17] It has been the subject of numerous works of art, a major symbol of the Georgian aesthetic. Hodges depicted it under construction as shown in Fig. 3.1.

Fig. 3.1 The bridge was depicted by William Hodges while under construction

As it approached completion, the management placed newspaper advertisements suggesting merchants use it in transporting goods from the west of London into the center. It was claimed the route was both more direct and the roads along the route were in better condition than the traditional route north of the river.

The financial administration was fairly straightforward. Dividends were paid every April and October and were started even as the bridge was being completed. The interest paid in October 1777 was £2/0/7, a fraction above four percent. An auction flyer from 1833 for one of the original shares stated the dividend had increased to £14/0/0 annually

[17] 48 *London Magazine* 417 (1779).

for the fifty-five remaining shareholders. A similar newspaper advertisement in 1852 indicated four nominee/shareholders were still alive, each receiving £200 a year.

The Richmond Library holds two pamphlets published in 1829 and 1843 recording the names of the nominees who were still alive. In 1829, this encompassed 116 shares based on the 114 nominees of the first tontine who were still alive, and twenty shares based on nineteen lives in the second. The figures for September 1842 are twenty shares based on nineteen survivors from the first and five in the second.

The two tontines were not merged but were treated as separate financial entities. This accurately implemented the investors' understanding of their situation; their chances were tied only to the lives of the pool of nominees named in each instrument. Per *Richmond and its inhabitants from the olden times:*

> The surviving nominee of the first tontine died March 3rd, 1859, at the age of eighty-six, having for the last five and a half years of her life received the sum of £800 per annum. The latest survivor on the second tontine died in August, 1865, aged ninety-one years, having received for the last nine years of his life the yearly income of £200.

The Commission husbanded its income effectively in the subsequent years, investing its surplus income in Consols. It was estimated in 1854 that the income from the Consuls was enough to provide for the maintenance of the bridge in the future when the tolls could be eliminated.

Enabling Act: 13 George III, Chapter 83

The eighty-three Commissioners named in the statute included a mix of Richmond locals, miscellaneous members of Parliament, and other parties, some of whom clearly had an interest. They included David Garrick, the Actor/Impresario; Daniel Giles, a Director of the Bank of England; James Rees, Mayor of Richmond; Edward Collins, a Richmond brewer and landowner; James Crokatt, a leading London and South Carolina merchant, whose daughter's family lived in Richmond; William Stallard, who had testified in the committee proceedings; William Adler, a local builder; three Cavendish brothers representing Twickenham interests; and the Hobart brothers, George and Henry. George later became the Earl of Buckinghamshire. James Paine, who was the architect of the bridge, was a commissioner, as was Kenton Couse, a colleague of Paine's at the Board of Works, and the Landscape architect, Launcelot 'Capability' Brown. Some had connections on multiple levels: the Commissioner John Boddington was not only the owner of a mansion in Richmond, but a high official in the Board of Ordinance and thus experienced in the realm of government contracting.

Twelve of the Commissioners bought shares in the Richmond Bridge Tontine.

Shareholders and Nominees

One hundred forty-four shareholders bought a total of 250 shares in the combined first and second tontines. They are named in the pamphlet *A list of the subscribers and their nominees in the Richmond Bridge Tontine.*[18]

The only location provided in the list is that of the nominees, whose home parish is listed. The parish was important because the minister or churchwardens of each nominee's parish had to certify the continued life of the nominee before the shareholders could receive their dividends. Richmond and Twickenham show up as the homes of many of the nominees. The various parishes of London, Westminster, and Middlesex provide the bulk of the rest. However, some were further from London. including Bedfordshire, Chester, Hampshire, Kent, Norfolk, Nottingham, Somerset, Suffolk, Surrey, Sussex, Wiltshire, two from Ireland and one from Paris. One family group included a son up at Jesus College, Oxford, and James Paine's son was studying in Rome at the time.

Three shareholders named the Prince of Wales as the dependent life, and one selected Frederick, Bishop of Osnaburgh, the second son of George III, as the nominee. The choice of public figures in a tontine nomination had two likely benefits. The rigmarole of having to provide proof of continued life would not be necessary, as the public figure's status would be common knowledge. Secondarily, there may have been a gamble that the health care for a prince would be better than that for the average citizen. Both boys lived into the 1820s.

[18] London: H. Reynell, Printer to the Commission, 1777.

The listing also indicated the familial relationship between the shareholder and the nominee if there was one. Most of the multiple shareholder groups were familial. For example, the largest shareholder was James Crokatt, who bought one share each in the names of his eight grandchildren.[19] In many cases, the nominee received ownership of the tontine share as a legacy on the death of the original purchaser.

Twenty-nine of the 144 subscribers were women.

Financial Context of these Shares

The subscribers were people who could afford to invest a minimum of £100 in 1774. Using the very conservative Retail Price Index, this is the rough equivalent of £15,000 in 2022.

It is likely that for the local shareholder who could afford it, the primary motivation for purchasing the tontine shares was participating in local civic improvement. The bridge was seen as an economic boon for the community. However, there were plenty of shareholders who did not have a direct interest in the community.

The four percent interest rate was standard for turnpike bonds at the time and was a point higher than the nominal rate for the most widely held government fund, the three percent consolidated annuities, or 'Consols.' The Consols traded around £88 in May of 1774, so the real interest rate was roughly 3.4%, still lower than the tontine share. Also, the banking Panic of 1772 may have made people wary of government securities.

There were no decent savings alternatives at the time. A fad for annuities companies the previous decade had fizzled out with most of the new commercial annuity companies failing due to poor underlying mathematics. Savings banks did not exist yet and life insurance had not yet become widespread. Tontines at the time were also seen as an intergenerational support tool, as most nominees were children or grandchildren of the shareholders.

Three aspects of the overall investor pool reflect the role of the tontine share as a serious investment: one was the purchase of multiple shares and another was how many of the investors bought into other tontine schemes. The third was the large number of subscribers with sophisticated financial backgrounds.

[19] Crokatt was a very rich trans-Atlantic Merchant. For a period in the mid-1700s he was the agent for the Province of South Carolina in London.

Significant Subscribers

George Bristow became a Director of the South Sea Company; Josiah Brown, a barrister, was a Director of the Equitable Assurance Company; William Curtis was an MP and London Alderman and a Commissioner for the issuing of Exchequer Bills; Duncan Dallas was a Sworn Broker, which was an elite financial group; Richard Gravatt was a Fleet Street banker; Jerome Knapp, barrister and judge, was the Treasurer of Middle Temple; William Leeves was one of the Lottery managers; William Plumley a watchmaker and silversmith was a projector of the Rational Annuity Society, a 1771 annuity scheme that seems to have lasted about six months; Sarah Roads was the daughter and sister of officials in the East India Company's London operations; Daniel Stump was a sworn broker and lottery ticket seller; Benjamin Tebbs, goldsmith, was later elected Sheriff of London, and G. Woodward Vane was a Director of the Million Bank.

Others had court and government connections: John Boddington ultimately became the Secretary of the Board of Ordinance; Kenton Couse and Thomas Fülling worked along with James Paine at the Board of Works; Catherine Dashwood was 'bed chamber woman' to the Queen; Gideon Dare was a tinplate manufacturer with the Royal Warrant; James Evelyn had been an MP and was an active magistrate; Samuel Firmin was a button manufacturer with many government contracts; Thomas Handley worked in the Six Clerks Office in the Chancery; Charles Hawkins was later surgeon to 'His Majesty's Household' and involved in the treatment of George III's mental health problems; the Hobart brothers were politically engaged aristocrats; Isaac Mark was a server in the Great Chamber of the Lord Chamberlain's Office; John Mitford was Clerk of the Inrolments in the Court of Chancery; the Third Earl Poulett was a member of the House of Lords; Alexander Stiell had several roles in the household of the Duke of Gloucester; and Henry Wheelwright was Second Clerk of the Kitchen in the royal household.

Subscriber Participation in Other Tontines

Lewis Robert Allen nominated himself in the Richmond Bridge Tontine and a daughter Susanna in the First Class of the National Tontine of 1789.

John Beckford, a natural son of William Beckford, one time Lord Mayor of London, was a £300 subscriber to the Irish Tontine of 1773.

Edward Collins, the local brewer, bought three shares nominating his three children. He also held one share in the Earl of Cork's Tontine (1789) in the name of his son.

Samuel Firmin, a button manufacturer who supplied the military, took one share each for his five children, two boys and three girls. In the Irish Tontine of 1775, he bought three £200 shares, nominating his three daughters.

Lady Fludyer, the widow of Sir Samuel Fludyer, also once Lord Mayor of London, bought one share nominating her son, George. He was also nominated for an investment of £1000 in the Irish Tontine of 1773, an unusually large investment. Sir Samuel, a silk merchant, was one of the richest men in London at his death in 1768.

Henry Frances nominated his son, also Henry, for the Richmond Bridge share. The son was also a nominee in Irish Tontine of 1777.

Richard Heaviside, a wealthy timber merchant, nominated his son, also Richard. He earlier nominated his daughter, Susannah, to the Society for Annuities Encreasing to the Survivors, Third Class.

Henry Hobart also nominated one of his daughters, Maria-Ann, in the Irish Tontine of 1777.

Henry Malpas, a haberdasher who was appointed as one of two 'Meal-weighers' in London for more than fifteen years, bought two shares in his own name and one share in the National Tontine of 1789 in the name of his wife.

Miles Poole Penfield, who appears to have invested in the Richmond Bridge Tontine in his own name, was also a nominee in the Irish Tontine of 1777. His brothers, Thomas and John Wornham, were nominees in the Society for Annuities Encreasing to the Survivors, Third Class.

Abraham Prado, a resident of Twickenham and a bread and forage supplier to the British Army, held three shares in the Richmond Bridge Tontine and was a £500 subscriber to both the Irish Tontines of 1773 and 1775 in the name of his son Samuel. He also left a share in the tontine known as Society for Annuities Encreasing to the Survivors to his wife via his will.

Alexander Stiell, House Steward and Clerk of the Stables to the Duke of Gloucester, held one share of the Richmond Bridge Tontine in the name of his daughter. She was also the beneficiary of a share in the Society for Annuities Encreasing to the Survivors.

Shareholders with Multiple Shares

Some of the multiple share purchases can be traced back to the number of children named as nominees. There are many two or three share purchases, almost invariably family situations. The Crokett example given above was the largest. Benjamin S. Bradbury, a haberdasher with a shop in Covent Garden, bought one share each in the name of his seven children. Others were more complicated. John Boddington nominated his wife for two shares, his daughter for one, and two sisters-in-law for one each. The brother and sister Jerome and Rebecca Knapp bought seven shares between them. Jerome nominated his children, and Rebecca nominated two sons of George Wakefield, the Richmond parish priest. George Wakefield himself bought two shares nominating two other sons.

The saddest story is that of Thomas Nettlesford, nominee of his father, a landowner in Twickenham. In 1835, he was found dead, a presumed suicide, in the Thames near Hampton. The report of his death included details of an inheritance of £30,000, constant racecourse gambling, and finally working as a racecourse tout and living in a workhouse.

The Primary Broker

The advertising of one of the designated brokers, Robert Withy, shows he had a business based in Baker's Coffee House, Exchange Alley, where he bought and sold "by Commission Estates, Mortgages, Life Annuities, Reversions, and all Kinds of Government and other Securities, also the same valued, and Lives insured, on the most reasonable Terms." He was a sworn stockbroker and a member of the Stationer's Company. While he was not a founder of the Laudable Society for the Benefit of Widows, established in 1761 in March of 1774, he served as Chairman of a group fighting a petition to Parliament to dissolve the Society, which had been in trouble at least since 1772. That fight succeeded, as the Society lasted to at least 1795.

Mr. Withy also appeared as the broker of another tontine scheme. In June 1774, the first of a number of advertisements appeared for a tontine based on 'the funds' comparing itself to the Richmond Bridge and Irish Tontines. It was to have three classes of £10,000 each, aged one to thirty, thirty to fifty, and fifty and above, with the capital devolving to the last five survivors among the nominees in each class. There are no further traces of this scheme besides the newspaper advertisements of the proposal.

Aftermarket Information

Robert Withy advertised a single share of the Tontine for sale in June 1774. It is not clear if this was a remaining undistributed share or the first aftermarket sale. In September, he then posted a very unusual advertisement looking to 'purchase a few shares' in the Tontine. A purchase advertisement was very rare and may be unique.

When shares for the Richmond Bridge Tontine were later offered at auction, the advertisements sometimes included the current interest being paid. In 1794, it was £4/15/10 annually. In 1796, it was £4/15/0. In 1802, one confusingly worded advertisement listed the income as £11/14/0, but since it indicated the share depended on two lives, which was impossible, it was likely half that, i.e., £5/17/0. An ad from 1833 indicates dividend had reached fourteen percent per annum. A similar advertisement in 1852 indicated four tontineers were still alive, each receiving £200 a year.

Administration of the Tontine

Keeping track of the owners and nominees was a complicated task. Shareholders lost their rights if the dividends were not claimed by a certain time. The management was very careful to make sure before declaring a person divested of their rights since it affected both the payments to the shareholder and the pool of survivors. Examples of the ads included notices attempting to trace John Lucas and Elizabeth Jane Finlason in 1828, and William Walter Vane in 1838.

The Commission existed for the duration of the tontine. They were the ones who decided to cancel the tolls after the death of the last shareholder in 1859. There had been pressure beforehand to eliminate the tolls on all the London Bridges, provoking a Parliamentary Select Committee review in 1854. The removal of the toll barriers on March 25th, 1859, was a ceremonial public event, with much speechifying and cheering.

Fig 3.2 Richmond Bridge by Gordon Home

Richmond Bridge as depicted in Fig. 3.2 has served its purpose ever since 1777. The only significant change was a widening executed in late 1930s into the 1940s. The engineers of that project were diligent in preserving the original design in the process, so it looks today much as it did 245 years ago.

CHAPTER 4

The Society for Annuities Encreasing to the Survivors

On August 25th, 1759, an advertisement in the *London Chronicle* announced a new broker looking to buy 'Annuities for the seller's lives' and reversions. Interested parties were directed to seek out a Mr. Siprut at his office in 'Freeman's Court, opposite to the Rainbow Coffee House in Cornhill.'

Ads of this sort were relatively common in the newspapers of the time. This was a regular business. The process provided ready money for people whose assets were tied up in property that would only provide payment in the future. For example, if a widow were left a portfolio of annuities which would pass to her son on her death, the son could sell his rights to those annuities to a broker for a discounted amount in immediate cash, rather than waiting for his mother to die. Reversion was the generic term for these expectations, which covered real property as well as financial instruments.

In 1763, Jacob Siprut moved his activities to the Carolina Coffee House. This too was relatively common. A businessman would pay a small annual subscription, often just one pound, and he would have a place to be contacted, hold meetings, and receive mail.[1] Between 1759 and 1771,

[1] See the introduction to *Joshua Johnson's Letterbook, 1771–1774*, London Record Society, #15, 1979, at footnote 30.

K. McKeever, *The Role of Tontines, 1750–1800*, Palgrave Studies in the History of Finance, https://doi.org/10.1007/978-3-032-12849-2_4

at least 500 Siprut ads appear in the London papers. This coffee house was his working location for the rest of his life.

On April 1st, 1768, this advertisement announcing a new scheme appeared in *Lloyd's Evening Post*:

> ANNUITIES for Joint Lives and Survivorships
> SUBSCRIPTIONS are now open at the CAROLINA Coffee-house, no.25, in Birchin-lane, Cornhill for raising the sum of £50,000 on joint Lives and Survivorships by Way of Annuities of Three percent Capital Stock, in five different Classes of £10,000 each, every Class consisting of One Hundred Shares of £100 each whereby every Annuitant, from an infant of one year old to a person of fifty becomes intitled to an equal Chance of the Benefit arising herefrom, in Proportion to such Annuitant's Life.

The advertisement then goes on for seven paragraphs. Following French revenue models, the five classes are defined by ages: one year to ten, ten to twenty, twenty to thirty, thirty to forty, and forty to fifty. A deposit of ten percent is required to be deposited with "Sir George Amyand, Staples, and Co. Bankers, at No. 50, Cornhill. Subscribers are limited to two shares per person."

A Trust was to be created, and trustees named. The capital stock was to be deposited in Chancery and the dividends were to be paid every six months at the Bank of England. If an Annuitant shall die within a dividend period, the guardian, heir, or executor shall be entitled to the whole six months dividend:

> That on the Demise of any of the Annuitants the Interest arising from the said Capital be divided among the survivors of each Class, Share and Share alike until the number of Annuitants be reduced to five; in which case the whole Capital to be sold out or transferred by the Trustee or Chancery, and to be divided among the Survivors in equal shares. --- So that besides the great Increase of Interest each Annuitant may be intitled to by the Demise of the others, the last five Survivors of each Class will become also intitled to upwards of £2000 Capital Stock of Three percent for their own Shares.

The final paragraph indicated that Mr. Siprut was available from 11 AM through 2 PM at the Carolina Coffee House. It concluded with a line indicating he would continue to be available for other 'Money Business, for the Nobility and others, intitled to Incomes for Life, Reversions, &c.'

Without actually using the word, Jacob Siprut had created a tontine.

Formal Creation

Per the 1769 *deed of settlement*,[2] there were to be six classes within the Tontine. These were allotted to nominees aged one to ten, ten to twenty, twenty to thirty, thirty to forty, forty to fifty, and fifty to 'the extremity of life.' The original proposal had just five classes, but an additional class encompassing the oldest group was added later. Shares cost £100, so the overall target was £50,000. Each class represented a separate pool of £10,000. The "last-five Survivors of every Class will become also intitled to upwards of £10,000 Capital Stock among themselves." The capital is to be invested in "Three percent consolidated annuities of the Bank of England or in some other Government-security…."

The First Class, the youngest group, filled out its allotted 'century' of 100 shareholders quickly, so a second century within the First Class was created. A second century for the Second Class was created later.

The Trustees were:

Roger Staples, Esq., a banker and Vice President of Equitable Assurance; Joseph Creswicke, Esq., a Director of the East India Company, 1765–1768; John Woodhouse Esq., also a Director of the East India Company in 1768 and for subsequent irregular terms, and a founding director of the Public Annuitant Society in 1771; and Hananel Mendes DaCosta, Esq., a Merchant based at No. 23 Mincing Lane.

An additional trustee, John Andrews Baker, Esq., was listed in some advertisements but was not listed in the deed of settlement. He died in October 1768.

Jacob Syprut was named the Secretary of the Tontine. The printed deed of settlement spells his name that way although all the advertising spelled it 'Siprut.' He was to be paid £20 a year per each century, although he had to put up a bond of £200 for each century as well.

The bankers were Sir George Amyand and Staples and Company. Sir George inherited his partnership from his father and passed it on to his brother, John, in 1774 when George took on the name (Cornewall) and

[2] *The deed of settlement of the Society for annuities encreasing to the survivors. Together with the declaration of trust to be entered into by the trustees for the same*, London: [The Society], 1768 (Gale database Eighteenth Century Collections Online).

estates of his wife's family. He later became a Member of Parliament.[3] The Staples partner in the bank is Roger, who also served as one of the Trustees. The bank later evolved into the larger private bank known as Staples, Baron Dimsdale, Son, and Company.

The deed of settlement included a Sixth Class although the early advertisements do not. The deed is dated May 22nd, 1769, although the date on the cover of the printed pamphlet of the deed is 1768. Later tontines of this kind tended to have a small fee associated with the initial investment to cover the costs of creating and executing the tontine. This Tontine does not.

The seat of the business was the Carolina Coffee House on one of the small streets adjacent to the Exchange Alley complex in Cornhill. This coffee house was known as one of the primary gathering places for brokers and other merchants doing business with the Southern American colonies. James Crokatt, a South Carolina connected merchant and a Commissioner and subscriber in the slightly later Richmond Bridge Tontine, listed this coffee house as his place of business. Another business operating out of the Carolina Coffee House was the wine and brandy merchant, A. G. Karr. The same street, Birchin Lane, was also the address of a number of private bankers of this period, as well as Mr. Clark's Annuity Office, at number ten.

Subscriptions for the first century came in swiftly. The *Stamford Mercury*[4] printed an equivalent of a modern press release in June 1769, reporting that £10,900 of three percent Consolidated Annuities had been purchased by the Society for Annuities Encreasing by Survivorship.

The first dividend, to the closed 'First Century' of the First Class, was paid in August 1769[5] even though not all of the classes had filled. An advertisement in July 1769[6] gave a count of the state of the rest of the subscription books. Eighty in the Second Class, seventy in the Third, sixty-nine in the Fourth, eighty-two in the Fifth, and fifteen in the Sixth Class.

[3] https://www.historyofparliamentonline.org/volume/1754-1790/member/cornewall-sir-george-1748-1819.

[4] June 29th, 1769.

[5] *Lloyd's Evening Post,* August 14th, 1769.

[6] *Gazetteer and New Daily Advertiser*, July 29th, 1769,

On February 22nd, 1770, the *Gazetteer and New Daily Advertiser* published a letter, perhaps paid for, commenting negatively on the recent arbitrary edict from Paris (issued on January 18th, 1770) converting French Government Tontine shares into simple life annuities. The letter describes tontines generally and concludes with praise of Siprut's Tontine in that the capital reverts to the final survivors and not the government and that the whole project is private, controlled by the trustees and not subject to the 'caprice of government.'

Per the March 3rd, 1770, issue of the *Gazetteer and New Daily Advertiser*, on March 8th a share in the First Class was to be offered at auction at Garraway's Coffee House, by the executors of Michaels Salomons. The nominee is not named in the advertisement.

After the relatively quick completion of the first century, filling the rest took some time. The Tontine was advertised quite heavily—over 100 times—through 1773.

Sadly, Siprut himself died on January 24th, 1771. A. G. Karr, the wine and brandy merchant whose business address was also the Carolina Coffee House, took over as Secretary.

A status report was advertised in May 1771[7] which showed the capital of the completed centuries to be £10,969/16/0 in the First Class and £12,280/12/2 in the Second Class. Note that that the £10,000 target for each century was technically exceeded in the first two classes completed. This was the result of the subscribers' contribution of £10,000 in each class being spent on Annuities that were selling below par.

In mid-June 1769, when the purchase of stocks for the First Class was announced, the Three Percent Consols were trading around £89–90. £10,000 would therefore purchase Annuities to the value of £10,900, as reported. The £12,280 in the Second Class was probably the result of £10,000 spent at a market price averaging roughly £81¼. In theory, the tontine members would be getting dividends based on £12,280, not £10,000, although records that could confirm this have not been located.

An advertisement from August 1771[8] indicated the number of subscribers was needed to complete the other classes. Five were needed in the Third Class, eight in the Fourth, and thirteen in the Fifth. The Sixth

[7] *London Evening Post*, May 2nd, 1771.

[8] *London Chronicle*, August 10th, 1771.

was not mentioned, although later advertisements still included it in their overall descriptions.

Advertising, focusing on the Third Class in particular, continued to appear. One from January 1773[9] included a short excerpt from the work of Dr. Richard Price. He was a member of the Royal Society who was a critic of the many fly-by-night annuity schemes of the period and extremely influential in developing mortality tables and implementing policies based on them.[10] It reads: "It is proper, I should add, in order to prevent mistakes, that the Society for Annuities Encreasing by Survivorship, goes on a Plan different from any I have considered, and the Nature of which implies Safety." The advertisement even cites the page number of the text quoted from Price's *The Supplement to the Doctrine on Annuities.*

It is notable that none of this advertising indicates an interest rate or dividend amount. Presumably, the initial rate could not be more than three percent, since that is how the capital was invested. While there would have been setting-up costs, it is possible that the difference between three percent on £10,000 worth of annuities and the actual amount accumulated in each class, for example the £10,969/16/0 in the First Class, covered these. If so, this meant the subscriber would get the full three percent generated by the underlying annuities.

Also in 1773, new trustees had to be elected.[11] Joseph Creswicke had died and Hananel Mendes DaCosta had announced his resignation. Six months later Mendes DaCosta was in bankruptcy proceedings. The two new trustees were Charles Gould, Esq., and Daniel Mildred. Mildred had served as one of the two auditors before that.

By October 1773, the Third Class had been fully subscribed and its capital of £11,629/10/0 invested in Old South Sea Annuities.[12] These paid the same interest rate, three percent, as the Consolidated Annuities and may have been the best price or the easiest to buy as a group when the decision was taken to capitalize the class.

It is uncertain whether any other classes or centuries were completed. A notice of a meeting in January 1774 indicated some centuries had yet to fill. It was aimed at the Fourth and Fifth Classes and the second centuries

[9] *Public Advertiser*, January 19th, 1773.

[10] *Dictionary of National Biography:* https://doi.org/10.1093/ref:odnb/22761.

[11] *Public Advertiser,* February 3rd 1773.

[12] *St James Chronicle*, October 19th, 1773.

of the First and Second Classes. The Sixth is not mentioned and may have been abandoned earlier. The agenda was to decide whether to go ahead with only fifty members in the classes or to return the subscribers' money. When the winding-up notices appeared, in 1827, 1838, and 1847, only the first three classes are traceable. Presumably, the others had been abandoned.

That was the last report having to do with the formation of the Society for Annuities Encreasing to the Survivors. The silence of the record can be taken as a positive sign as it indicates there were no public complaints or lawsuits.

General Administration

The Society next appears on the record in 1788 when a meeting is announced to select new trustees to replace Roger Staples and Daniel Mildred, both of whom had died. The location of the meeting, the Pennsylvania Coffee House, was either adjacent to the Carolina Coffee House on Birchin Lane or an extension of the Carolina Coffee House space. It is possible they are the same building at different points in its history. Karr may have been part of the coffee house management. A slightly earlier letter from Benjamin Franklin, then in London, to David Hall dated January 12th, 1765,[13] reads in part: "Mr. Karr of the Pennsylvania Coffee House desires you would send the Papers to him directed agreable to the enclos'd." Franklin was referring to newspapers from Philadelphia being delivered to London.

The aftermarket for Society's shares is found in auction advertisements in the years following the creation of a tontine. There are advertisements in 1776, 1784, 1788, 1796, 1801, 1803, and 1808. The notices rarely provided many details, but the 1796 announcement described the participants of the first century of the First Class as numbering between seventy and eighty. The 1801 notice was for a share in the first century of the Second Class stating there were 'about 70' shareholders, and indicated the interest was £4/11/0 at that point. The 1808 auction was the result of the failure of the Staples bank.

At some point, the business of the tontine had shifted to the Jerusalem Coffee House. A notice in *The Times*, on August 3rd, 1802, announced

[13] https://founders.archives.gov/documents/Franklin/01-12-02-0007.

a new Secretary, Samuel Hollingsworth, Karr's son-in-law, a stockbroker, and a new location, No. 2, Great St. Helen's, Bishopsgate Street, which was presumably his office.

In 1804, Hollingsworth, from a different location in Tokenhouse Yard, Lothbury, published a ten-page pamphlet entitled *A List of the Surviving Members of the Third Class of the Society for Annuities increasing* (sic) *to the Survivors...*[14] a copy of which is held in the Hertfordshire County Archives. The Third Class is the group that would have been between twenty and thirty years old in 1769, or born around 1750–1760. Of the 100 original members of the 'century,' 64 were still alive thirty-five years later. This is the only formal record of any of the participants that has been located.

Informally, shares can be traced through wills. An example is John Worham Penfold's will,[15] drafted in February, 1782, which reads: "I also give and bequeath to my sons Thomas Penfold, John Wornham Penfold, Darius Penfold, and Sarah Penfold my daughter one hundred pounds each now standing in their names paid in by me to the Society for Annuities encreasing to the Survivors." Thomas and John appear in the 1804 list, Sarah and Darius do not. The bequeathing of the shares to the nominees was standard behavior within tontines. However, many of the wills traced to the shareholders in the 1804 list make no mention of the Society.

The will of Abraham Prado,[16] who had invested in the Richmond Bridge Tontine and in the Irish Tontines, also revealed his ownership of a share of Siprut's Tontine, although the description is unusual in that it names the trustees, but not the Society:

> ...One hundred pounds on the life of Esther the daughter of Francis and Sarah Salvador in a subscription raised under the Direction of Roger Staples Joseph Cresswicke John Woodhouse and Hanamel Mendes daCosta...

Prado died in July 1782. The bequest of the tontine share was to his wife, not the nominee, who was his step-granddaughter. It is conceivable that the naming of the trustees and not the society was punctiliously legal in

[14] London: Printed by R and H Causton, 1804. Hertfordshire County Archive Reference Number 14994.

[15] UK National Archive, PROB-11-1128-306.

[16] UK National Archive, PROB-11-1094-221.

that technically the trustees 'owned' the capital property of the Society, since it was created by a deed of settlement and not via incorporation.

A third will shows how administering a tontine could be a headache. Joanna Kellow, a 'Spinster' of Maker, in Cornwall:

> …Also, I give and bequeath to my said niece Joanna Kellow the Principal or Capital sum of one hundred pounds which I have sometime since subscribed upon her Life a certain Stock or Fund of a Society known or distinguished by the name of the Society for Annuities increasing to the Survivors together with all interest that shall arise or grow due for the same and all benefit advantage or increase that may happen arise or be made by survivorship or otherwise howsoever…

The initial subscriber and the nominee/legatee had the same name.[17]

Final Distributions

The Society was wound down class-by-class when each class was reduced to ten members, not the five as originally proposed in the deed of settlement. Legal notices were printed when a given class was reduced to ten members. The Third Class (twenty to thirty year-olds) was wound up in 1827,[18] the Second Class (ten to twenty year-olds) in 1838.[19]

The first century of the First Class (one to ten years old in 1769) lasted until August 1847.[20] The initial winding-up step was an announcement in *The Morning Chronicle* and *The London Gazette,* a journal whose purpose was to print government and legal notices and advertising. The actual distribution was to take place a year later after a series of notices were published to make sure there were no lingering claimants. The amount distributed was not stated, but it should have been slightly more than one thousand pounds for each survivor.

This is roughly what £100 a year compounded at three percent for seventy-seven years would produce. Note that that figure does not take into account the annual dividends. As an estimate of inflation over that

[17] Nat'l Archives, PROB 11/1126/270.

[18] *London Gazette,* June 29th, 1827.

[19] *London Gazette,* November 13th, 1838.

[20] *London Gazette,* August 6th, 1847: *Morning Chronicle*, July 2nd, 1847.

time period according to the conservative retail price index, something that cost £100 in 1770 would cost slightly more than £150 in 1847.

The Personnel

The 'projector' or founder of the Society was Jacob Siprut de Gabay. The family name 'de Gabay' was never used in everyday business, only on official documents. 'Siprut' was sometimes spelled 'Syprut.' He was born in Amsterdam in 1731. His family was listed in the Amsterdam records as Portuguese-Jewish. This community was formed by refugees from the Catholic Inquisition. The extended family was an important one in the London Jewish community as well. Jacob Siprut was the future Prime Minister Benjamin Disraeli's grand-uncle.

There were other family members acting as merchants in London by 1745. Once Jacob appeared, he initially made a living in the financial world, buying and selling Annuities, Reversions, and the like from a succession of locations in Freeman's Court and Michael's Alley, in both the Cornhill and Exchange Alley area. In 1763, he moved to the Carolina Coffee House on Birchin Lane in the same area which is the location given in most of his advertising. Between 1759 and 1771, at least 500 Siprut ads appear in the London papers with some of the texts combining Siprut's regular business with text focusing on the Society for Annuities Encreasing to the Survivors offering.

Siprut's name appears as a prisoner for debt in *The London Gazette* of August 22nd and *Public Ledger* of November 26th, 1761. The compelling creditor was a John Wade and the prison was the Fleet Gaol. This is probably misleading as to Siprut's true financial condition. The Insolvency Act of 1761 included a 'Compulsive Clause' that contained a loophole enabling quick movers to go through a sham demand from a friendly creditor that had the effect of wiping out their debts. The clause was repealed a year later. Siprut is likely to have been taking advantage of this unusual opportunity.

In 1765, Siprut approached the 'Court' (Board) of the relatively new Equitable Assurance Company to ask if they would be willing to pay him a commission if he sold their life insurance policies. They decided no.[21] However, two of Siprut's trustees for the Society for Annuities

[21] Ogborn, M. E., *Equitable Assurances*, Abingdon: Routledge, 1962, reprinted 2003, Page 58.

Encreasing to the Survivors were directors of Equitable, Messrs. Staples, and Woodhouse. Siprut died around January 24th, 1771.

The Original Trustees

Roger Staples was a partner in the bank that served as the Society's bank. He was also a founding Director and Trustee of the Society for Equitable Assurances on Lives and Survivorships in 1762. It was the first mutual insurer. He was an 'Assistant Governor' of the Mines Royal and Mineral and Battery Works, which was the equivalent of being a member of the Board of Directors. He died in 1778.

Joseph Creswicke was a Director of the East India Company 1765–1768 and had a position in the Receiver-General's office at the Customs House.

John Woodhouse was later elected one of the Directors of the East India Company as well as being a Director at the Equitable Assurance Company.

Hananel Mendes DaCosta was a merchant whose business included tobacco import/export. He also served as a Steward of the Hospitals for Small Pox and Inoculation. He acted a number of times as an intermediary between the merchant community and the Admiralty on convoy preparation matters during the American Revolution. A bankruptcy notice for him appeared in *The London Gazette* for June 12th, 1773.

John Andrews Baker died in his chambers at Gray's Inn in October 1768 as the Society was still in formation. He owned an estate in Penn, Buckinghamshire. He had been plain John Andrews, but after inheriting the Baker family estate as a surviving nephew, the King authorized the addition of Baker in 1767.

Later Trustees

Daniel Mildred was from a Bristol Quaker family and was a partner in Masterman, Peters, Mildred, and Masterman, Co., bankers. He was also a ship owner. He served as Vice President of the General Dispensary. Originally, one of the Auditors of the Society for Annuities Encreasing to the Survivors, he was elected a trustee in February 1773. He died in February 1788.

Sir Charles Gould was also elected as a replacement in 1773. He was the President of Equitable Assurance Company (of which Woodhouse and

Staples were on the board) from 1773 to his death. He was a Member of Parliament for Brecon (1778–1806) and the Judge-Advocate General in the Army. He became a Privy Councilor in 1802. He took the name Morgan ('with the King's permission') when his wealthy and landed brother-in-law died without issue. He died in 1806.

At least three additional trustees can be traced, although their times in office cannot.

Henry Thornton Esq., MP, came from a Russia and Baltic trading family, but shifted to banking, becoming a partner in Down, Thornton, and Free. Thornton was the Member of Parliament for Southwark from 1782 to 1815. He was a significant contributor to the development of economic theory during his lifetime, principally through a text, *An Enquiry into the Nature and Effects of the Paper Credit of Great Britain*, which blamed the economic problems of Great Britain on the expansion of paper credit and currency during the Napoleonic Wars. As an MP, he wrote an important committee report on returning to the gold standard, which in fact took place in 1821. He was an abolitionist, a cousin of William Wilberforce, and one of the founders of the Sierra Leone Company, established to create a place in Africa where enslaved people who had been freed could find a home.

Thomas Henry Hume, Esq., was a cleric and Treasurer of Salisbury Cathedral. William Masterman, Esq., was the son-in-law and banking partner of Daniel Mildred, above.

Others Connected with the Society

The bank known at the time as Sir George Amyand, Staples, and Co. managed the Society's funds. Amyand married into the Cornewall family and in 1771 the King authorized a name change to Cornewall (also sometimes spelled Cornwall) and he ultimately became Sir George Cornewall, Baronet, MP. He was also the nominee in a share of the Third Class of the Society. In 1804, the share was owned by the assignees of the widow of Roger Staples, Amyand's banking partner. He died in 1819 at the age of 71.

Arthur George Karr, Esq., the second secretary of the Society, appears in a 1786 directory as a Wine and Brandy Merchant whose business address was the Carolina Coffee House. He died in 1802 with his will[22] indicating at that point his business address was the Jerusalem Coffee House. The will specifies his shares in the tontine are to be given to his wife, Martha. He was successful enough to also leave her two thousand pounds in the stock of the East India Company as well as a house in Highbury Grove. Martha's shares, in which she was also the nominee, are on the 1804 list.

Karr's will also mentions benefits for his daughter, Martha Elizabeth, and her husband, Samuel Hollingsworth. Hollingsworth also took over as Secretary to the Society, and he is the one who published the 1804 list.

Subscribers and Nominees

The only vaguely formal record of any of the participants in the tontine is the 1804 pamphlet, *A List of the Surviving Members of the Third Class of the Society for Annuities increasing (*sic*) to the Survivors.* It is unusual as it lists both the current shareholder, nominee, and their residences, as well as providing a separate short list of the names of the nominees who have died. Since the other classes are not represented, this shows only a third of the subscribers.

While most of the subscribers were from London and surrounding counties, in the Third Class there were participants from Canterbury, Bath, Nottingham, Maker in Cornwall, Barrowley, near Grantham in Lincolnshire, and Oldham, Lancashire.

Participants and Their Connections Who also Held Shares in Other Tontines

John Bridges, Esq., of Charter-house Square is also listed as the nominee for shares numbered 59, 60, and 79 of the 1789 English Tontine.

Sarah Halsey, nee Crawley, was also a nominee for five shares numbered 44–48 of the Third Class of the 1789 English Tontine.

Charles Blicke is in the list of survivors of the Second Class of 1777 Irish Tontine in 1810 published by Parliament as part of a review of the administration of the Irish Tontines. The listing reads 'Charles Blicke

[22] UK National Archives PROB-11-1374-204.

surgeon – (33) – parish of Allhallows Staining in the city of London…' as a £100 shareholder.

Elizabeth Godin, 'Widow, Daughter of Henry Lond, Gent., late of Holborn' is shown as a holder of two shares in her own name in the pamphlet. The list of survivors of the Second Class of 1777 Irish Tontine in 1810 shows a £100 share nominee as: 'Elizabeth Godin–(34)–parish of St George Bloomsbury Middlesex…eldest daughter of Henry Long….' Presumably, the pamphlet's spelling is a typo.

Richard Heaviside, a wealthy timber merchant, nominated his daughter Susannah. He nominated his son, Richard, in the Richmond Bridge Tontine.

William Taylor Money aged ten and his brother James Money aged seven appear as surviving £100 nominees of the Third Class of the 1777 Irish Tontine. Their mother, Martha Money, of St. Andrew, Holborn, was a shareholder in the Society for Annuities Encreasing to the Survivors.

Mrs. Ann Ommanney, a £200 Participant, is reported in the pamphlet as having died in 1801. The 1777 Irish Tontine Third Class nominees list includes "Ann Ommanney – (10) – parish of St Botolph Aldgate eldest daughter of Edward Ommanney of the said parish, merchant, by Anne his wife." She held £200. Edward Ommanney was a naval agent for, among others, Admiral Collingswood, second in command at Trafalgar. Advertisements for his office's distribution of prize money to crews regularly appeared in contemporary newspapers.

The Society annuitants, the Penfold brothers, Thomas and John Wornham, had a brother, Miles Poole Penfold, who was a nominee in the Richmond Bridge Tontine.

Mrs. Barbara Sherwin, sister of John Sherwin, Esq., appears twice in the list. The list is in alphabetical order but both of Sherwin's listings are out of that order. The first time is amid the 'Ds' and the nominee is a Robert Dennison of Nottingham, so it is likely that the share was originally purchased by someone named Dennison. Mrs. Barbara Sherwin also appears in the 'M' section of the list as a shareholder whose nominee was John Musters, Esq., of Colwick Hall, Nottinghamshire. In the list of surviving nominees of the First Class of the 1777 Irish Tontine, a £100 share is shown as owned by 'Barbara Sherwin spinster–(51)–Parish of St. Mary in the town of Nottingham; eldest daughter of John Sherwin of the same parish by Barbara his wife.' From the context of the list, the age given is the age of the participant at the time of the purchased, the late 1770s. Barbara Sherwin died in 1809, aged eighty.

Alexander Stiell first appears in the contemporary London Directories within the household of the Duke of Gloucester, the younger brother of King George the Third. In *The Court and city register, or, Gentleman's complete annual kalendar, for the year 1771*, he is one of the 'Pages of the Back Stairs' and the 'Clerk of the Stables.' By 1790, he had become 'House Steward and Clerk of the Stables.' In the early 1770s, Stiell invested in a number of tontines. In the name of his daughter Catherine, he purchased one share (number 91) in the Third Class of the Society for Annuities Encreasing to the Survivors. At roughly the same time, he bought one share (number 121) in the Richmond Bridge Tontine, nominating another daughter, Caroline, born c. 1769 as the life the share was based on.

Samuel Waring, Gent., was listed as a shareholder in the pamphlet. The nominee was his wife, Frances. He ran a brewery in Lambeth. In the list of survivors of the First Class of the 1777 Irish Tontine in 1810, a £100 share is shown as owned by "Samuel Waring, brewer–(40)–parish of Lambeth in the County of Surrey; first son of Joseph Waring late of the said parish, brewer, and Margaret his wife, both deceased." Frances Waring, aged twenty-seven, the nominee, is also shown as a surviving nominee for a £100 share in the Second Class of the 1777 Irish Tontine with the appropriate details of identity. A Samuel Waring, aged five, the only son of Samuel Waring, brewer of Lambeth, is listed as a £200 nominee in the 1777 Irish Tontine survivor list, Third Class. Samuel Waring, aged 51, son of Joseph and Margaret, deceased, but with an address of Kinghorne, Gloucestershire, is listed as nominee for share number twenty of the Fifth Class of the 1789 English Tontine.

This shows that roughly ten percent of the Third Century shareholders had other tontine investments in their financial portfolios.

Conclusion

The purely financial tontines can be seen as the ancestors of our mutual funds. The Society shareholders were investing in the standard securities of the period, but without the bother of having to pay attention to the market and going to the Bank for their dividend payments a couple of times a year. They were also protected against the volatility of the prices of the annuities, since the annuities paid their interest based on the par value of the stock, not the market price.

They received an additional benefit of an increase in their dividends as their co-adventurers died off. And for the ten percent of each 'century' who were the survivors, the final prize of £1000 was substantial. On the downside, it is likely the investors assumed the death rates would be faster than they were.

There are three main precedents for the Jacob Siprut's Tontine. The English government had tried to create a tontine within the budget loan of 1765, but it was disastrously undersubscribed. At the deadline, only thirty-seven people were reported to have signed up. The government substituted Three Percent Annuities of essentially the same price although the government did allow subscribers who wanted to stay with the tontine form to keep them. Only one hundred eighty shares were kept in the tontine.

At roughly the same time, starting in the 1760s, Great Britain went through a kind of bubble relating to annuities being provided by private companies designed for that purpose. Annuities themselves were an old business, issued by governments, sold by individuals, and provided by organizations to support their members in old age. What was relatively new was the creation of commercial companies whose purpose was to provide annuities. Virtually, all of them failed within a few years due to an inadequate understanding of the mathematics involved. While a tontine is not exactly an annuity company, a financial tontine had similar aims. The successful issuance and survival of Siprut's Tontine stands in stark contrast to most of the annuity companies of the time.

A third strand in the pre-history of Siprut's Tontine can be found in the Netherlands. Starting around 1670, Dutch merchants created tontine-like investment funds initially based in the stock of the Dutch East Indies Company (VOC). A share in these funds was cheaper than a share in the VOC itself. The generic name for them was *contracten van overleving* or 'contract for survival,' and were common enough to use pre-printed forms with blank spaces for specifics. At least 250 were created between 1670 and 1765.[23] A contract of this sort created in Groningen in 1763, featuring eleven classes and a pamphlet listing all the subscribers and nominees, is reproduced in Google Books. Given Siprut's background

[23] Wagenvoort, Hermann, *Tontines, een onderzoek naar de geschiedenis van de lijfrenten...*, Diss. Utrecht, 1961, pp 126 et seq. See also: K. Geert Rouwenhorst's *The Origins of Mutual Funds*, Yale School of Management—International Center for Finance, working paper 04-48.

and community, he would have been aware of these schemes. Siprut's offering was very similar to the Groningen example, but simpler.

The market for this private Tontine may have been particularly favorable, as the Government had developed a process for paying-off accumulated Annuities in the years after the end of the Seven Years' War. In the language of the time that meant 'money' was available. Filling the classes for older participants proved understandably difficult and abandoning them made sense. However, for the remaining three hundred subscribers and their nominees, the Society delivered what it promised, increasing dividends as time went on and a pot of gold for the lucky few.

CHAPTER 5

The Ipswich Universal Tontine

In the latter half of the 1780s, the annual discussion of the budget and loan for the coming year occasionally included suggestions for a nation-wide tontine instead of the usual annuity offerings. This culminated in a National Tontine in 1789 which is the subject of Chapter 8. In the penumbra of this process, suggestions appeared for local, private tontines that were purely financial, as opposed to supporting a specific project.[1]

These took two forms. One aimed for the richer investor, with shares priced around £100 each and tied to the lives of nominees. The other schemes aimed for a broader market, with small weekly contributions and dispersal of funds after a short term, usually five or seven years. The former model was best exemplified by tontines based in Ipswich and Doncaster.[2] The small-sum, short-term tontines are reviewed in Chapter 9. This chapter will focus on the Ipswich Universal Tontine of 1790.

The first advertisements for the Ipswich Universal Tontine appeared in the *Norfolk Chronicle* on March, 13th, 1790, and the London *General Evening Post* of April 3rd, 1790. In various forms, similar ads were published in papers in Ipswich, Chester, Leeds, Stamford, and additional

[1] Examples can be found in the *Northampton Mercury* of June 20th, 1789 and the *St James Chronicle* of June 30th, 1789.

[2] A full advertisement of the Doncaster Tontine can be found in the *London Packet* of October 29th–31st, 1788.

K. McKeever, *The Role of Tontines, 1750–1800*, Palgrave Studies in the History of Finance, https://doi.org/10.1007/978-3-032-12849-2_5

London papers through March 1793. Subscriptions closed March 25th, 1793, known at the time as 'Lady Day' and commonly used as a key date in legal settings.

The advertisements stated the scheme was created with the "Trust, Management and Direction of Sir John Rous, Sir Thomas Charles Bunbury, Sir Gerard William Vanneck, Sir Robert Harland, and Sir William Rowley, Baronets," and nineteen others in the County of Suffolk. In the language of the time these men were the 'projectors.'

This was a financial tontine as opposed to one supporting a construction project. The basic proposal had several steps. The subscriber paid a set amount and named themselves or another person, often a child, as the life during which dividends would be paid. The contributions of the subscribers would be used to create a capital fund by purchasing government debt, in the form of the standard annuities. The dividends paid by the annuities would be pooled and distributed to the subscribers each year during their lifetimes. As the pool of shareholders shrank due to the deaths of the nominees, the interest paid to each surviving beneficiary would increase. The capital would be distributed to the remaining shareholders when their numbers shrank to the point where each one would receive £1000.

To ensure a rough sense of fairness, the original French tontines had age class structures, so that each sub-pool consisted of people of like ages, usually in ten-year groupings. As tontines were adopted in England, some of the earliest followed this model. The Ipswich Tontine came up with an ingenious way to create a single pool—much easier to administer—by discounting the original subscriptions based on age. Only the shares with nominees aged five to twelve paid the full £100. There were fifteen bands, with nominees aged one and younger charged only £78 and those over sixty-seven were charged only £40 pounds. The dividend paid to these discounted subscribers was the full amount based on £100 a share.

It may seem strange that an older person would be the nominee or dependent life since their life expectancy would be comparatively short, but the actual interest paid for that band was close to ten percent a year. No other contemporary security paid anything near that. Six out of 511 nominees were in the classes that paid less than fifty percent to purchase under this scheme. However, the disproportionate dividend to share price ratio for that group may be a factor in the tontine interest payments remaining relatively flat for the first twenty years.

The advertisement specified that the money was to be invested in the Four Percent Consolidated Annuities. It did not specify an interest rate for the annual dividends. The shares were transferable, although the nominee had to remain the same. A common practice was for a shareholder to leave the share to the nominee, usually his or her own child, as a legacy.

The Deed of Trust[3] specified that Rous, Bunbury, Vanneck, Harland, and Rowley would be the Trustees. The other nineteen names listed in the advertisement would be the directors, and Emerson Cornwell would be the 'Actuary or Secretary.' The subscribers or shareholders were referred to as the proprietors.

The local bankers were the Ipswich firm of Alexander, Cornwell, Alexander, and Spooner.[4] London investors could have their interest payments made via the bank of Barnett, Hoare, Hill, and Barnett. The London broker was Thomas Ellis.

To deal with the initial administrative costs, there was an entry fee of £0/10/6. To nudge laggard subscribers, there were late fines, rising to £15 shortly before the deadline in May 1793. These fines did not go to the projectors. They were included in the dividend distribution for the first two years.

The actual legal form of the Ipswich Universal Tontine was a trust, with a small number of trustees holding the shares on behalf of the shareholders. The state of the law at the time made creating a company both difficult and expensive. The underlying Deed of Trust had already been drafted by the time the tontine was first advertised. The names of the attorneys who drafted the Deed of Trust were specified, as was a promise to enroll the Deed in the Court of Chancery as required by the Annuities Act of 1773. Copies of the full Deed were to be viewable at the Bank and at the office of the Clerk of the Peace for the County of Suffolk.

The lengthy advertisement ends with a single line "N.B. No Foreigner, resident Abroad, can be admitted." While this was likely to keep administration simple, it may also reflect the heavy participation of Swiss investors in the Irish Tontines of the 1770s.[5]

[3] Suffolk Archives Ref HD 827 1 1 3 3 1 1-3. The Shropshire Archives holds an abstract, Ref 484/506.

[4] Colloquially known as the 'Yellow' bank, due it being the Whig bank in Ipswich. Malster, Robert, *The Wharncliffe Companion to Ipswich*, Wharncliffe Books, 2005.

[5] Gautier, Charles, Un Investissement Genevois: La Tontine d'Irlande de 1777, 10 *Bulletin de la Société d'Histoire et d'Archéologie de Genève*, 53–68 (1951).

As promised in the advertising, the first dividend of £4/2/9 was announced July 1791.

The two key documents from creation process were the formal 'Deed of Trust' and 'The Abstract of the Deed of Trust for establishing a Universal Tontine…' which translates the very legalistic and formal Deed text into something much clearer for the layman. Both were printed for distribution to the participants and the Deed of Trust includes a notice of the acknowledgment on March 29th, 1792, before (Thomas Foster) Notcutt, an Ipswich solicitor acting as a Master Extraordinary of Chancery.[6]

In 1793, a list of participants was published. Note that this is a list of the nominees, not the purchasers. The list included a summary financial statement of the funding of the tontine. The Four Percent Annuities were bought in three batches in June 1791, 1792, and 1793. The first batch was bought fractionally below par, the second at four percent above par, and the third at seven percent below par. £66,575/11/7 was spent for a total of £68,000 in Four Percent Annuities. The final number of shares was 790, with 511 nominees.

The paper share receipts distributed to the participants were comparatively simple, modeled on the government annuity receipts. Earlier tontines tended to have large indentures drafted in the legalese of the period as the representation of share ownership.

The dividends of 1792 (£8/4/0) and 1793 (£8/2/0) were both artificially high, as they included the money paid in fines by late subscribers. A July 1794 letter in the Fletcher-Tooth collection of the University of Manchester Library[7] from Elizabeth Ritchie to Mary Fletcher mentions the effect of this 'bonus.'

> The Ipswich Tontine that last year yielded a dividend of £48/12/11 has sunk to £19/19. The organizers have written to say that 'it was the premium money which for two years raised it so high and that now it will only be increased by deaths.' This is a disappointment to me as the

[6] Useful files related to the Ipswich Universal Tontine are found in the Lincolnshire County Archives (Ref E34430-KJ, multiple administrative texts), the Shropshire Archive (Ref 484/506, Abstract of deed of trust), and the Suffolk County Archives (Ref. HD1656/1Triennial statement, HD 827/1/1/3/3/1 Deed of Trust).

[7] Item Reference number GB 133 MAM/FL/6/7/2.

end I had in sinking near £600 there was to increase my present income rather than with an eye to the future.

The subscriber list shows four shares bought by Elizabeth Ritchie in her own name. It also shows one share each bought in the name of two others in the household, likely a niece and a nephew, which explains the 'near £600' investment. Ritchie was a significant figure in the development of the Methodist Church and lived until 1835. She was also a nominee in the Third Class of the National Tontine of 1789, holding share number 57.

After that initial bump, dividends fell to £3/6/7 in 1794 and stayed below four percent until 1810.

This extended period of initial low returns reflects one of the underlying problems with tontines. Statistics as a subject was just developing and understood only by practitioners in the insurance and allied professions. The knowledge at that time of aggregate lifespans was flawed. Mortality tables were improving but were still inaccurate. The retail purchasers are likely to have anticipated a greater death rate than was realistic. This was especially true because of the number of children in the pool of nominees.

The first Secretary of the Ipswich Universal Tontine was Emerson Cornwell, one of the bank partners. He earned £0/3/6 per subscription per year through to his death in 1819. At the beginning of the Tontine, this would have brought in around £140 a year.

Dividends rose to above £5 in 1817, and £6 in 1823. The Tontine was then faced with a dilemma. The British Government decided to eliminate the Four Percent Annuities. The government was trying to reduce the overall interest paid on the National Debt and gave the owners of the old Four Percent Annuities the choice of accepting a one-for-one substitute in Three and a Half Percent Annuities or being bought out at par, i.e., £100 when the Four Percent Annuities were trading at £102. The purchase offer was made unattractive by paying only one-third of the value immediately, with the rest to be paid in unspecified future installments.

In March 1824,[8] a meeting of the Directors of the Ipswich Tontine was called "to decide on the Chancellor of the Exchequer's offer of 3 ½ per Cent. in lieu of 4 per Cent. Annuities." The Triennial Statement of the Tontine for March 25th, 1826, records the change from Four Percent

[8] Notice of meeting, *Ipswich Journal*, March 6th 1824.

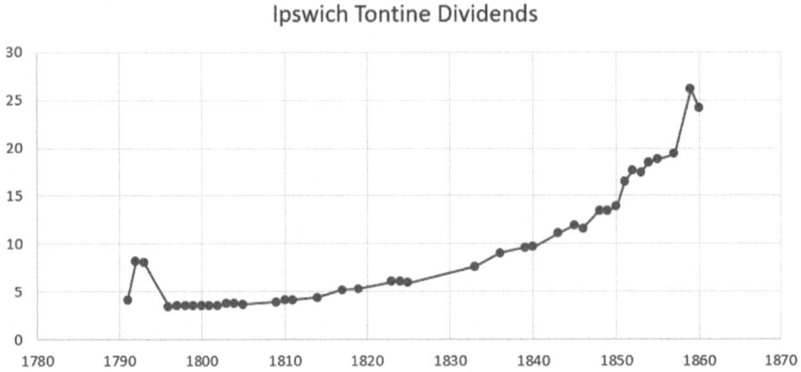

Fig 5.1 Ipswich Tontine Dividends from 1780–1870

Annuities to Three and a Half Percent Annuities and the ensuing drop in the dividend from £6/1/11 to £5/18/5.

Twenty years later, a second Government-induced reduction in the income is reflected in the notice of the dividend (£11 11s 6d) for 1846 in the Triennial Statement. It reported "The Dividend this year is less than last, in consequence of the reduction of the Interest of the £3 10s 0d per Cents, in which the Capital is invested, from £3 10s 0d to £3 5s 0d."

In 1850, one of the costs of not having a corporate form became apparent. Instead of the capital stock being held in the name of a corporation, it was held in the names of the trustees. New trustees had to be appointed and all the annuities had to be transferred formally into the names of the new personnel. This involved broker commissions of £42/12/6, and a solicitor's bill for a new trust deed of £45/14/4. These charges effectively wiped out any dividend gain that year from participant deaths.

The overall progression of dividends is shown in the chart seen in Fig. 5.1. The left column represents pounds and the horizontal line represents years.

The Tontine was wound up in 1860. The Actuary or Secretary of the Tontine at that point, George Josselyn, was also the Mayor of Ipswich. The final annual dividend before distribution was £24/4/0. The dip from the previous year's dividend of £26/2/6 is attributable to the winding-up costs being accounted for at this stage rather than being deducted from the distribution of the final amount. The costs included a solicitor's bill of

£120/1/4 and banker's and broker's fees of £69/13/9. The sixty-eight remaining nominees received £1000 each.

Aftermarket

Sales and auctions of shares in the Ipswich Universal Tontine occurred in desultory way during its existence. Three shares were offered at an auction in 1796. Newspaper notices for sales also appeared in 1816, 1832, 1841, and 1852. Unfortunately, while the auctions were advertised, the prices the shares sold for were almost never reported. An exception occurred in 1846 when a share of the tontine came up for auction at Garraway's Coffee House in London. The *Law Times* reported the sale price as £290/0/0.

The purchaser paid £290 for one of the 179 remaining shares which were paying £11/11/6 at that point. That comes to roughly four percent annual interest on the purchase price, and a 68 of 179 or thirty-seven percent chance of holding one of the £1,000 shares at the final distribution. The distribution point was fourteen years in the future, but that would not have been known at the time.

Another transfer ended up in court. A debtor in a bankruptcy proceeding, Robert Cana, an auctioneer in Woodbridge, Suffolk, had to surrender all his real and personal property to creditors. He attempted to hold on to an Ipswich Universal Tontine share, number twenty-four. The share was originally owned by his wife, nee Maria Gooch, and Cana took control over it on their marriage without a formal transfer. Cana was requested to endorse the transfer voucher for the share to his creditors to settle his debts and he refused stating it was not his property, but his wife's. He was ordered to make the endorsement.

Personnel

The 'Projectors'

While headed by aristocrats, the list included a number of local businessmen.

Sir John Rous, Baronet, later 1st Earl of Stradbroke (1750–1827), was a British aristocrat, racehorse owner and Member of Parliament for Suffolk from 1780 to 1796. Sir Thomas Charles Bunbury, Baronet (1740–1821), was a British politician who sat in the House of Commons for Suffolk between 1761 and 1812. He was very involved in horse racing and his horse Diomed won the first Derby in 1780. Sir Gerard William Vanneck, Baronet (1743–1791), was a British merchant and Member of Parliament for Dunwich between 1768 and 1790. He also served as a Parliamentarily appointed Commissioner for the Richmond Bridge Tontine of 1774.

Sir Robert Harland, Baronet (1765–1848), was the son of an Admiral. He served in 1st Regiment of Dragoons, Lieutenant of Division of the Ipswich Volunteers, 1803; he was appointed Sheriff of Suffolk in 1817; and he built Wherstead Park, Ipswich. And Sir Joshua Rowley, Baronet (1734–1790), was a Vice Admiral who retired to Tendring Hall, Suffolk. He also served as a Parliamentarily appointed Commissioner for the Richmond Bridge Tontine of 1774.

The rest of the projectors were a mix of lesser aristocracy and local tradesmen. Philip Bowes Broke, Esq., was a scion of a local important family; William Middleton, Esq., was Member of Parliament for Ipswich, 1784–1790; Philip Champion de Crespigny, Esq., (1738–1803) was a British lawyer and politician who sat in the House of Commons for Aldeburgh between 1780 and 1790; William Rowley, Esq., was likely the older brother of Joshua Rowley, above; Mileson Edgar, Esq., was from an old Suffolk family, knowns as the 'Edgars of the Red House' in Ipswich.

John Ford, Esq., appears in the local news as a businessman; Nathaniel Turner, Esq., died just as the tontine was being formed in 1791 at Stoke Hall near Ipswich, aged 53; the Rev William Fonnereau was from an important local family, including relatives who had earlier been MPs for Aldeburgh; Richard Savage Lloyd, Esq., was an former Member of Parliament for Totnes, 1759–1768; Edward Goate, Esq., was the owner of Brentely-Hall, Suffolk, aka Brent-Eleigh Hall.

William Whitby, Esq., was the owner of Raydon, Hadleigh, Suffolk; Robert Trotman, Esq., was Bailiff for Ipswich in 1790 and High Sheriff of Suffolk in 1783. He also served as Commissioner for the Land Tax for Ipswich.

William Ivory, Esq., was a significant architect of Norwich; he also served as a Parliamentarily appointed Commissioner for the Richmond Bridge Tontine of 1774; William Beeston Coyte, Esq., was a local doctor, noted for developing a Botanical Garden which had been started by his uncle, Dr. William Beeston. He wrote several books on botany. Richard Powell, Esq., was a Collector of Taxes.

Mr. John Cobbold, local brewer and malter, was from an old and significant Ipswich family. He bought the Holywells estate in 1780. He also became a local banker of the 'Blue' or Tory bank in 1786. Mr. James Willett was another local brewer.

Mr. John Kirby was an attorney in Ipswich who supervised the execution of the Deed of Trust of the Tontine.

Mr. Emerson Cornwell, an Ipswich banker, was probably the main projector of the Ipswich Tontine and acted as its Secretary until his death. Note the advertising does not list him as an 'Esquire,' but many other contemporary sources do. In 1780, Cornwell was involved in another tontine proposed to construct a 'House of Industry' (i.e., workhouse) for the 'Hundreds of Hartsmere, Hoxne, and Thredling' in central Suffolk. It was likely inspired by the successful tontine used to create the poor-house in Forehoe in Norfolk in 1776–1777. The Hartsmere plan did not succeed. In 1786, he was one of a small group that attempted to start an Ipswich-based Greenland Whale fishery endeavor, but failed in a year of two. In 1781, he was a £20,000 subscriber to the Government Loan that year.

Cornwell's obituary in the *Gentlemen's Magazine* of March 1819 stated he was 'for many years' a partner in the Ipswich and Needham Market Bank, also known as S.D. and S. Alexanders and Company. A large portion of his 'immense' property was bequeathed to a nephew living in America. Cornwell bought one share in the Tontine in his own name and one in his wife's name.

Cornwell was also the Treasurer of the Ipswich Public Dispensary. In what is likely an oblique homage, or perhaps a tease, Cornwell's name was used as a name in a model writ for a securities dispute in John Wentworth's *A complete system of pleading: comprehending the most approved precedents and forms of practice...* (1799).

This list of potential trustees and directors conforms to the common practice in schemes of this period. Tontine and company offerings of all kinds tended to have a list of people who may or may not have been actively involved in the development and execution of the tontine. Their names provided a sense of probity. In this case, the first five names became the trustees and the other nineteen names on the list became the directors.

The 'Proprietors' or Subscribers

Note that the list published in 1793 is of the nominees, not the subscribers or purchasers. In many cases, for example within families, the actual subscriber can be guessed at, but it would not be a hard fact. The context can only go so far. For example, the listing for the share that nominated 'Sarah Young, daughter of Sir William Young, Bart.,' might be read to assume William Young was the subscriber. But a later unclaimed dividend notice shows the subscriber's name to be Ann Lawrence.

Of the projectors, only John Cobbold, Emerson Cornwell, W.B. Coyte (five shares for his daughter), and John Kirby (via two of his children) bought shares.

The local bankers for the Ipswich Universal Tontine were Alexander, Cornwell, Alexander, and Spooner. Besides the Cornwell purchase mentioned above, Dykes Alexander, the second in the partnership, bought a share in his own name and three shares in the names of his sons. Spooner bought a share in his wife's name. The London bankers were Barnett, Hoare, Hill, and Barnett. Benjamin Barnett subscribed for two shares in his wife's name and two shares in his daughter's name.

Thomas Ellis, Esq., was the London-based broker for the tontine. A Thomas Ellis, Esq., stockbroker in London, is shown as having bought one share for each of his daughters. B. Colchester, who served as the Deputy Secretary of the tontine, bought one share in the name of his newborn daughter.

Of the 511 nominees, 273 were women. There were several groupings that appear to be sisters, with the same surnames, place, and designation 'spinster.' Most of the women were listed as the wives or daughters of the presumed subscriber.

While most of the subscribers came from Norfolk, Suffolk, and Essex, the pool was national. Bristol, Bath, and the London area provided many of the subscribers. Others came from all over the country, from Whitehaven to Hull to Plymouth. There were a few from Wales, and a couple from Lanarkshire, in Scotland.

Largest Holdings

There were twenty-two subscriptions of five shares or more. These were either in an individual's name or in family groups.

The largest tranche was fifty shares nominating Helen Jekyll, aged nine. She was the daughter of Joseph Jekyll, Esq., of Spetisbury, near Blandford, Dorsetshire. Joseph served with the East India Company in Bengal and Patna. One auction advertisement in 1832 mentioned the recent death of a subscriber holding fifty shares. It had to be Ms. Jekyll.

Jane Jekyll, nominee for ten shares, was the daughter of the Rev. John Jekyll. She was the likely stepsister of Helen Jekyll, above, as Joseph Jekyll married John Jekyll's widow.

Sarah Cambel of Westminster and her four children owned fourteen shares.

The Reverend H. J. Close of Hitcham in Suffolk bought eighteen shares, two each for his three sons and three each for his four daughters. The children ranged in age from under one to nine.

Thomas Ellis, Hopfactor in Borough (Southwark), bought nine shares, nominating his five children, including five in the name of a newborn son.

Thomas Jackson, Esq., of Bedford, age 72 bought fourteen shares. He would have paid only £40 a share, thus received a return of almost ten percent annually on his investment. He was one of six who paid less than fifty percent per share.

Samuel Spencer Skinner, Esq., aged sixty, bought twelve shares, and six more in the name of his wife Isabella, aged fifty-six. They were Loyalists from New York who ended up in England after the Revolution.

A nominee entry for five shares reads "Pretyman, William Edward, son of George, Lord Bishop of Lincoln, Buckden Palace, near Huntingdon." The elder Pretyman, although an important cleric, had been a standout mathematics scholar at Pembroke College in Cambridge. He was the senior wrangler of his year and won the Smith Prize in Maths. He was also William Pitt's tutor at Pembroke College. Pretyman, who later took the name Tomline as the result of a legacy, became an unofficial private secretary and close financial advisor to Pitt, actually living at Downing Street before being named Bishop of Lincoln. That someone with as sophisticated a financial background as Pretyman felt investing in a tontine was sound can be seen as yet another endorsement of the concept.

William Edward, two years old at the time of the Tontine, ultimately became a Member of Parliament for constituencies in Christchurch, Truro, and Minehead.

Finally, there was only one nominee with a surname beginning with 'N,' Wedd William Nash, which seems statistically improbable.

Shareholders with Connections to Other Tontines

The Forehoe Tontine of 1777 shared some subscribers with the Ipswich Tontine. It was created to build a 'House of Industry,' i.e., poorhouse, in Forehoe, fifty miles north of Ipswich, near Norwich. Ipswich nominee two-year-old Charlotte Browne was the daughter of Henry Browne of Diss. In the list of subscribers to the Forehoe Tontine, Henry Browne of Diss is shown as a subscriber for his one-year-old son, Harry. Likewise, Thomas Slapp of Botesdale subscribed for one share in the Ipswich Tontine for his son Thomas, aged twelve, and one share in the Forehoe Tontine for his daughter Charlotte, eight years old in 1777. John Darby of Diss nominated his son John, fifteen, in the Forehoe Tontine, and then young John, aged twenty-eight, bought shares for himself and his wife in the Ipswich tontine.

Some of the Ipswich nominees were also owners of shares in the 1785 Covent Garden Theatre Life Tontine or had connections to them. Sarah Cambel and her four children owned fourteen shares of the Ipswich Tontine. Betty Freeman, the daughter of Covent Garden Tontineer George Bridges Esq., of Mistley held two shares of the Ipswich Tontine. Edward Griffiths Esq., of Carnarvon, Wales, owned three shares, and Catherine Hodges, wife of Wickins Hodges, held two shares.

Mr. Thomas Ellis, Hopfactor of Borough, held five shares in the names of his five children. His wife was a nominee for one share in the Second Irish Tontine of 1775, as was his son, Thomas. His son, James, was a nominee in the First Irish Tontine of 1773.

Helen Senior, a nominee for ten shares, was, as 'Hellen' Senior, also a nominee for two shares (£200) of the Third (youngest) Class of the 1773 Irish Tontine. Her younger stepsister was nominee for three shares. Her father, Ascanius W. Senior, served in the East India Company and was back in England by 1771. He had Company connections to Joseph Jekyll, above, and was referred to in the Parliamentary trial of Lord Clive and the investigation into the finances of the East India Company in 1772–1773.

Three members of the Trustee/Director list were also Commissioners of the Richmond Bridge Tontine. They were Sir Gerard Vanneck, Sir Joshua Rowley, and William Ivory.

Was It Worth It?

One hundred pounds at four percent compounded annually is £1,560 after seventy years. However, the interest rate on the underlying capital was reduced twice during the life of the tontine. The result is that the compounded total would be only £983.

The surviving tontineers received dividends for each of the seventy years of the life of the tontine. The opportunity for compounding was foreclosed by distributing the interest each year. An actual accumulated interest figure can be arrived at by extrapolating from the incomplete data available. The sum of the accumulated paid interest over the seventy years amounted to approximately £608. Adding that to the £1000 final distribution gives a result of £1,608. This is significantly more than the compound interest result.

According to the Measuring Worth website, using the conservative Retail Price Index (RPI), a £100 annuity bought at par in 1790 had a value of £128 in 1860. Another way to look at it is to see the figures in 2020 prices. According to the RPI, the relative cost of the 1790 investment of £100 in 1790 was roughly £12,200 in 2020. The 1860 final dividend of £1,000 was worth £96,000 in 2020 pounds.

As to the non-finalists, even from the beginning, by investing in the Four Percent Annuities, the subscribers received more than they would have received from the more common Three Percent Annuities. If you survived to around 1805, you at least got your investment back. By 1820, the tontine shares were paying more than most common securities. If the tontine is seen as a proto-pension system, this is also the point at which the participants might start to need the higher payments.

Another benefit that is hard to articulate with specificity was the reduction in the complications of owning annuities directly. The participants did not have to deal with brokers on their own, nor did they need to make a trip to the Bank of England to pick up their dividends. For non-Londoners, there would have been rigmarole involving a power of attorney before the Bank would issue dividends to an agent. The banks and the tontine administrators took care of all that for the subscribers.

Given the depression in the financial markets during the wars with France, the shares in the Ipswich Universal Tontine were a perfectly respectable investment in awkward times.

CHAPTER 6

The Covent Garden Theatre Life Tontine

With the American Revolution drawing to a close, the discussions of the budget in 1783 took on a 'peace benefit' aspect. In the newspapers, the debate was often expressed through simple isolated paragraphs that suggested various options. The Navy Bills, the credit structure that sustained the Royal Navy during the war, were well behind in payment and a way to pay them off as soon as possible was a major issue.

The Morning Chronicle, in particular, pushed the notion of a tontine as part of the annual Loan. On April 14th, 1783: "A Tontine, it is said, will make a part of the next operation of finance; and from the success of the Irish scheme of this nature, much may be prognosticated in its favour." On October 27th, 1783: "In the loan of next year, it cannot be too often repeated, that a *tontine* should be a part of the Ways and Means; by experience it is proved to be everything that can be wanted or wished in an operation of finance, acceptable to individuals, and advantageous to the public!" On June 11th, 1784: "From the extreme avidity, with which the Richmond Bridge Tontine, and yet more, the Irish Tontines, were bought up, it certainly seems advisable for a Tontine; to make part of the present year's finance." And on November 22nd, 1784: "In the provision to be made for the remaining load of unfunded Navy debt, a tontine is very properly in contemplation as part of operation of finance."

Ultimately, no government tontine was created, but the Loan of 1785 included a new high interest security known as the Navy Annuity. It

K. McKeever, *The Role of Tontines, 1750–1800*, Palgrave Studies in the History of Finance, https://doi.org/10.1007/978-3-032-12849-2_6

paid five percent, well above the three percent that was standard for the Consols.

Within this environment, on November 20th, 1784, a small advertisement appeared in the *Gazetteer and New Daily Advertiser* for a private tontine, with the contact details of Farrer and Lacey, solicitors. It was repeated at least twenty times by the end of the year. This is the first public appearance of the Covent Garden Theatre Life Tontine.

> LIFE TONTINE / To be purchased a very advantageous Life Tontine, well secured. For particulars apply to Messrs. Farrer and Lacey, Bread-street-hill.

This did not come entirely out of the blue. A tontine-supported new theatre had been proposed earlier, but apparently the project sputtered out. This had appeared in the *Public Advertiser* of February 3rd, 1783: "The Project of a new *Theatre in Grosvenor Place* is revived —The Plan is to raise £40,000 by Shares of £250 each entitling each Subscriber to his proportionate Share of the Profit and, in the Manner of a Tontine, such share of Profit increasing by Survivorship." A handbill, a copy of which is held by the National Library of Scotland,[1] also advertised the project. The tontine proposed had a term of only twenty-one years. Readers were directed to Henry Holland, the architect, and a Mr. Smith, of St Mary Axe, for particulars of the scheme.

The 1784 proposal was less ambitious. It was a means by which Thomas Harris, the impresario, obtained additional operating funds for the financially fragile Covent Garden Theatre.

The Covent Garden Theatre Life Tontine

The Covent Garden Theatre Life Tontine, created via an indenture[2] dated June 17th, 1785, consisted of two fifty-person Classes, the First for nominees under thirty and the Second for those over thirty. Shares cost £250 and the First Class paid six percent per annum and the Second Class

[1] A Plan for the Improvement of Theatrical & Other Public Entertainments..., Shelfmark/reference number: 5.1835(6).

[2] A manuscript working copy of the Indenture is held by the London Metropolitan Archives, among the Duke of Bedford's papers. Reference E/BER/CG/E/08/10/002. The Duke owned the land on which the Covent Garden Theatre was built.

paid 6.4%. Those figures are comparatively high and made the investment attractive for the period. The text also expresses an intention to enroll the Indenture.

The Indenture outlines the steps to be taken to transfer money from the Theatre to the 'receiver' for the Tontine for distribution. The capital was to revert to Thomas Harris after the last death in each class. In fact, there was no real capital fund, only a promise to pay a set amount to the benefit of the Tontine shareholders. In a standard project tontine, the income of the project, such as the tolls on a bridge, was committed to paying the tontine. In this case, only a relatively small part of the overall cash flow of the Theatre was needed to pay the tontine.

The Tontine scheme also included a bonus of a right to a seat at every performance at Covent Garden. This is similar to the rights associated with the standard 'Renter's Share' that financed the theatres of the time. The tontine share was represented by an indenture, and the commitment of a seat was a separate indenture.

The working copy ends with a detailed list of the subscribers. Both classes were fully subscribed. Internal evidence, primarily notations as to death and transfer information, indicates this copy is from the late summer of 1788 at the earliest. This list is unusual as it includes both the purchaser and the nominee, if there was one. Most of the shareholders, particularly in the over thirty class, nominated themselves as the dependent life.

Creating the Tontine

The formal creation of the Tontine involved three indentures signed on June 16th, 17th, and 18th, 1785.[3] The first indenture cleared an accumulated debt of £24,500. The second indenture of the 17th June was the 'constitutional' document of the Tontine, creating a trust to manage it. The third indenture (18th June) was a loan from Hugh Dive, seemingly a bridging loan for the overall process.

There were five trustees. The first named was Robert Burton, MP for Wendover from 1784 to 1790. He was knighted in June 1800. He was a

[3] The details of these are found in an 1835 (!) case before the Court of Exchequer called Bayley v Longman, later called Bayly v Harris. Bayly was the assignee of the debt referenced in the third indenture. The transcript is found in the imaging project known as the Anglo-American Legal Tradition. The first page of the Bayly case is found at http://aalt.law.uh.edu/AALT6/E126/E126no55/IMG_0063.htm.

Treasurer of Gray's Inn and a Tax Commissioner for Huntingdonshire in 1798. Burton died in 1810. The second trustee was Rowland Stephenson, Esq., MP for Carlisle 1787–1790. He was a banker, first as a clerk in Martin's Bank, in 1752, then partner in the firm of Batson, Stephenson, and Hoggart from 1766 on. They served as the bank for the tontine. Stephenson was an owner of enough East India stock to be entitled to have a vote in the Board elections. He was also a Trustee and Banker for the Universal British Tontine Society, a successful small-sum, short-term scheme in 1791. His bank was also involved in other tontine offerings of this era. He died in 1797.

The third trustee was James Farrer, Esq., a solicitor, practicing from the Bread Hill Street address since the mid-1760s. He was qualified as a Solicitor & Proctor and served as a Secondary Deputy in the office of the Clerk of the Pipe within the Exchequer Office. He was also the Solicitor for the Foundling Hospital by 1810 and a stockholder of the East India Company in 1792. The fourth was Thomas Longman, Esq., an 'Eminent Bookseller' in Paternoster Row. The firm ultimately became Longmans, Green, & Co, and merged into the Pearson conglomerate, who still maintain a Longman imprint. He was also the brother-in-law of Thomas Harris. He died in 1791.

The final trustee was Hugh Dive, Esq, who was a senior Clerk within the office of the Comptroller of Duties on Houses, Tax Office. He subscribed £2000 to the loan of 1781 and appeared on the published list for unclaimed dividend for single share of Three Percent Annuities in 1797. He was reported as having inherited £800 per year in 1792 but died the same year.

Structure

The underlying source of the annual dividends paid by the tontine was the income generated by "all those said 7/12th parts of & singular said 2 letters patent Leases Theatre Buildings & other the … theatrical property assets…." The manuscript this is taken from is hard to read at points. The seven-twelfths was the extent of Harris's majority shareholding in the Theatre.

After the last death in each Class, the rights reverted to Thomas Harris or his heirs. There was no final large prize to be hoped for by the participants. The rate of return, six and 6.4%, was comparatively high, thus attractive. The dividends, of course, increased with survivorship. Capitalized at £25,000, the Tontine had to pay out £1,625 each year.

The Tontine shares were half the price of the standard theatre shareholding, known as a 'Renter's Share.' These had an initial value of £500, and, instead of a formal interest rate, paid a per performance royalty. They also included a free admission right. The Renter's Share royalty was converted to a five percent dividend in 1808. These shares were sold for a term matching the 99-year lease of the grounds from the Duke of Bedford. Like the Renter's shareholders, each Tontine subscriber had a right to a seat at every performance at the Theatre each year. Although no Tontine share certificate has been traced, two copies of the Admission Indenture have been turned up via County Archives.

A 'Deed of Privilege of Free Admission into Covent Garden Theatre' is held by Berkshire Record Office[4] citing a price of five shillings. Note that five shillings was often the price cited during that period for any transactions that in reality were transferred without a charge. The admission right could be valued at roughly £20 a year if the holder attended every performance. It is not a simple share statement, but a full-fledged formal indenture. It is pre-printed with spaces left for names, dates, etc. Thomas Harris is the party of the first part, the five trustees are parties of the second part, and Robert Palmer, the subscriber, is the party of the third part. The nominee was the twenty-year-old son, also named Robert Palmer. The shareholder had a right to a seat at any performance except on the stage or in the owners' boxes. The indenture ends with a statement of the terms by which it can be assigned to another.

On the reverse is an endorsement indicating the assignment from Robert Palmer to Henry Hakewill, Architect, registered on June 18th, 1799, by Covent Garden's treasurer. Since the original Robert Palmer died in 1787, this transfer would have been from the nominee/heir. The endorsement is accompanied by a handwritten memorandum acknowledging the assignment to Hakewill but acquiescing in the original grantee's occasional use of the admission right.

[4] Reference D/EE/F10/1-2.

As was typical of all tontines, the shareholders had to prove the life of their nominee in order to collect the interest payments. An advertisement from *The Morning Chronicle* of February 9th, 1816, reads:

> COVENT GARDEN THEATRE TONTINE -- The SUBSCRIBERS to the TONTINE on this Theatre, may receive a Half year's Annuity due at Christmas, by applying to the Treasurer, at his Office, on the South side of the Portico in Bow-street, Covent garden, on Monday next, the 12th instant, on Tuesday the 13th, on Wednesday the 14th, on Thursday the 15th, and on Friday, the 16th, between the hours of Twelve and Three. Those subscribers who have subscribed for the lives of Nominees, are to appear with such Nominee, Or Certificates from the Minister or Church-Wardens of the parish where they reside, of their being alive. It is requested that in case of death, notice may be given as above for the further Benefit and Regulation of each class.

The Tontine scheme did not supplant the standard, older form of what would be considered stock in the Covent Garden Theatre. These 'Renter's Shares' were initially sold at £500. Trusler's *London Advisor and Guide*,[5] published in 1786, estimated the current price to be around £300. The income and benefit to owning a Renter's Share were (1) income of two shillings per performance in the Theatre and (2) the right of free admission to every performance. With roughly 200 performances a year, the income would be around 400 shillings, or £20, which amounts to a four percent return. They were sold by the major theatres for terms of years, typically ending when the theatre's lease on the property ended. Over time, the Covent Garden royalty of two shillings a performance evolved into a straight £25 a year for a £500 share. During the financial troubles in the early nineteenth century that was reduced to £12/10/0.

Evidence that the shareholders' rights to a seat were exercised fairly steadily is provided by this excerpt from *The Times* of April 15th, 1785. It is a complaint about the reduction in takings from a performer's benefit production, which was a standard way for the actors to earn a bonus.

[5] Trusler, John, T*he london adviser and guide: containing every instruction and information useful and necessary to persons living in London…*, London printed for the author, No. 14, Red Lion-Street, Clerkenwell, 1786.

> A correspondent assures us, but we can scarcely give credit to the assertion, that most of the hundred subscribers to the Covent Garden Tontine, as well as the old renters, avail themselves of their freedom, and go into the Theatre on benefit nights. This, continues our correspondent, is a hard case on the performer, who pays a hundred guineas into the treasury for his benefit, which is purchasing the sole use of the House for a night and as that hundred and five-pounds constitute part of the subscribers and renters security, they ought to protect, not injure the performer.

Note that this reference to the Tontine shareholders' use of the seating privilege comes some months before the execution of the official indentures. A sense of the income of the theatre can be gained by this report.[6]

> The receipt of Covent Garden Theatre, on Monday evening, was on the first account £347 cash. exclusive of those persons who are free on the tontine; and during the evening, the performance brought full £400 into the treasury.

The Tontine started making payments immediately, as indicated by an advertisement in *The Morning Chronicle* of June 25th, days after the execution of the founding documents. This means the indentures were not issued until there were already a reasonable, if not full, number of subscribers.

Advertisements announcing interest payments appeared in the newspapers every January and June through 1817. They were also later announced, at least through 1813, via Montefiore's *Original Canal and Dock List, &c*, a broadsheet of stock prices and other miscellaneous information. They were initially paid via Farrer's office, then through Stephenson's bank, and lastly though the box office of the Theatre. Stephenson's bank created printed receipts for this purpose, illustrated in Fig. 6.1.

Note this reflects an annual interest of £16/13/0. Steers was in the Second Class, earning 6.4% originally, or £16 annually on the £250 investment.

The Tontine was a reliable payer at least through roughly 1820.

[6] *Morning Post*, Oct 19th, 1785.

Covent Garden Theatre, Life Tontine.

RECEIVED this 30th Day of Jan. 1795 of ROWLAND STEPHENSON, Esq. the Receiver appointed of the above Tontine, the Sum of Eight Pounds, Five Shillings & 5 Pence being for Half a Year's Annuity, due to me at Christmas 1794, as Subscriber of the Second Class thereof, upon the Life of myself

Witness.

Fig. 6.1 A 1795 receipt from Covent Garden Theatre for £8/5/5 for half a year's annuity

The Covent Garden Theatre Life Tontine in the News

In an article describing the development of tontines in the magazine *All the Year Round* in 1872, this text appears:

> At one time, Covent Garden Theatre was the subject of a Tontine with Mr. Cooke, of the Exchequer Office, as manager. A story is told of an apothecary, one of the members or Tontineers, who was always asking Mr. Cooke whether any of the other members had departed, expressing his disappointment by saying, "What! nobody dead yet!" The apothecary, as matters turned out, was the first to go.

Among the death notices in *The Times* of August 17th, 1787, was this statement:

> Wednesday, Mr. Yale, apothecary and surgeon, formerly of Catherine-street, after a very short illness. This is the first decease of the subscribers to Mr. Harris's Tontine.

The text validates the ironic anecdote in *All the Year Round* mentioned above and the death is also noted in the Duke of Bedford's working copy of the Indenture. Yale was shareholder number thirty in the Second Class.

On January 17th, 1788, *The World* carried this:

> In the Covent Garden Theatre Tontine, two lives have dropt – one in each class: and with an exactness that is very accurate, the encreased interest now paid, is three shillings and three-pence to each person.

The Times of June 14th, 1789, has a short reference:

> The Covent Garden Theatre Tontine has made an increase of a few shillings in each dividend.

The World of January 20, 1789, reports:

> On the COVENT GARDEN *Tontine,* one life more has dropped in the lower class.

The World, as part of a campaign to get a different Tontine to raise its proposed interest rate, published a note on June 15th, 1789, showing comparable initial interest rates or dividends:

> RICHMOND BRIDGE Tontines were 4 per cent. – KEW BRIDGE 5. – COVENT GARDEN Theatre 6l. 10s. besides the freedom, which was a saleable *bonus.* – LORD CORK's scheme 5l. 10s.
> The Uxbridge scheme failed.

The 'freedom' mentioned above is taken to mean the free admission right.

Tontine Aftermarket

Auctions involving the Tontine shares occasionally turned up amid a more active market for the Renter's Shares.

The language used to advertise the Renter's Shares could be confusing, using the term 'annuity' where we would use the term 'dividend.' There were tontine shares offered at auctions in 1786, 1789, 1792, and 1804. By 1804, roughly twenty years after the creation of the Tontine, the interest payment had risen to only £17/10/0 a year, or around seven percent, at the most a six percent increase from the original payment. This is a good illustration of the comparative slowness of the increase of rate of return of the tontines of the period, which is likely one of the features which led to their decline.

The actual auction sale prices are just about impossible to trace. Renter's Shares seemingly held their value in auctions. A comparative example involves the auctioning of a share in the newly rebuilt Drury Lane Theatre in 1794, reproduced in Gale's digital *Eighteenth Century Collections Online*. The annotated auction particulars show a £500 share sold for £470. In the same auction, a turnpike bond with a face value of £300 sold for only £63.

The Final Erosion of the Covent Garden Theatre Life Tontine

After a fire on September 20th, 1808, the theatre was rebuilt. An isolated notice in the *Jack Johnson Collection of Ephemera* held by the Bodleian Library, Oxford, seems to be a valuation of a Covent Garden share dated October 15th, 1808, signed by William Morgan, a noted mathematician and the Actuary for the Equitable Assurance Office.[7] It states the share pays an annuity of £25 a year, so it should be seen as a Renter's Share not a Tontine share. It estimates the current value of a share to be worth £580/0/0, including the value of the right to a seat at every performance. This figure would indicate that Mr. Morgan simply took the par value as a current value, with no acknowledgment of current auction sales.

In 1812, an agreement was worked out among the six 'proprietors' and John Brandon, the treasurer of the company, as to who owned which portions and how the reconstruction and other debt was be paid and future profits disbursed. Thomas Harris, a half owner, under that agreement, maintained the day-to-day control of the theatre. In the following years, a number of the parties died, including Thomas Harris. His portion and role were taken over by his son, Henry Harris. Advertising of the dividend payment dates continued through at least March 1817. That was for the dividend payment due at Christmas the previous year. In the early days of the Tontine, that payment was advertised in the first week of January.

A notice was published in *The Times* of November 1st, 1821, which provides the first clear hint of trouble:

> COVENT-GARDEN THEATRE. — The PERSONS interested in the TONTINE ANNUITIES secured on the shares and interest of the late Thomas Harris, esq., deceased, in this theatre, are requested to MEET,

[7] Digitized in ProQuest; available through the Bodleian Library: https://www.bodleian.ox.ac.uk/collections-and-resources/special-collections/catalogues/johnson/finding-aids/digitised.

> at the Freemasons' Tavern, Great Queen-street, on Wednesday, the 7th day of November, at 12 o'clock, to consult on the proper Measure for obtaining Payment of their annuities. SCOTT and SON, Solicitors, St. Mildred's-court.

The finances of the Covent Garden Theatre were substantially reorganized in early 1822. That process included unilaterally dropping the Tontine dividend payments.

The rationale seems to have been a determination that the founding Indenture was not 'enrolled,' i.e., registered in the High Court of Chancery, so it could be treated as null and void. Since it was not enrolled, the Tontineers ('Annuitants') who were not parties to the founding indenture itself did not have a right to sue. The details of this are found in the record of the much later lawsuit over repayment of one of the other individual loans made in the refinancing of 1785.

A second agreement was drawn up in 1822 involving Henry Harris and some of the successors of the original parties. A representative of an heir who was not a party to the agreement noted the dismissal of the long-term treasurer and perceived that the distribution of income was being distorted to the favor of the other proprietors. He sued for the accounts of the theatre to be run according to the 1812 agreement and that a receiver be appointed to make sure this happened.

Ultimately, the court decided that the 1812 agreement had to take precedence and the Chancellor called for a meeting to appoint a new treasurer. However, the case seems to have petered out without any formal record of the subsequent steps being taken. Presumably, there was some sort of agreement made among the parties. At no time in the discussion of the issues of this case did the obligation to pay the Tontine debt come up. There are general references to the obligations and debts of the company, but nothing specific.[8]

Bayly v Harris, Court of the Exchequer, 1835–1837

In December 1835, both *The Times* and *The Sunday Times* have short reports of a preliminary stage of a case in the Court of Exchequer called *Bayley v Longman*. This gives details of the background of the Covent Garden Tontine. The articles garble the background to the case.

[8] *Const v Harris* Turner and Russell's Chancery Reports [ER 37] 496 (1824).

Bayly had ended up possessing the rights to the loan provided by Hugh Dive in the Third Indenture of 1785 and attempted to call it in. The defending parties, one of whom was a conflicted mortgage holder/ trustee, responded in part by claiming that all the Tontine annuitants would have to be added as parties and the expense of doing so would be beyond the value of the mortgage. The only point of the case at this stage was that it was decided the suit could go ahead without making the annuitants necessary parties.

The case, now listing Henry Harris as the defendant, was assigned by the Court to a Master, Jeffrey Spranger, Esq., A legal notice was published and ultimately a decision was reached in 1837. *The Times* report of July 4th provides more details. That decision's description of the original deal reads:

> ...[B]y an indenture of the 17th June 1785, [Harris] conveyed the patent to Messrs. Dive, Longman, and other trustees, upon trust, to grant tontine annuities to 100 subscribers of 250*l* each. On the following day the trustees accordingly granted annuities payable out of the produce of the patent, but which annuities were never enrolled.

The patent referred to was an old perpetual grant from Charles II licensing the right to present plays. There were very few of these (covering only the Covent Garden, Drury Lane, & Hay Market Theatres) and the patents had the effect of creating a lucrative if fragile triple monopoly. As to the reference about enrollment, enrollment of annuity-like schemes was required by a Parliamentary Act of 1777.[9] It is clear, from advertisements of other tontines created in the late eighteenth century that enrolling the trust or settlement documents in Chancery was a legal requirement and a standard practice.

The description continues:

> Dive and Longman afterwards became incumbrancers, subject to the tontine annuities. The patent was afterwards sold, and the produce invested in trustees (sic), by a deed which duly declared the trusts of the fund to be for the payment of the first annuitants, and afterwards for the payment of the subsequent incumbrancers.

[9] *17 George III, Cap xxvi, (1777).*

Bayly, the plaintiff, was the assignee of Dive's incumbrance interest and he wanted to be paid from the proceeds of the sale. The situation was referred to a master who decided all the tontine annuities were void and that Bayly was the prime 'incumbrancer.' The Court confirmed that decision.

> It is ordered by the Court that the report of Jeffries Spranger Esq the Master to whom this Cause stands referred bearing date the 16th day of June 1837 be and the same is hereby Confirmed And the court declare the several Grants of annuities under the deed of 17th June 1785 void for want of such grants having been inrolled according to the Act Parliament in that case made & provided.[10]

At this stage, at least two of the tontine annuitants, Ladbroke and Lalande, were represented in court. Their only consolation was that they were entitled to their costs. This decision had the effect of confirming the dropping of the obligation to pay the tontine dividends as executed in 1822.

In 1856, the Covent Garden Theatre was destroyed by yet another fire. A detailed assessment of the financial implications appeared in *The Times* on March 18th, 1856. It is a report of a meeting of interested parties and it does not mention a tontine. The interests involved include the land itself, owned by the Duke of Bedford; the physical theatre, owned by a group of shareholders in 110 shares (Renter's Shares); and what seems to be the business of the theatre, including the patent, owned by the estates of Charles Kemble and Thomas Harris. Harris's estate is described as hopelessly indebted.

The Participants

The working copy of the founding Indenture from the Duke of Bedford's Archives in the London Metropolitan Archives includes a list of purchasers and nominees. There were fifty shares in the First Class, i.e., nominees aged thirty and under, and fifty in the Second, for nominees over thirty. There were only ninety-three individual shareholders, however, because there were multiple share purchases and purchases on behalf of multiple

[10] Transcript page 179, toward the end of line 33 (AALT image 93). The lack of punctuation was standard in documents of this sort during that time.

children. The list includes a description of their 'Rank Profession or Trade.' Traces of many, but not all, of the participants can be found in contemporary newspapers and other digitized sources. Note that the figures below are not mutually exclusive.

Seventeen were listed as 'Gentleman,' eighteen were listed as 'Esquire,' and two were Baronets: Sir Henry Fletcher and Sir Henry Thomas Gott; one was an Earl: the Earl of Surry(sic), who became the Duke of Norfolk on the death of his father in 1786.

Eight were Members of Parliament: Miles Peter Andrew, Stephen Thurston Adey, George Barclay, John Dent, Sir Henry Fletcher, Robert Ladbroke, Rowland Stephenson, and Michael Angelo Taylor.

Seventeen were either directors, owned stock in, or worked for the East India Company. Ten were either directors, owned stock in, or worked for the Bank of England. Two owned stock in the South Sea Company, one of whom served as director. By that time, the South Sea Company had evolved into a financial company, not a merchant trading company.

Nine were directors, members, or worked for insurance companies. Nine listed themselves as bankers, but external evidence shows at least three others were bankers. Five listed themselves as attorneys or proctors but three more who listed themselves as 'Esquire' were also attorneys. One of them was Robert Palmer, the lawyer for, and executor of, the Duke of Bedford's estates. The property on which the Theatre stood was owned by the Duke of Bedford.

Two were clergy and four were surgeons. Eleven were female.

A number listed a trade in the description: Bookseller, Draper, Druggist (2,) Factor, Haberdasher, Merchant (10,) Stockbroker (2,) Tea Dealer, and Tallow Chandler, albeit Master of the Worshipful Company of Tallow-Chandlers in July, 1787. Note that 'merchant' at this time was an evolving term that could describe a traditional general or commercial trading house or, increasingly, a business that offered some sort of financial services.

Some held Civil Service positions: Edmund Armstrong, a regimental agent, was the 'Husband of the Four and One Half Percent Plantation Duty' in the Customs Office. Francis Barker was a 'Groom of the Great Chamber,' Daniel Cabanel, a sometime poet, was 'Clerk Assistant of the House of Lords,' and Wm James Cooke was 'Accountant, Office of Exchequer Bills.'

The vast majority were from the modern greater London area, listing an address in London or Middlesex with a small number from nearby

Surrey, including Borough, East Sheen, Lambeth, Snows Fields, and Walworth. One came from Shrewsbury. The most distant was Edward Griffiths, of Carnarvon, North Wales. Two gave an address from the area around Manningtree in Essex. One listed a Winkfield, Berkshire address. Three came from Grove Place, Hampshire of whom two were husband and wife, and the third, by name, appears to be a relative of the wife.

Sixty of the participants named themselves as the 'life' on which the share depended. This is very unusual and likely reflects the desire for the seat entitlement outweighing any investment or generational transfer motives.

Multiple Tontine Ownership

At least nine had shares in, or connections with, other tontines.

Irish Tontine, 1773: Catherine Jenkins was the nominee of a £200 share held by her mother, Elizabeth. The Irish report her as still living, Christmas, 1810.

Freemasons' Tontine of 1775: Nominees Elizabeth Maria Bathurst and Catherine Jenkins.

Irish Tontine of 1777: Harriet Peach, daughter of Rev. Samuel Peach, a £100 nominee; Thomas Conway, who held two £100 shares in the name of his seven-year-old daughter; and the Earl of Surry, nominee for one share. Possibly Philip Antrobus, whose name is written on a 1777 Share certificate as a secondary purchaser, February 1813.

Sheffield Inn Tontine, 1782: The Earl of Surrey (Charles Howard) via Vincent Eyre, £300 (the Earl of Surrey owned the land the Sheffield Tontine Inn was built on, Charles's brother, Henry, resident in Sheffield, also subscribed).

Earl of Cork's Tontine of 1789: Edmund Armstrong had one share each for the lives of the same three children he nominated to the Covent Garden Tontine.

The National Tontine of 1789: Edmund Armstrong had one share each for the lives of the same three children he nominated to the Covent Garden Tontine; the shares numbered 643, 644, 645. Sarah Ann Sherson Belcombe, aged five, a daughter of William and Mary Ann Belcombe, was the nominee for share # 1528 of the First Class. The address given was Geneva. Note the Belcombes had petitioned the King to approve the change of name from Bulcock. Also the Earl of Surrey, Joseph Hurlock, Clement Strong, who had two shares nominating himself and his son, and Richard Stone, who had nine shares split among his wife and two children.

Ipswich Tontine of 1791: Sarah Cambel wife of John Cambel, and her four children owned fourteen shares of the Ipswich Tontine. Betty Freeman, the daughter of George Bridges Esq., of Mistley held two shares, Edward Griffiths Esq., of Caenarvon, Wales, owned three shares, and Catherine Hodges, wife of Wickins Hodges, held two shares.

Three were 'projectors' of other tontine schemes: the bankers Stephen Thurston Adey, Rowland Stephenson, and his partner, Edward Buckley Batson.

Two became bankrupts soon after this Tontine was created. Thomas Conway's wife died in the spring of 1786, and his property, including shares in the Covent Garden Theatre Life Tontine, the Irish Tontine, and a Renter's Share in the Opera House appeared in auctions soon after. He was declared Bankrupt in 1788.

Similarly, Charles Dale's wife died in the summer of 1786 and he was declared bankrupt in 1788. The working copy list records Dale's share as 'Sold by the Sheriff to Allan, by him to Ro Williams.'

Another, the banker Moses Staples, went bankrupt in 1796 and the advertisement below of a sale of his assets from *The Times* of September 27th includes his Tontine share as Lot 2. The image is blurred and seems to read:

> A clear ANNUITY of £15 per annum well secured, and regularly paid half yearly out of the Theatre Royal, Covent Garden, with the benefit of survivorship to the sum of £750 held for the above life, aged 31.

The sum should be £250 and it is difficult to see if the figure in the image is a typo or bad reproduction.

Some of the Tontineers can be seen in contemporary portraits: Charles Howard, the Earl of Surrey, was the subject of a portrait by Gainsborough. Robert Palmer was also painted by Gainsborough and Richard, his son, was painted by Romney. The nominee of George Bridges, his son, was painted with his family by Constable. There is an anonymous portrait of Henry Fletcher in the Museum at Greenwich.

Notable participants in the Tontine:

Philip Antrobus was one of the leading stockbrokers of the period. He represented Coutts Bank, where his brother Edmund was a partner. Philip became a Freeman of London in 1786 via the Goldsmiths' Company, via redemption, i.e., by buying his way in. In 1797, he took over '…the agency for negotiating the Exchequer Bills for the service of Government, lately held by Mess. Goldsmid….' It was reported that Goldsmid charged a quarter percent commission, while Antrobus charged a flat one shilling. He took £250,000 in the Loyalty Loan of 1796–1797 and was a four-vote proprietor of Bank of England stock. Messrs. Goldsmid and Antrobus and Wood were also Government brokers of Navy Bills.

John Antrobus, seemingly no relation, was a major Tea Merchant who supplied the Royal Court with tea.

Edmund Armstrong, Esq., at one point a Grand Warden of the London Freemasons, was an agent for three regiments (8th, 32nd, 54th Foot) in the Army and the Hertfordshire Militia, in the Army. He served as a Captain in, and the adjutant of, the Eastern Regiment of the Middlesex Militia, a volunteer unit, in 1778. In 1794, he was promoted to be 'Groom of the Privy-Chamber' from his previous position as 'Gentlemen Usher Quarter Waiter' in the Lord Chamberlain's office. He bought Forty Hall in Enfield, North London, in 1789.[11] In a report dated July 1797, he is listed as 'Husband of the 4½ Percent Duty from the Plantations' in the Customs Office.

William and Mary Ann Bulcock, who changed their names to William and Mariana Belcombe, appear in a webpage presenting potted family histories of the people mentioned in the diaries of Anne Lister.[12] A second Mariana, the daughter of Mary Ann, was one of Lister's primary lovers. Lister's life and secret diaries are considered important elements of modern Lesbian history.[13] William was a noted surgeon, developing techniques as a Naval surgeon later adopted back in England. While the Belcombe family lived in Geneva, they became acquainted with Jacob Schweppes and helped him establish a bottling business in England.

John Cambel, Major, Army Corps of Engineers, was assigned to North America from 1772 through 1794. An accumulated pay warrant record of 1795 indicates he was commanding Engineer in North America, 1779–1794. He contributed to the mapping of North America.

George Curling later served a term as Chairman of Lloyd's.

[11] The Armstrong family has a connection: https://www.fortyhallestate.co.uk.

[12] https://sjriocain.wordpress.com/the-sherson-family-of-fetcham-surrey/ and https://sjriocain.wordpress.com/belcombes/.

[13] See the Dictionary of National Biography, https://doi.org/10.1093/ref:odnb/37678.

Sir Henry Fletcher was one of the first of the returning East India merchants ('Nabobs') to set up a country estate on his return to England.

John Hopkins, Alderman, and then Lord Mayor of London, 1792.

Charles Howard, Earl of Surrey, renounced his Catholic faith to be able to serve in Parliament, became Duke of Norfolk in 1786. The name often appeared as 'Surry' at the time.

Robert Ladbroke was a banker and a Member of Parliament. His father had been Lord Mayor as well as an MP. Ladbroke's nominee was Felix, his son, who later ran the banking firm and was one of the intervenors in the Bayly lawsuit. Felix and his brother Henry were managers of Sun Life Assurance Society, but Felix is most famous as a cricketer.

Thomas Lewis, a Director of the Bank of England, 1801–1815.

Thomas Longman, a trustee of the Tontine and brother-in-law of Thomas Harris, was the transformational developer of the important publishing company Longmans, now part of Pearson.

Charles Steers was a London stock jobber during the latter part of the eighteenth century. He worked alongside his brother James in the consortium brokering government loans known to economic historians as Barnes-Steers-Ricardo.[14] Yes, David Ricardo. The Museum of London holds Steers's Broker's Badge (Accession No. A22407). As a broker, he advertised sales of Hudson Bay Company stock during the 1770s. He died in 1810.

Christopher Taddy, a druggist of Paternoster Row, served on the 'special jury' that convicted Tom Paine *in absentia* of Treason in 1792.

Edward Topham was a society figure, well-regarded adjutant in the Life Guards, and occasional playwright (including *Laura*, produced at Covent Garden in 1786). (Hmmmm.) In 1787, he founded and edited *The World*, a London Newspaper, along with fellow Covent Garden tontineer, Miles Peter Andrew MP.

[14] Parys, Wilfried, *David Ricardo, the Stock Exchange*... University of Antwerp, Department of Economics, Research Paper 2020-009 at page 10 and following. https://repository.uantwerpen.be/docstore/d:irua:3740.

Conclusion

The Covent Garden Theatre Life Tontine should be considered a successful venture, on the whole. It provided additional funding without diluting the Renter's Shares. It received this encomium in the *Public Advertiser* of July 1st, 1785:

> The Covent Garden Tontine has succeeded so well, answering equally the purposes of both buyers and sellers, that it is said Drury-lane and the Opera property go upon a similar scheme.

The finances of the Drury Lane Theatre and the King's Theatre, which produced the Opera, were as precarious as those of Covent Garden. However, neither ever proposed a tontine.

The only serious criticism came many years later. Strife between the management and performers as to changes in customs within the theatre resulted in a pamphlet in 1800 by J. H. Johnstone entitled *A Statement of the Differences Subsisting between the Proprietors and performers of the Theatre-Royal Covent-Garden,* etc.[15] Actor's Benefit performances were a serious part of major actors' income expectations and the management had been making them less and less profitable. On page sixty-six there is this reference: "The Tontine alone introduced at one time *an hundred additional persons* with the right of occupying seats gratis on each Actor's Benefit" (italics in original), thus significantly reducing the actor's take from benefit performance proceeds.

While the price, £250, was steep, likely the highest of any tontine of the period, it was only half that of the Renter's Shares. The interest rate was unusually high, especially when combined with the value of the free admission right. The tontine also likely benefitted from the social attractiveness of the free admission bonus and the general social cachet of association with the highest levels of society.

The additional benefit to Thomas Harris was that the expiration of the Tontine involved no final large payment. This was an element that was used to support using tontines as revenue tools at the municipal and national level.

The negative aspects included the standard complication of regularly proving the continued life of the nominee, although many of the

[15] London: Printed by J. Davis, Chancery-Lane, for W. Miller, Old Bond-Street, 1800.

subscribers nominated their own lives. And, as was standard with all the Georgian tontines, the growth in interest was slower than generally anticipated.

The fatal flaw for the subscribers, in the long run, was the failure to enroll the initial annuity offering in the Chancery, as required by law. This had the effect of preventing legal standing for the subscribers as the administration of the Theatre tried everything to cut their costs in the 1820s. The question remains as to whether this was deliberate or simply forgotten in the process of getting the project off the ground.

CHAPTER 7

The British Government Tontines, Part One

It is curious that in an environment with so many successful tontines, the British Government Tontines tended to be failures. None of them were fully subscribed and substitute schemes had to be improvised both to achieve the desired income for the government and to allow the subscribers to receive their dividends.

It must first be noted that the UK Treasury's borrowing system, which was dependent on variations of the Consolidated Annuities, was oddly open ended. While in theory the Consols were redeemable at the whim of the Government, they were rarely redeemed, so the national debt just carried forward from year to year.

Theoretically, if annuities were to be redeemed, they had to be redeemed at par. But they were rarely issued at par. They were issued at roughly the current market price each year, usually below par during the latter part of the eighteenth century. So, besides the annual interest payment, redemption would involve an additional loss. In practice, however, when there were rare attempts to reduce the debt, the Government bought securities on the open market at the current market price, almost invariably lower than the par price.

In contrast to this, the Long and Short Annuities, which never represented more than a small fraction of the net borrowing, the termination date meant the amount paid out as dividends evaporated at that point. A

K. McKeever, *The Role of Tontines, 1750–1800*, Palgrave Studies in the History of Finance, https://doi.org/10.1007/978-3-032-12849-2_7

tontine had the same attraction in that it comes to an end, albeit many years in the future.

The Million Act, 1693

Although the French national government used tontines regularly, the English rarely did so. The first, in 1693 attempted to raise a million pounds and the Tontine raised only slightly more than ten percent of that figure, £108,000. The rest of the money raised was through annuities paying an interest rate of fourteen percent, an enormous premium. This failure was alluded to every time a later tontine was suggested. The 1693 Tontine is the focus of a book by Moshe Milevsky published in 2017[1] and will only be discussed peripherally in the detailing of later schemes.

Tontines would occasionally be mentioned in budget speculations of the late 1700s. Here is an example from the *General Evening Post* of March 7th, 1776:

> A tontine is talked of among the ways and means for raising the supplies for the present year. There has been no Tontine in England (by Government) since the year 1698, and what is very remarkable, seven lives are now remaining of that subscription.

Two points are interesting in this extract. One is the knowledge that there were still subscribers receiving income from the 1693 Scheme. Second is the ignorance of the proposed Tontines of 1757 and 1765.

A near-to-last death within the 1693 pool was reported in 1779, in the *St. James Chronicle* of Sep 16th:

> Friday died at Enfield, aged 87, Benjamin Boddington, Esq. formerly an eminent Turkey-Merchant,[2] and one of the Survivors in the Annuities granted by King William the Third, who received £1000 clear yearly Income; they are now reduced to three. For some Years past the Surplus of the Interest, by the original Constitution of the Tontine, has been applied to the Uses of the Government.

[1] Milevsky, Moshe A.,*King William's Tontine: Why the Retirement Annuity of the Future Should Resemble its Past*, Cambridge Univ. Press, 2017.

[2] Country, not bird.

1757

Contrary to the unstable government financing in the 1690s, the proposal for a tontine in 1757 was introduced into a relatively stable regime of government loans, involving annuities and lotteries, various forms of which were traded on the stock market of the period. However, the Seven Years' War had just started and the target amount, three million pounds, was a million more than the loan for the year before.

On May 26th, 1756, a text suggesting a tontine appeared in the *Gazetteer and London Daily Advertiser.* Citing Graunt's 1662 mortality data, a crude scheme was outlined including the suggestion: "Suppose that for each of these 100 children…£100 was paid in; this would amount to £10,000 which at 3 per cent would produce £300 to be divided annually between the children and the survivors of them…." Using Graunt's data, it further states that after six years there would be only 64 survivors, after sixteen years only forty, etc. The word tontine is never used: it was a 'Scheme to raise Money for the Service of the Publick.' Without stating it clearly, the description implies the scheme would repeat in perpetuity, creating and then extinguishing the debt over time.

The assumed mortality rate was much faster than any tontine ever experienced. Later investigators produced more accurate tables later in the century.

This seems to be the first hint that a tontine might be under discussion in England. The Mr. Graunt referred to is John Graunt (1620–1674), an early investigator in what would become demography and statistics and author of *Natural and Political Observations Made upon the Bills of Mortality*, London: Thomas Roycroft, 1662.

In the late winter and spring of 1757, the newspapers reported a range of different proposals aiming at a loan of roughly three million, the most detailed of which appeared in the *Public Advertiser* of February 18th and the *London Chronicle* of March 19th.

The 'Annuities on Survivorship' scheme proposed at that stage involved a four percent interest rate for a class with no age limitation, although aimed at children. The tontine effect increase would cease after sixty years. There were to be four additional classes. For subscribers whose nominees were above twenty years old, the interest rate was 4.25% and the capping point came after fifty years. Similarly, subscribers with nominees above thirty received 4.5% interest for 45.5 years; above forty the interest rate was 4.75 capped at 38.5 years, and for those above fifty, the rate was five percent limited at thirty-five years. In the alternative, potential subscribers were also offered simple term annuities whose interest rate depended on the length of the term, from thirty-six years and nine months to sixty-six years.

The proposal evolved, ending up with two and a half million pounds being raised via term annuities and a half million via survivorship life annuities roughly as outlined above. Subscription books based on this framework were opened at the Bank of England in mid-March. However, on March 31st, the *London Evening Post* printed a clarification of the terms. The First Class was not confined to those twenty or under. 'The First Class comprehends Persons of any Age, promiscuously.' At the end of the sixty years, all those left in the class would continue to receive the original annuity plus the augmentation due to the deaths of the other participants. However, there would be no further increase on the deaths of the other participants. The dividend would then be static until the participant's death.

In late April, the Loan framework was changed into the more classic and straightforward Three Percent Annuities with a small Life Annuities sweetener. A few years later Thomas Mortimer, in the 1761 edition of *Every Man His Own Broker*, makes reference to the failure of the project for a reason that will be echoed in 1789:

> The year 1756 or 1757, I think furnished us with an instance of this kind, when a scheme for raising the supplies on a new plan, admirably calculated to prevent the increase of the national debt, and as advantageous to the public, as any that has since been accepted, lay at the Bank for several days unfilled; and was obliged to be laid aside, for no other reason that ever I could find, but, because the Brokers universally cried it down, and advised all their clients to have nothing to do with it for this obvious reason; that the whole transaction was to be betwixt the people and the government; and these gentlemen could reap little or no profit from it.

The London Gazette for April 30th confirmed the change. The Bank Annuity subscription totaled £2,186,900 with Life Annuities issued to a value of £1/2/6 for every £100 subscribed. The would-be tontine portion was converted to this framework. Besides establishing the terms of the conversion for abandoning the Survivorship scheme, this notice provided for a further £500,000 of Bank Annuities to be made available. This brought the revenue to an even three million pounds.

At no time was the word 'tontine' used to describe the offering.

1765

Another tontine issue was attempted in the mid-1760s. A rumor in the *Gazetteer and London Daily Advertiser* of February 1764 stated: "It is confidently said, that a lottery, attended with annuities for life, the proprietors of which are to enjoy the benefit of survivorship, will soon take place, in imitation of the Tontines of France."

On December 19th, the *Gazette and New Daily Advertiser* had a somewhat confusing paragraph using the term lottery to describe a proposed tontine without using the word tontine. The lottery tickets were to cost £100 and the prizes would start at £5 per annum with lives to be designated by June 1767. It continued: "The great objection to a lottery upon lives is, that great frauds have been formerly committed by foreigners (who never die). If such lottery should take place, suppose it was confined to Great Britain and the British islands in Europe. These loose thoughts are thrown together, in hopes that was it may occasion some able calculator to send us a scheme on the above plan."

The Loan that was proposed[3] was originally arranged per £1000 as follows:

£400 as Three percent Annuities, valued at 86	£344
£200 as Tontine shares, valued at 87	£174
40 Lottery Tickets, valued at 12/2/0	£484
	£1002

The Tontine shares were to pay three percent, the same as the standard annuity, but with the increases that would be due to the tontine effect as time passed. There were six classes and individual payouts were to be limited to £1,500. The attraction for the government was that once the pool of tontine owners had died, the debt was extinguished, while regular annuities retained their value on a perpetual basis. If they were ever redeemed, the Government had to pay par value no matter what

[3] *London Evening Post,* March 26th, 1765.

they were sold for or trading for at the time. They were discounted at a rate roughly equivalent to the Consols in the same offering.

This loan was also aimed at reducing the pool of outstanding unpaid Navy Bills accumulated during the Seven Years' War, which had just concluded. This was noted in the *Leeds Intelligencer* of March 12th, 1765:

> Yesterday the Bank of England agreed to lend the Government £1,000,000 at three per cent. by way of annuity lottery, and tontine or survivorship. The possessors of the navy bills are to have their preference of subscribing their bills in first.

The price of shares in the Tontine shows up, either as 'Survivorship' or 'Tontine' in the newspaper stock quotations in late March. Ultimately, 'tontine' became standard. *Lloyd's List* on April 2nd, 1765, using the term 'tontine,' shows trading around 91 and a fraction. When traded during April, it bounced between 89 and 90. However, for many days there are no trades reported. By early June, it dropped to 87. It crept back up to 89 in early August but was still rarely traded. It reached 90 in early September but was back at 89 in December. The last price quoted was on May 2nd, 1766, when it traded at 88 and a quarter.

The deadline for enrolling in the Tontine was noted in *Lloyd's Evening Post* as May 6th, 1766. Lloyd's then reported that "There not being nominees enough to form a class in the Tontine, it is thought it will be altered into transferrable stock redeemable by Parliament." At that time, it was reported only thirty-seven investors signed up for the Tontine.[4] Ultimately, 180 tontine shares were purchased and treated as a single class. Many would-be purchases were reported as having been converted into 'Reduced Annuities,' also paying three percent.[5] The Lloyd's List 'Tontine' entry is dropped in the May 9th issue. The Three Percent Reduced Annuities were also trading for 88 and a fraction at that time, providing a rough equivalence.

The 'List of Unclaimed Dividends' of the Bank of England printed in the *Public Advertiser* of June 16th and 17th, 1791, showed twenty-seven 1765 tontineers among the neglectful investors.

[4] *Gazetteer and New Daily Advertiser*, May 9th, 1766.

[5] The 'reduced annuity' was one of the standard funds of the time.

A much later analysis, printed in the *Morning Post* of October 8th, 1898, reported that the subscriptions amounted to only £18,000, creating a dividend pool of only £540, 'an amount insufficient to complete even one of the six classes contemplated.' Sir C. Yorke and Sir William de Grey, Law Officers of the Crown, decided that: "even the first class could not be completed by reason of the paucity of subscribers, yet these were entitled to the benefits for which they had subscribed, and directions were accordingly given by the Treasury on July 26, 1766, for carrying the provisions of the Act into execution. One hundred and thirty-eight lives were nominated in respect of the 180 shares subscribed." The final survivor was Lieutenant-General Sir John Slade, who "died on August 13, 1859, after having enjoyed the whole of the annuity of £540 for about four years."

This illustrates the sense of obligation the government felt toward the subscribers who insisted on keeping their tontine shares, in contrast to French edicts abrogating the tontine elements of their schemes four years later.

The statute that is recited in the text seen on the receipt shown in Fig. 7.1 is the Loan Act of 1765. The payment is to Thomas Somers Cocks, an attorney (who lived at 12 Downing Street, two doors down from the Prime Minister's residence/office.) It states it is 'during the life of Mary Cocks.'[6] It is dated December 2nd, 1782—the second printed '7' in the form is overwritten an '8'. The payment is for the sum of £1/15/5¼, which would amount to £3/10/10½ per year on a security which was sold at three percent. If it were not a tontine, the payment would have been a flat £3. Seventeen years after the purchase, the dividend has increased by ten shillings ten and a half pence, just over eighteen percent. The only reason for that would be the Tontine effect.

Noted on the back of this receipt is 'Survivorship 1766 4th Dec. 1782 Paid £3.10.10½.'

[6] Thomas Somers Cocks's third daughter, Maria, is reported marrying an Admiral Harcourt in 1811. The oldest and second daughters were each nominees in the Irish Tontines of 1773 and 1775.

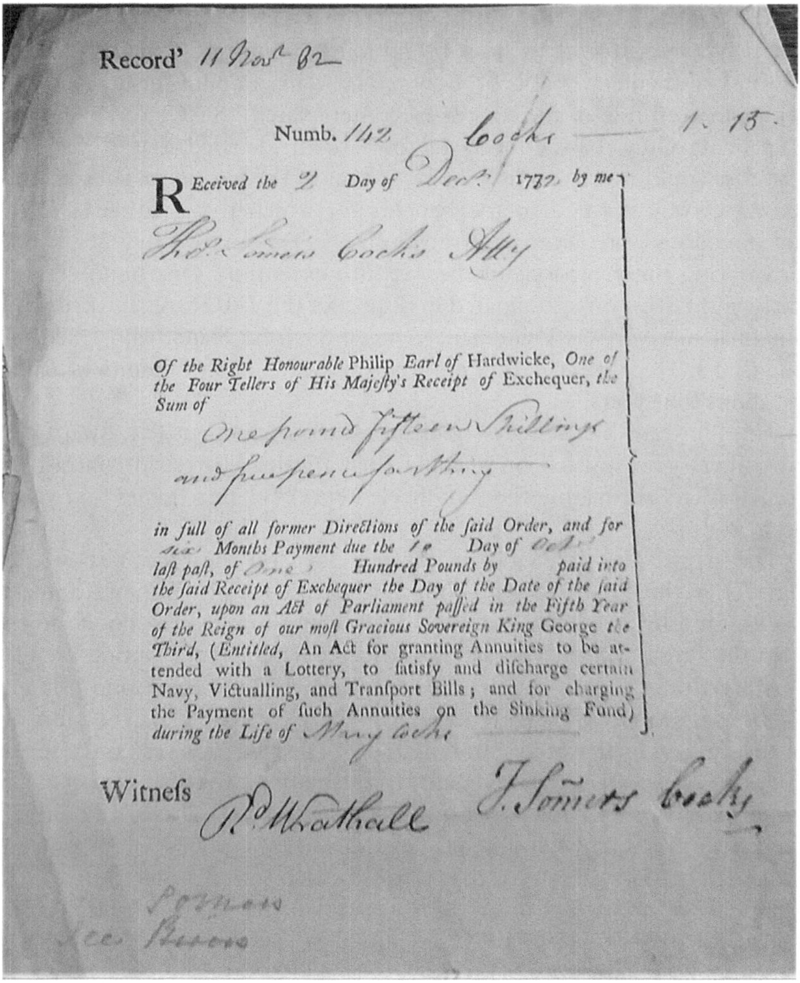
Record' 11 Novr 82

Numb. 142 Cocks — 1. 15.

Received the 2 Day of Decr 1772. by me

Thos Somers Cocks Att^y

Of the Right Honourable Philip Earl of Hardwicke, One of the Four Tellers of His Majesty's Receipt of Exchequer, the Sum of

One pound fifteen Shillings and fivepence farthing

in full of all former Directions of the said Order, and for six Months Payment due the 10 Day of Octr last past, of One Hundred Pounds by paid into the said Receipt of Exchequer the Day of the Date of the said Order, upon an Act of Parliament passed in the Fifth Year of the Reign of our most Gracious Sovereign King George the Third, (Entitled, An Act for granting Annuities to be attended with a Lottery, to satisfy and discharge certain Navy, Victualling, and Transport Bills; and for charging the Payment of such Annuities on the Sinking Fund) during the Life of Mary Cocks

Witness R^d Whathall T. Somers Cocks

Fig. 7.1 The receipt is for a payment on this Tontine

A Digression: The Irish Tontines

The Irish economy in the eighteenth century was never stable, as it suffered from its subordinate status in relation to Great Britain. One solution attempted three times in the 1770s was the creation of general revenue tontines. They were successful in the sense of their being fully subscribed, but the amount of money raised was not enough to keep the government in the black and the last one, in 1777, was predicated on a ruinous seven and a half percent interest rate. In 1780, the Irish Government opted for an annual lottery.

One unusual aspect of the 1773 Tontine was that the annual interest payments to subscribers were capped at the amount of the purchase. The dividends on a £100 share could increase to £100 over time, but would never go above that, no matter how small the pool of survivors became. This did not pass unnoticed, per this from the *Daily Advertiser* of December 8th, 1773:

> A letter from Dublin mentions, that the raising of present taxes by Survivorship in Ireland, is looked upon in so advantageous a light for the Subscribers, that very near the whole of that money (£265,000) will be filled up by the principal persons of that Kingdom, without the interference of the People of England; there is an additional clause, however, that makes this Scheme not altogether so advantageous to subscribers, as appeared upon the first sketch, which is, that no survivor (though he may be the last) can be entitled to more than the same sum *annually*, which he originally subscribed.

Contrary to the expectation indicated above, the majority of the subscribers were from England.

The 1777 Tontine attracted a very sophisticated group of investors from Geneva who tried two significant approaches to reduce the risks. They selected as nominees, following medical advice, young women of long-lived families. They then pooled their shares in an early form of a derivative so the loss of income from the early death of a nominee was shared by all the participants, but all of the participants continued to have the income from the remaining nominees. The primary broker for this process was the Genevan-born Peter Thellusson (naturalized in London in 1762), although David Duval and Martin and Co had Swiss clients as well.

Irish accounts indicate a sum of slightly over £46 was spent advertising the Tontine in Holland and London. Thellusson was the primary agent for more than £100,000 of the total.

A report in the *Times* of December 17th, 1927 claimed: "The sole survivor of the tontine, an old lady living in Switzerland, lived to receive a sum of no less than £7,784, 3s, 11d, as one half year's dividend."

Administrative Headaches

The post-issuance selling of tontine shares generated an additional problem in maintaining the records. The text of the 1793 letter below, from a Scottish merchant in London, G. F. Kinloch to a Chas. Buchan, Esq., in Ayr, is a good example of the difficulty in maintaining contact with a nominated 'life' after the transfer of ownership of a share in a tontine:

> We rec'd for some years an Irish Tontine in the principal sum of £100 for the late Provost David Fergusson who died considerably in our debt on the life of his Daughter Mrs. Stevenson, but no certificate of her life has been transmitted to us since the Provost's death. We shall be obliged to you therefore to procure us a certificate signed by your Minister agreeable to the enclosed form as after the expiration of three years from the last receipt there may be some risk of its being forfeited. We hope you will excuse and believe us very much at your service in any similar election...[7]

Fergusson was Provost in Ayr, Scotland, and died on March 3rd, 1791. *Musgrave's Obituaries*[8] lists him as Collector of Customs. Kinloch was a multiple share shareholder in the Bank of Scotland.

Another aspect of tontines was the occasional nomination of a public figure as the nominee of a shareholder. The most likely reason for this was it eliminated the necessity of having to constantly affirm the life of one's nominee. A public figure's life was common knowledge. The following aftermarket advertisement from *The Times* of June 1816 shows an extreme version of this:

> By Mr. ADAMSON, at the Auction Mart, on Tuesday, June 11, at 12, in 7 Lots, by direction of the Assignees of Mr. Alex. Anderson
>
> > Lot 1. ONE HUNDRED POUNDS DEBENTURE on the Life of his Royal Highness the Prince Regent, with the benefit of survivorship, the last half-yearly dividend being £4/16/10 sterling.
> > Lot 2. One ditto half-yearly dividend on his Royal Highness's life, being £4/3/0 sterling.
> > Lot 3. One ditto, ditto, ditto, £4/3/0.
> > Lot 4. One ditto, ditto, ditto, £4/3/0.
> > Lot 5. One ditto on the life of the Duke of York, £4/3/0.
> > Lot 6. Ditto, ditto, £4/5.0.

[7] Collection of the author.

[8] Musgrave, William, and G. J. Armytage, *Obituary prior to 1800*, London, 1899–1901.

Lot 7. Ditto, ditto, £4/8/0.

Particulars may be had at the Mart: of Mr. Osbaldeston, solicitor, Loudon street, Fenchurch-street; and of Mr. Adamson, 58, Fenchurch-street.

The Prince Regent became King George IV, who died in 1830. The Duke of York died in 1827.

In a punctilious contrast, the death of a very public nominee to the Freemasons' Tontine of 1775, King George III, in January 1820, did not preclude the Secretary of that Tontine from including the King in a nudge advertisement in *The Morning Chronicle* for information on two of the nominees in that Tontine six months later, on June 20th, 1820.

In 1812, there was a Parliamentary investigation[9] of the administration of the Irish Tontine dividends. The initial complaint involved "...disappointment that the Dividends had not advanced in proportion to the general opinion of the probabilities of the deaths of the Nominees." The primary *Report* concluded: "...a want of method, laxity of regulation, and negligence, prevailed to a most culpable degree; owing to which many payments were made, in cases where the Claim of the Proprietors had been long since forfeited. With a view to prevent such abuse, the attention of the Irish Government had been applied in forming and prescribing new Regulations for the future conduct of the Office."

The report does not go into any questions as to the statistical accuracy of the dividends and their slow increase. However, the Appendix of the second Report is a rich source for everyday execution of the clerical tasks involved, and how they could be abused. The acme of that situation was the admission by the office manager that a clerk who had embezzled from them was still working in the office!

What became of Carr? —Carr still continues... ...he is very clever in some parts of the business, and it is a difficult task to arrange and-conduct it properly; I was obliged to continue Carr... ...I did not intend to take Carr back; but necessity compelled me to it; there was no Clerk could do the business.

[9] The key texts are Great Britain, House of Commons, Select Committee on State and Management of Tontine Annuities granted in Ireland in 1773, &c., *Report*, and Select Committee on State and Management of Tontine Annuities granted in Ireland in 1773, &c., *Second Report*, Appendix, 1812–13.

A clerk who was truly good with numbers was astoundingly valuable.

The Times of June 1st, 1871, contained a report based on a later Parliamentary document that displays the classic nineteenth-century attitude regarding tontine information only as a matter of amusing curiosity:

> The surviving annuitant in Dublin of this class of the tontine of 1778 was a widow lady named Wade, who was 44 when nominated, and she appeared personally at the age of 96 to receive her annuity, then £730. 7s. 5d. in return for the original subscription of £100... ...The second class comprised persons who were between 20 and 40 when nominated; and the youngest possible ages of the last survivors were 97 and 99. The third class comprised persons under 20 when nominated: and the last return describes a survivor of the tontine of 1778 still remaining who has received the annuity for 92 years.

Irish Tontines as a Precursors to the British Tontine of 1789

The seeming success of the Irish Government tontines should be seen as a large part of the background to the decision to attempt a British Government tontine in 1789. The Irish annuities were fully subscribed to and had a record for reliable payment even when the payment system did get confused in the early 1800s.

The report below, from *The Times* of July 4th, 1787, gives the status of the three offerings at that point. This particular news story is worth recording in full because it represents one of the best presentations of tontine mortality rates available to the public in the run-up to the National Tontine of 1789.

> Irish Tontines
>
> The following state of them which may be depended on as minutely faithful, will, no doubt, be acceptable to the numerous Subscribers and the Public:

TONTINE OF 1773

Youngest Class		
Shares that have dropped are		85
Do.	remaining	1612
Middle Class		
Shares	dropped	92
Do.	remaining	639
Old Class		
Shares	dropped	18
Do.	remaining	223

TONTINE OF 1775

Young Class		
Shares that have dropped are		60
Do.	remaining	1090
Middle Class		
Shares	dropped	31
Do.	remaining	364
Old Class		
Shares	dropped	21
Do.	remaining	184

TONTINE OF 1777

Young Class		
Shares	dropped	85
Do.	remaining	2201
Middle Class		
Shares	dropped	30
Do.	remaining	473
Old Class		
Shares	dropped	8
Do.	remaining	203

The interest in the Tontine of	1773 began at	5 per cent
Do.	1775	6 per cent.
Do.	1777	7/10/0 per cent.

In the last Tontine, the first offer to the Public was at six percent, but the combined fleets at the time appearing in the Channel, an alarm spread and only £60,000 were subscribed.

£300,000 were wanted, and to supply this want, Government raised the offered interest to 7½, at which terms the loan was instantly complete; and the alarm soon giving way to good preparation, each subscription got 11 per cent above par.
Peter Thellusson was the greatest gainer on Paris,[10] to the amount it is said of near £20,000. Brown and Company, Nesbitts, one of the Clements, and Latouche, also profited much.
Of the Subscription last mentioned, above six-fifteenths are in *foreign names*, and chiefly the Swiss, and from Geneva.

The penultimate survivor of the third tontine was James Martin. His dividends from 1854 through 1871 culminating in a six-month dividend of £3,891/10/2 are noted in a history of Martins Bank,[11] whose street sign was a golden grasshopper. The final survivor was a Genevan woman.

A Digression: The Million Bank

There is one earlier scheme, unrelated to a tontine, that might be seen as a precedent for the Geneva-based program: the Million Bank. It was unrelated to the Million Act Tontine of 1693. It was founded in 1695 with a capital based on the Million Pound Lottery that year wherein the non-winning tickets were also annuities that paid interest through 1710. As the lottery-based pool of income expired, the bank reconfigured itself, shifting into a complex scheme which, oversimplified, traded shares in itself plus a regular five percent dividend for the rights to individual fourteen percent government long term or Life Annuities issued in the early 1700s. This was possible because the life specified by the annuity did not have to be the owner of the annuity. In effect, annuity holders could stretch their participation beyond the deaths of particular lives. They received a perpetual transferable share with a reasonable dividend rate. The bank also bought life insurance on the annuity lives, thus earning a cash bonus as the annuity expired.

As the eighteenth century progressed and the annuity lives slowly expired, the capital was again shifted, this time to the standard securities, the South Sea and Consolidated Annuities, and South Sea Stock in

[10] Likely a typo for 'par.'

[11] Martin, John B, *"The Grasshopper" in Lombard Street*, London: Leadenhall Press, 1892 at page 100.

addition to the increasingly smaller core of the pool of Fourteen Percent Reversions. When the lives or terms entitled to the Fourteen Percent Annuities were exhausted, in the early 1790s, the bank was wound up via an Act of Parliament, the Million Bank Act 1796, *36 Geo. III. Cap. 91.* The conversion of the individual Annuities into a basis for a shared profit pre-figures a key element in the Geneva scheme for the Irish Tontines.[12]

[12] A good summary is found in Fairman's *The stocks examined and compared*, 1796 edition, at pages 52–3.

CHAPTER 8

British Government Tontines, Part Two

Great Britain Tries Again, 1789

After the three successful tontines issued by the Irish Government in 1773, 1775, and 1777, and the rise of private tontines, the English government decided to attempt a National British Tontine in 1789. It was designed to provide virtually all the borrowing necessary for that fiscal year. This was something of an experiment to see if the tontine could work as a substitute for the annuities which had been the core of budget financing since the 1720s. One major attraction was that as the tontine pools dwindled, the loan itself was extinguished. With the standard annuities, the capital had to be eventually repaid to the purchaser, even though in practice they rarely were. While small amounts of the Loan were covered by short-term annuities and the annual lottery, the tontine was designed to provide the core one million pounds.

Background

In the spring of 1780, a report[1] on the annual loan negotiations included this isolated line: "His Lordship [Lord North, the Prime Minister] said he could have wished to have made 3 per cent. with a small tontine of 5s the basis of the agreement between him and the subscribers but that the

[1] *Whitehall Evening Post*, March 7th, 1780.

K. McKeever, *The Role of Tontines, 1750–1800*, Palgrave Studies in the History of Finance, https://doi.org/10.1007/978-3-032-12849-2_8

latter were of a different opinion…." It is not clear what was meant by a five-shilling tontine.

A similar snippet about a possible government tontine in 1782 attributed a proposed tontine element in the next Loan to Sir Grey Cooper. He served in the House of Commons from 1765 through 1790 and was the Secretary of the Treasury from 1765 to 1782. It was not implemented.

In 1782,[2] there were hints in the London newspapers that the next Prime Minister, William Pitt the Younger, was contemplating a tontine to pay off a large portion of the accumulated Three Percent and Four Percent Annuities. After the end of the American Revolution, the government apparently had a surplus in its budget and that provoked discussion on how best to exploit it.

The April 16th, 1785, issue of *The Morning Chronicle* suggested a tontine for the next annual loan. "…[W]e cannot help but suggest a TONTINE. Among the various modes of borrowing, none offer,[3] which could be so greedily caught at by the people. If the Minister be properly attentive to contemporary occurrences, we cannot fail in knowing, with every other observer, the event of two extensive private negotiations, in which a tontine was the plan for raising the money, and it was all raised before the proposals were made publick."

The two tontines mentioned in the third paragraph remain unidentified. It is probable that one was the Kew Bridge Tontine (begun in 1783) for which no advertisements seem to have been printed. It is possible that the other was the Covent Garden Tontine (1785), which was lightly and anonymously advertised, and through which participants were receiving benefits before it was formally established.

Amidst the flurry of tontine rumors, on December 15th, 1785, the *St. James Chronicle* reported: "At a meeting in Downing-Street on Monday-Night, at which the ablest Calculators in the Kingdom assisted, a Plan for Converting into a Tontine Fifty Millions of the 3 per Cents. was submitted to the Minister's Attention and, as it is *reported* actually approved of." However, *The Morning Chronicle* of the very same date stated: "We can assure our readers, that Ministry have no idea of aiming

[2] *The Morning Chronicle*, April 16th, 1782.

[3] Likely a typo for 'on offer.'

at the attainment of any national benefit, by the Tontine scheme so frequently mentioned in the publick prints."

The London Chronicle on December 20th, 1785, reported: "The much talked-of plan of a tontine, for the redemption of the public debt, it is now believed, will not take place; the monied men disapprove of it (perhaps from interested views)...." This echoes earlier and later similar statements of opposition by the brokers to a tontine, in that it was perceived as a deal between the government and the people, not giving much flexibility for middlemen to make a profit.

The back and forth continued. In January, 1786, the *Public Advertiser* stated: "The idea held forth lately of a tontine, is complicated absurdity".[4] But later in January the *London Chronicle* responded: "The scheme of a tontine is again revived for subscribing 25 millions of 3 and 4 per cents. into life annuities; and so far from any fear of its not filing, it is supposed, from applications already made, that twice the sum will be subscribed. It is to be divided into many classes to accommodate all ages."[5] *The Times* had a similar 'most confident report' on January 21st.

In the first week of February, the *Public Advertiser* reported the tontine idea had been dropped. "The idea of life annuities, or a tontine, is entirely abandoned; but the surplus is to be applied in purchasing two millions of Stock in the market...."[6] Stock in this case means Government annuities, and the hint is that this might be a very rare occasion when government actually redeemed some of the annuities.

Other Tontines of That Period

Besides the Irish Tontines, in the 1770s and 1780s a number of successful smaller tontines had been created, including the ones used to build Richmond Bridge, Kew Bridge, and the Freemasons' Hall. A purely financial one, the Society of Annuities Encreasing to the Survivors, or Siprut's Tontine, had also proven successful. There were also failures, most notably the Uxbridge Tontine of 1785.

In 1789, a number of other municipal or non-governmental tontines were advertised. They included schemes based in London, Bath, Bristol,

[4] *Public Advertiser*, January 4th, 1786.

[5] *The London Chronicle*, January 17th, 1786.

[6] *The London Chronicle*, January 17th, 1786.

Doncaster, Exeter, Glasgow, Gloucester, and, based on Irish properties, Lord Cork's Tontine. The year before, Middlesex County created a Tontine to build a 'House of Correction.'

The Times reported rumors of a large private tontine on July 15th, 1789, amid the debate over the government's tontine proposal.

> A private loan is now subscribing in the City, to the amount of one hundred thousand pounds, by the way of Tontine, said to be for the use of three gentlemen at the West end of the town, to be paid off when either shall arrive at his paternal inheritance. The medium terms of the above loan are seven years purchase; and one gentleman in the City has already bought in seven hundred a year for seven thousand pounds.

This story was copied in other papers, but no other record of this has been uncovered.

The Reappearance of a National Tontine

Pre-budget tontine rumors were slim in 1789. In April, a comment appeared in *The World*[7] which was seemingly directed at the smaller tontines, but it might also have served as an indirect hint to Pitt and his circle:

> Tontine Schemes/By various Adventurers, in various modes, are now attempting about the country. To all of them it should be known that the last granted Tontine, secured by no less than the PARLIAMENTARY FAITH of Ireland, STARTED AT 7½ PER CENT. encreasing by Survivorship.

In early June, the same newspaper stated 'A TONTINE SCHEME is in consideration, as part of year's Budget.'[8]

The next day the *Morning Star* reported that "MR. PITT is to raise a million by a Tontine for the service of the current year. The principal Bankers have been in treaty on the subject with the Chancellor of the Exchequer all the week, and a meeting was held for this purpose in Downing-street yesterday."

[7] *The World*, April 8th, 1789.

[8] *The World*, June 4th, 1789.

Note this is for the annual operating loan, not a special proposal to reduce current debt by substituting the Tontine for outstanding Consolidated Annuities. In early June, *The World*[9] published a rumor on debt reduction: "Mr. Pitt will introduce new improvements in the revenue not only by a tontine at present, but by using the same operation of finance more largely, and converting some of the perpetual Funds into Life Annuities of which a Tontine is obviously the most enticing."

Pitt had a significant financial advisor during this time, George Atwood, who had taught natural sciences—Physics—at Cambridge during Pitt's time there. A later short biographical note on Atwood stated:

> At these lectures, which were largely attended, the younger Pitt was, for several terms, one of Atwood's most constant and attentive auditors, and the future statesman entertained a high opinion of the natural philosopher's ability and integrity. When, in 1784, the son of the great Chatham became the head of the English administration, he employed Atwood as his private secretary for financial affairs; and most of the details, if not the principles, of the various schemes for raising money for the public service were laid down by him.[10]

In any case, in June 1789 a Tontine was finally incorporated into the Annual Budget. The text below appeared in the June 9th *The World.* "One Million is to be thus raised… …Mess, Angerstein, Johnson, and Devaynes have this loan – For it they give a premium of a quarter per cent. which on one million is £2,500." The description of the survivorship element states the dividend is never to go beyond £1,000, with a nomination deadline of October 1790. The six classes were described, and the interest rates are given for each class, from £4/3/0 per hundred for the youngest through £5/12/6 per cent, for the nominees over sixty. The announcement ends with the installment payment deadlines.

The proposed interest rates for the various classes of the Tontine are higher than the basic Consolidated Annuities (Consols) but were not extravagant. There were no Consols offered in the loan package for this year although a small amount of Short Annuities (£14,000) were included, taken by the banker Thomas Hammersley, whose clients

[9] *The World*, June 8th, 1789.

[10] See also *A new catalogue of living English authors*, London: printed for C. Clark, 1799, Vol. 1, pages 115–118.

included the Prince of Wales. The annual Lottery was subscribed by E.P. Solomons, T. Solomons, and Thomas Cope.[11] Lottery tickets were valued at £15/8/7½ each for a pool of £200,000.

It is worth noting that in past years, the Consols offered in the annual loan package were discounted to reflect the market rate at that time. The Tontine shares were not discounted but were taken by the subscribers at par plus a tiny premium. This was probably one of the main attractions of a tontine scheme for the government. The government received a full one hundred pounds for their interest payments instead of a discounted market price.

The underwriting bankers for the Tontine were John Julius Angerstein, a major broker who was later the Chairman of Lloyd's; Godschall Johnson, who was one of his associates; and William Devaynes, who was a Director and sometime Chairman of the East India Company, a Member of Parliament, and was named a Baronet in December 1790.

The World, in particular, seemed to have an interest rate obsession. It commented the day after the announcement comparing Pitt's scheme to the Irish Tontine of 1777: "Say nothing of the Tontine – for the last Tontine on Parliamentary faith, the Nation paid Seven and a half per cent. – where here they pay only Four Pounds Three Shillings! –N.B. ANGERSTEIN, JOHNSON, and DEVAYNES, are too well known to be run down."

The Response

The Tontine shares immediately started being traded in the stock market. It was actually scrip, i.e., the result of the first installment payment, although not described as such. The brokers didn't know how the retail market would work, since there was no market price in the traditional sense.

The first appearance on *Lloyd's List* on Friday, June 12th, shows them trading at a quickly rising price. The Thursday column showed the price as a percentage premium on the par value. The Friday column showed the actual prices. The Tontine was allocated space at the bottom of the list of stocks.

[11] The first Solomons is likely a typo. It was likely the banker Eleazer Philip Salomons and associates.

Lloyd's report was published before the first payment was due on the Tontine shares and before the enabling bill was passed into law. This may have been simply the standard behavior of the stockjobbing community, making time bargains without actually owning any of the underlying stock. However, at a meeting later in June, the subscribers were reported as saying they had '...suffered only small sums of the loan to come into the market....'[12] The added complications of the 'life' nominating process and the certification of the lives of the nominees in order to receive the dividend were in the future. Participants forfeited their rights if the affidavit testifying to the continued life of a nominee was not submitted in time. At this early stage, that rigmarole had yet to be fully understood.

The trading took place even though part of the appeal of the Tontine was that its shares would not be part of the rough-and-tumble of the exchange, as suggested by this from *The World:* "Mr. Pitt's Tontine, besides its first obvious benefit to the Revenue, will have this secondary good consequence – it will prevent individuals from suffering by the various hedge schemes, now so rife about the country."[13]

Contrariwise, the following snippet, from *The Oracle* dated the same day, June 12th, 1789, hints at stockjobbing shenanigans, oddly naming the wrong lead subscribers:

> An astonishing fluctuation took place yesterday at the Stock Exchange; considering the space of time, and that the public were in possession of the facts some days ago it may be considered as unprecedented in the annals of stockjobbing. The premium on TONTINE opened in the morning at five-eighths, or 12s 6d per cent. rather heavy; but on closing at three, the premium had risen to 4 per cent. which on the whole million would have produced an immediate fortune of FOUR HUNDRED THOUSAND POUNDS to the Contractors, Messrs. COPE and SOLOMONS had the whole sum been sold at the same rate.

A few days later, *The Oracle* reported a new high price for the Tontine Shares, five percent above par, dropping to four and three quarters at the close.[14]

[12] *Whitehall Evening Post*, June 20th, 1789.

[13] *The World*, June 12th, 1789.

[14] *The Oracle*, June 16th, 1789.

Then a disagreement arose between the government and the subscribers. The subscribers were counting on interest payments for the whole offering starting after the payment of the first installment as had been the practice in the past for the standard annuities. The government wanted to pay interest on each installment only as it was paid for.[15] A meeting on this issue was the subject of a seemingly candid report in the *Whitehall Evening Post* of June 20th:

> When they [Angerstein, Devaynes, and Johnson] made the bargain it was agreed that the subscribers should have four per cent. until the nomination of the Annuitants in the month of October 1790; and the purchasers understood that this loan was to be like all former bargains, namely, to bear interest on the whole sum from the day of the payment of the first installment. The first payment of ten per cent. took place last week. On the issuing the receipts the subscribers found, to their astonishment, that their receipt was to bear interest only for £10 and not the £100 which it ought to have done agreeable to the constant custom of former loans.

In attempting to resolve the dispute, the Minister turned to the subscribers to the Lottery, Solomons and Cope, who had been in the room as the original deal was worked out. Unfortunately, Solomons agreed with Angerstein *et al.*, and Cope sided with Mr. Pitt. The meeting did not reach a resolution.

The misunderstanding became the subject of a Parliamentary debate, as reported in *The Times*, *The Oracle*, and *The World* of June 26th. Pitt introduced a bill to accommodate the subscribers. He stated that while he had understood the proposal as not providing full interest right away, he was willing to concede that the subscribers had understood the traditional custom applied and he, Pitt, could live with that. The MP (and playwright) Richard Brinsley Sheridan complained it would throw the budget off by £10,000, but Pitt felt the anticipated taxes would be enough to handle it. Another MP, William Hussey wanted to know if Pitt had been shown the calculations made by the subscribers in arriving at their bids, and Pitt indicated he had.

The dispute was resolved in favor of the 'Monied Men.'

The formal Bill passed the House of Lords in late June and was enrolled as 29 George III Cap XLI. It was a typical revenue bill, a detailed

[15] *St. James Chronicle*, June 23rd, 1789.

and dense text of forty sections, taking up ten pages (534–544) of *The Statutes at Large: From the Twenty-sixth Year of the Reign of King George the Third to the Twenty-ninth Year of the Reign of King George the Third* (Vol. 15). M. Baskett. 1789. Nationwide advertising for it started immediately, starting with the formal announcement in *The London Gazette* of September 12th–15th, 1789, pp. 597–600, which served as the model for all the newspaper notices.

The Tontine consisted of 10,000 shares costing £100 each. It had six classes divided by age with dividends increasing with each class:

First class	Birth to 20	£4/3/0 annual dividend per £100
Second class	20–30	£4/5/6 "
Third class	30–40	£4/8/6 "
Fourth class	40–50	£4/13/6 "
Firth class	50–60	£5/2/6 "
Sixth class	Above 60	£5/12/0 "

The Tontine paid four percent until the subscriptions were complete. The nomination deadline was on October 10th, 1790. Payments could be made in £15 installments roughly monthly. Foreigners need not apply.

A comparison to the Consols was included in the advertising: "The Average of this Table will be found to be 4/12/0 per Cent. which estimating the 3 per Cent. Consols, without the Dividend, at the present Price 75, is worth £117/10/0." That is to say, one would have to own £117 ½ worth of the Consols to earn the same interest as the Tontine.

The increase of payments due to the tontine effect was capped at one thousand pounds. Interest payments were to be made twice a year, available at the Exchequer every Midsummer and Christmas. A final note in the advertising indicated the shares were sold on the Stock Exchange.

A Predictive Assessment

On May 1st, 1790, *The World* published a short report on the Irish Tontines that could be taken as an indicator of the likely mortality rate of the 1789 Tontine. It provided information on the individual classes, but the gross totals show that, as of Christmas, 1789, 92.8% of the nominees of the 1773 Tontine were still alive, 91.2% of the nominees of the 1775 Tontine were alive, and 94.1% of the nominees of the 1777 Tontine were alive. A reasonable reader could have worked with these figures as an indication of the probable mortality and rate of increase of the returns on the National Tontine of 1789.

Encouragement

This extended text in the *Public Advertiser* of June 19th, 1790, is essentially an exercise in public relations or advertising, not a piece of reportage:

> Notice having been given in the Exchequer for the holders of Tontine to give in the names upon whose lives they wish to have the annuity granted, will now give vigour to the Tontine, and be the means of compleating the nomination of the whole million long before the 10th of October.
>
> According to the Act of Parliament, all persons nominating before the 10th of October, in case the party so nominated should die, may take a fresh name or even change one nomination for another before the said 10th of October next, if they think proper.
>
> No person can have more than £1000 a year upon one life; but if any person chooses to nominate ten or fifteen lives in one class, and there should be £10 or 15,000 a year in that class, he may have £1000 a year for every name that survives; or if he takes his own life ten times over, he may have £10,000 a year upon it.
>
> To single women of small fortunes, a Tontine is peculiarly enviting, because every hundred pound laid out must give a very large income in the course of a few years, and may give £1000 a year.
>
> The Irish Tontine bore a premium of 20 percent within a few days of the time appointed for nomination, and it is generally expected that those who have waited to buy cheap, as the time approaches in the English Tontine, will be very glad to give 110 for shares which they now neglect at 98. According to Mr. Pitt's calculation, the Tontine is now worth 104 per cent. as there is 4 percent interest due the 24th of this month.
>
> There is no comparison between the Irish and English Tontine; the Irish Tontine was filled with foreign names, which never die; whereas the Government Tontine now on sale must be filled by natives, and residents in Great Britain. Foreigners are excluded altogether.

> It is possible that one class may engage so many nominees as for the interest to amount to £20 or 30,000 per ann. in which case two or three persons holding ten shares a piece, may have £10,000 a year each.
>
> By the Last Act of Parliament, the whole million of Tontine: must be completed, that is, the whole £10,000 shares must be nominated; for all that the public does not take, will be taken by the Lords of the Treasury, who are empowered to nominate English, Scotch, and Irish Peers, their children and grand children, the Baronets of England and Scotland, Bishops, Deans, Archdeacons, Prebendaries, the Governors of the Charter-House, the Governors of the Foundling and Christ Hospitals, &c. &c. &c.

The whole tone of this piece reflects the overly optimistic increase in returns to be expected via a tontine. The failure to meet these expectations is likely one of the primary reasons for the eventual decline in tontines in the nineteenth century.

A similar optimistic note was struck in the same newspaper for July 13th: "The Tontine is in great repute abroad as well as at home. -- One of the first Brokers of the Stock Exchange has bought, for a French house, and an Indian connection, more than five hundred shares, and the sale increases daily."

The Plan Falters

By late summer there were signs of the Tontine's ultimate failure, based in part on it not developing a premium in the market and in part on its comparatively low interest rate. Per *The Times* of August 25th, 1789: "Those who took the whole purchase from Government (sic) went much upon the expectation that there would be large speculations on it, in which they have been greatly disappointed. Taking it by way of an annuity the interest is certainly not proportionable to what many other public bodies allow."

The next day this snippet on the Tontine's low interest rate appeared in *The Times* as well:

> The TONTINE is likely to prove a very heavy loss to the proprietors who farmed[16] it of Government. Not above one third of it is actually sold out of the Stock Exchange. The security is certainly the best, but the people who buy an annuity, look for a larger interest.

Additional critics of the scheme spoke up quickly when the market price did not increase. This attack in *The English Chronicle*[17] is fairly candid:

> Whoever recommends the Tontine is either a knave or a blockhead for he must do it with a view to deceive mankind with respect to its worth or he must be ignorant of calculation altogether: Tontine at the present price is near 20 per cent. above its value. The man who does not know this knows nothing.
> Those who sold Consols at 75, to buy Tontine at 105, which was never worth 90, have great reason to acknowledge an obligation to their brokers for they have gained a loss of 7 per cent. by so doing, and will probably be shortly inclined to sell Tontine at 90, to buy Consols again at 85.

The declaration of Tontine price being beyond its value is based on two possible analyses. One would be based on the then current rate for a standard life annuity. While the nature of the annuity trade meant rates were not a matter of a listing price, the formulas for pricing life annuities were well known and published in a range of mathematical/financial guidebooks. The second would be a comparison to the current market value of the Long Annuities. In fact, when the Tontine was later abandoned and subscribers were offered Long Annuities paying £4/5/0 annually as a substitute, the perception was the value of that offer was around £92/0/0 instead of the £100 Tontine par value.

By September, the Tontine was selling at a slight discount:

> The Tontine was yesterday done at a discount, that is at £100 and the original subscription was £100 and a quarter premium. They have lost this, therefore, and all the interest on the two payments already made. It will be down still further, for it will not stand the test of calculation. It might do for a club at an alehouse, where men agreed to subscribe a crown

[16] An obsolete use of the word, meaning those who took the financial instrument from the government to sell on the retail market.

[17] August 29th, 1789.

a week and the longest liver to take all – but for a national operation of finance, it is unworthy of our intelligence and resources.[18]

The passing reference to a 'club at an alehouse' is prescient because the fad for small-sum, short-term tontines that started in the early 1790s involved very similar schemes. These are reviewed in Chapter 9.

The World, on October 9th, printed this assessment of the key news of the market generally:

MONEY MARKET

The DIVIDENDS now in payment at the Bank, add above two millions of ready money to the market.

The TONTINE is the only falling stock, and that looks flatter and flatter.

The Corporation of BATH, for their improvements, are trying to raise money at 4 per cent.

The English LOTTERY is hurt a little by the Irish – But the Tickets in both, are far less heavy than last year.

The LOYALISTS DEBENTURES – Edge up, more and more.

The Loyalist Debentures were the result of Parliament having created a fund to compensate Loyalists for their property losses in the American Revolution. It resulted in payment warrants that traded like other government debt.

Then, on October 30th, 1789, *The World* published a letter that stated:

With every other PUBLIC SECURITY proportionately ADVANCED with the recovered character and restored resources of the country, how happens it that the TONTINE alone should FALL?

At 97 and a fraction – it is four per cent. below par!....

The fall is not from any fabrication of the Market – but from the natural working of causes, such as these:

1st The par price is found above its value.

The writer goes on to say it might have worked on a smaller scale.

[18] *The English Chronicle*, September 24th, 1789.

The *Public Advertiser*, on January 25th, 1790, included the sluggishness of the Tontine offering in a current assessment of the stock market generally: "The subscribers to the Tontine scheme have applied to the Minister for some relief, and it is said the subscription is to be turned into a 3 or 4 per cent. stock negociable at the Bank, like the other funds."

The payment on the Tontine due on January 29th was the final payment. There were complaints six months later that the bureaucracy needed to implement the final purchase of the Tontine shares and registry of nominees had not yet been set up.

On March 18th, the *Public Advertiser* complained the administration of the Tontine was poor:

> But for the supineness and inattention of the subscribers to the Tontine, every shilling of it would by this time have been disposed of – at an extraordinary premium. The public like it – the public want it –the public would readily purchase and nominate on almost any terms. But they are waiting month after month to see books opened at the Bank to receive their names... Therefore it is time the Minister comes forward, and declares, that if it is not accepted by the public as a Tontine, it shall be converted into a four per cent....

The English Chronicle was optimistic later that Spring, as this excerpt from May 11th, 1790 shows:

> Tontine is quite different from all the other funds for it is neither a perpetual, a long, or a short annuity – it is an annuity upon lives, for the benefit of survivorship, and is well worth 105 at this moment, as it was when consols were 80 – for it has nothing to do with the fall of Stocks – the Minister did not sell it as a stock, but as a thing which is always to be estimated at £100. This is a fact well known to every gentleman who attended when the bargain was made.

The Tontine was trading at 94 the day this was published. The last sentence in the quotation above is something of a dig at the top-level subscribers.

The following appeared in the *Public Advertiser*, also on May 11th, after a short text reporting how the rumored capture of the HMS Trusty had caused a fall in the Consols.[19] It is an extended argument in favor of the Tontine and is a good illustration of how tontines were generally perceived:

> Had every man who now holds £100 in the three per cents. laid out his money in Tontine, he would have escaped the fall. -- This is an argument of great weight, and deserving of the closest consideration, more especially as a war is much in favor of Tontine; as there is a greater probability of a mortality among the annuitants than in time of peace.
>
> A man has six children, and he can give them £100. a piece in the funds, say three per cents. -- This gives them three pounds a year a piece, and if they want to sell it or throw it away, they may lose 20 per cent. by the sale. Whereas by laying out the same money in Tontine, he prevents the sale, and secures them a great income in the end.
>
> There is a superior recommendation of Tontine in every view of it. Suppose for instance, a servant maid saves, in the course of years, one hundred pounds, and lays it out in a Tontine, if she marries a bad husband, he cannot touch it; whereas in Stocks he may sell all, and leave her a beggar. -- In another point of view, if a man buys a Tontine for a profligate son, he cannot sell it; but may perhaps in the course of years, after surviving his profligacy have a very handsome income. -- This is clear that one hundred pounds laid -out in 3 or 4 per cents. can never give more than 3 or 4 per cent. whereas one hundred pounds laid out in Tontine, must in a few years give double that sum, and may give one thousand pounds per annum.
>
> The public see Tontine in a very different point of view from every other fund -- they consider it as a life annuity, and calculate that by waiting till near the expiration of the time appointed for nominating they will be obliged to give a price very considerably higher than the present -- for as the shares are taken off the market, the value must encrease with the consumption, because the name being once fixt, the whole million will be lost sight of forever.

[19] The HMS Trusty rumor was false. A review of the newspapers published the same day shows that the Tontine was trading at £97 per *The Diary or Woodfall's Register*, £94¼ per *The English Chronicle* and £94 per the Gazetteer and Daily Advertiser and the *General Evening Post. The St James Chronicle*, the *Public Advertiser*, the *London Chronicle*,*Lloyd's List* and the *Whitehall Evening Post* all reported no price, normally an indication of no transactions on that trading day.

> The Irish Tontine rose near 50 per cent. within a few days of the time fixed for completing the nominating-and afterwards got up to 20 per cent. premium; and so will the British, unless the public are prudent enough to buy in time.

The phrase in the third paragraph in the excerpt above, '…must in a few years give double that sum….' is a reflection of the actuarially unjustified optimism about mortality rates that drove tontine sales. The interest for the first class did not double until around 1840.

And in the fourth paragraph note that the first buyer had time after the purchase and before submitting a nomination for the life to resell the share easily. However, once the life nominee had been named, a resale would involve the purchaser having to become the monitor of the life nominee, who was likely to be a complete stranger to the secondary buyer.[20]

On May 14th, 1790, the *Public Advertiser* printed this little boost:

> There have been more purchases made in Tontine within the last four days, than in the whole month preceding. This is partly owing to its extraordinary cheapness, being no more than 95, though intrinsically worth 100. If the present spirit for buying Tontine continues, there will very shortly not be a single share upon the market…. When the Minister made his bargain for Tontine, he did not regulate it by the price of the Funds. He sold his shares as bearing a certain premium above 100 pounds…. It has nothing to do with any other annuity existing.

That text was unduly optimistic. Interestingly, the criticism focuses on the financial aspects of the Tontine. This does not take into account the particular awkwardness of the secondary sales of tontine shares. The totality of tontine participation included the nomination of the lives on which the share was based and regular presentation of proof that the lives still existed. A secondary purchaser was saddled with maintaining the documentation requirement for nominees he or she likely did not know. This may be one of the reasons for the occasional nomination of the life of a public figure as the nominee in a tontine. The Irish Tontines of the 1770s had purchasers whose nominee was the Prince of Wales. This is likely due to the visibility of the life of the person, thus reducing the

[20] See the quote referenced at footnote 7 in the previous chapter.

burden of proof or selecting a nominee for whom healthcare would have been the best possible.

The constant need for proving the continued life of a nominee meant that tontine shares were not as easily fungible as the regular Bank Annuities.

Contrary to the enthusiasm shown above, the lack of retail investors became more apparent. The underwriting 'monied men' who bought the issue from the Government pressed for some sort of relief. This report on Parliamentary events is from the *St. James Chronicle* of May 20th, 1790:

> The Chancellor of the Exchequer stated, that the Tontine voted in the last year hung heavily on the heads of the subscribers, it not being yet nearly filled; it was his intention, therefore to accommodate them for the present, by enlarging the time for nomination from the 10th of October in the present year, to the 5th of April in the next. He moved for leave to bring in a bill accordingly.

However, this was followed a week later by capitulation:

> In a committee on the Tontine Act, came to a resolution proposed by Mr. Pitt, to enable the holders of Tontine to exchange it, if they thought proper, for Long Annuities. – Ordered the report to be made on the morrow.

The Solution to Weak Sales

The government's proposal to allow buyers to substitute Long Annuities for the Tontine shares was put on the agenda in Parliament. Debate followed, as reported in the *Whitehall Evening Post* of June 3rd:

> *Sir Grey Cooper* disliked the precedent of altering the situation of a bargain such as this, of which he knew no example, except in some few instances of Loans which happened to turn out infavourably. He then asked, whether the option of remaining in the Tontine, or of being transferred to the Long Annuities, was the desire of the original subscribers to the Tontine or of the subsequent purchasers? Whether the Public were to lose by the measure? And how many subscribers might be expected to remain?

> *Mr. Pitt* replied that the measure was adopted at the instance of the original subscribers who, from the occasional depression of the funds at this time, could not bring the Tontine to market with the advantage they must have expected. But Notwithstanding this, the subsequent purchasers were undoubtedly entitled to the same advantage of an option.... As to the number of Subscribers that might remain, it was impossible to form any estimate, for it was not likely that many would name [a nominee] till near the time in which it would be necessary.

An interesting administrative complaint addressed to George Rose, MP, Secretary to the Treasury, was printed in the *Public Advertiser*[21] at this point. It echoed the 'supineness' mentioned above. The letter raised the question of whether there was a deliberate delay in formally recording tontine sales at the Bank of England. This might have been at the behest of the initial subscribers, who wanted to see how the market treated the Tontine shares. Since the Tontine shares traded below par within months, they stood to lose money.

Apparently, the procedures and tools for implementing the Tontine at the Bank of England simply did not exist. No books were opened. There was no place to have nominees recorded. 'The want of books has brought the Tontine into discredit with the public.... ...from the moment the contract is made, Government discourages the sale of it.'

The London Gazette published this notice on June 29th, 1790:

> TONTINE, 1789
>
> *Exchequer Office, Palace-Yard,*
> *May 29, 1790*
>
> Notice is hereby given, that Books for the Nomination of Lives in the Tontine of 1789 are now preparing at this Office, and all Persons who mean to nominate Lives in the said Tontine are requested to give notice thereof, in Writing, to Mr. Paxton at the Exchequer, where attendance will be given each day (Sundays and Holidays excepted) between the Hours of Ten and One, or to Mr. Abraham Newland, at the Bank, Naming and describing the Person whose Life he, she, or they shall desire to have an Annuity, with the Benefit of Survivorship....

[21] June 15th, 1790.

The enabling statute was *30 George III, Cap XLV*. The corrective plan was announced and was described and criticized in a piece in the *Gazette and New Daily Advertiser* of July 8th, 1790:

> It was soon discovered that there were not ten thousand persons disposed to give a considerable premium on an *unsaleable article*.... The Tontine is to be filled up with *nominal* shares in order that the *few* adventurers may be placed on the same footing as if the whole had actually been disposed of. If therefore, one thousand real lives be named, there must be nine thousand *nominal lives* added, and the expence to the public will be as great as if the original plan had taken place.

The unsold shares were converted into Long Annuities with a dividend of £4/5/0 per year expiring January 5th, 1860. Those who had already purchased the Tontine were given the option of converting to the Long Annuities. The article contended the value of the Long Annuities substitute was only £91/18/1½, so the investors were being offered a significant loss. For the shares kept as Tontine shares, the article speculated it would be forty-seven years before the dividend doubled due to deaths of the real and nominal nominees. In the event, a relatively good prediction.

A couple of weeks later, on July 26th, the *Gazetteer and New Daily Advertiser* continued its attack:

> The contempt with which Mr. Pitt treated the understanding of the people of England, when he imagined there could be found ten thousand persons so foolish as to engage in a scheme so contrary to their true interest as a tontine for a million of money, exceeds all precedent, and sets at defiance every other transaction of the kind.
>
> In 1765 the late Mr. George Grenville attempted a tontine for a million, which of course was meant to contain the like number of shares with the present, and although every exertion was made by Government to carry it into effect there were found only one hundred and eighty persons, of the proposed ten thousand, who were silly enough to subscribe their money.

This is a very rare example of the experience with the 1765 Tontine being brought into the debate, although it misstates the amount. Grenville's proposal in 1765 was for a portion of the loan, not the whole loan. A tontine initially paying three percent was proposed for only 17.5% of a million and a half pound loan, not the whole sum. The rest was raised via Consols and a lottery. Also, Grenville priced his offering at a discount, close to the market rate for the Three Percent Consols at the time.

The critique goes on to derive a sense of future earnings from the experience of the Third Class of the Irish Tontine of 1773. It consisted of 1,697 shares of which 115 had 'fallen in' by 1790. It speculates, via applying the same mortality rate to a like number of shares, that in 1807 the increase in the dividend "of six shillings and one halfpence to each share, generating an annual dividend of £ 4/9/0½ instead of £4/3/0."

Making the Numbers Work

A later writer, William Fairman, summarized the conversion of the Tontine this way:

> As the plan of this Tontine was not generally approved, the subscribers were afterwards allowed to exchange their shares for Long Annuities of £4:5 for 69¼ years; and, in order to place those persons who retained their shares of the Tontine on the same footing they would have been if the whole number had been filled up, the commissioners of the Treasury were empowered to nominate lives for the shares exchanged, who were to be selected from the peers of Great Britain or Ireland, baronets, justices of the peace, governors of public charities, &c and to be distributed among the several classes in the same proportion as the nominees appointed by the subscribers.[22]

Grellier[23] reported in 1799 that 'a greater part were in the following year exchanged….' Although other variables might affect individual decisions, arguably, the split might be taken as a poll on the perennial issue of whether a tontine was an investment or reckless gambling. Fewer than five percent stayed with the Tontine.

The first modern English Census did not take place until 1801, so compiling the names and data on the nominal lives was awkward. A hint on the means of creating the list of names was revealed in this from the *General Evening Post* of September 21–23rd, 1790:

[22] Fairman, William, *The Stocks examined and compared….*, 3rd Edition, London: Galabin, et al., 1798.

[23] Grellier, J J, *The terms of all the loans which have been raised for the public service during the last fifty years….*, London: Galabin, et al., 1799.

> Mr. G. Atwood is appointed by the Lords Commissioners of the Treasury, to collect certificates of the residence and births of all persons born since the year 1765, who may come under the following description. viz, children and grandchildren of Peers of Great-Britain or Ireland; children of Baronets of England or Scotland; the children of Lords of Manors of England or Wales; and children of persons named in the Commission of the Peace for any County or Riding in England or Wales; he has in consequence sent a printed requisition to the Minister of every parish in Great-Britain, for certificates of the above.

This was supplemented, perhaps for the older classes, via the process reported in the *Gazetteer and New Daily Advertiser* of October 2nd, 1791:

> The Mininster's eagerness to fill the *Tontine* Loan with *names* has carried him further than to the London Assurance Societies. The Country Benefit Clubs, those in Sussex especially, have received orders to send up lists of their members.

George Atwood, Esq., a mathematics prodigy, former tutor at Cambridge University, and member of the Royal Society, became acquainted with Pitt at Cambridge and later served as a kind of special advisor to the government. A no-show sinecure was originally found for him in 1784 as a 'Patent Searcher'[24] in the Customs Office, but in July 1790 he became the Inspector of Tontine Certificates.

A more detailed description of the creation of the pool of artificial government nominees can be found in Cornelius Walford's *Insurance Cyclopedia*, volume five, published in the 1870s in London:

> These were chosen as follows: the class under 20 consisted of the children of the nobility and gentry, whose names, age, parents, and residence were returned by the clergy of the several parishes. The other elder classes consisted of well-known free-holders of property, persons insured in the Amicable Office, and so on. From the whole, the numbers deficient in each class were drawn by lot, viz. 4,831 lives.

Walford goes on to state how the artificial lives were tracked:

[24] Patent in this sense has to do with the process by which he was appointed, i.e., via a 'patent' or appointment from the Prime Minister rather than a civil service commission.

> Justice to the contributors required that the officers at the Exchequer should discover every such date with the utmost accuracy, and they paid a small reward for each parochial certificate of such an event. In fact … …they had never once lost sight of the nominees for a period of 40 years—knowing perfectly well their residences, professions, etc., which was not difficult, since they were mostly people of considerable note in life. The death, it was admitted, might not be known immediately on its happening, but it was always very soon known, and then its real date and other necessary particulars to enter on the register were obtained. Hence it was 'quite clear from the separate observation on the mortality of this class that there can be little if any error whatever in this respect.'[25]

Only shares amounting to £42,802/1/6 remained as Tontine shares. This amounted to roughly four percent of the initial offering. The rest of the loan was raised as Long Annuities.

The creation of the artificial shares included counting those putative shareholders as annuitants, although the government did not pay them anything. The dividends were calculated based on the combined pool, but the government only had to pay the dividends to the contributors' nominees! The long-term effect of this solution was to slow down the rate of increase of the dividend and to allow the government to keep more than half the proceeds each year.

The interest was calculated using a pool of both the real and artificial nominees which shrank proportionately more slowly than if the pool consisted of only the 'real' nominees. The mortality rate was a function of 9,952 shares rather than 4,219. To make things worse, there were more artificial nominees than there were real ones, 5,733 shares versus 4,219.

For example, in 1840 in the first class there were 1,501 'real' shares and 2,214 'government' shares extant. If the pool of £28,307 were divided among the 1,501 'real' shareholders, the dividend would have been roughly £18/17/0. But it was divided among 3,715 shares for a dividend of only £7/14/5, for a rough total of only £11,630! The government was underpaying by more than fifty percent.

[25] See also: *Tontines and life annuities: copy of the report and observations of Mr. Alexander Finlaison, actuary of the commissioners for the reduction of the national debt, relating to tontines and life annuities, and to the duration of life among the nominees* /ordered by the House of Commons, to be printed, 25 August, 1860, London. Pages 12–13.

Since this was easily the most visible tontine of the period, the slow rise in the dividends may have had a discouraging effect on future proposals.

Glitches and Completion

It turns out that the final deadline of October 10th, 1790, for purchase and nomination fell on a Sunday. The Exchequer Office was obliged to remain open. In December, *The Times* commented: "The Lords of the Treasury have before them a fine piece of drudgery -- the signing of upwards of five thousand skins of parchment, on which the name of the holders of shares in the Tontine are enrolled." The traditional Annuities did not involve this step.

On February 19th, 1791, a notice appeared in *The Times* acknowledging that 'several' tontine certificates were granted but not delivered to the Office of the Auditor of the Receipt of His Majesty's Exchequer. This had the effect of cutting off the subscribers' benefits. A meeting at Peel's Coffee House in Fleet Street was announced to give the affected parties the opportunity to have their situation rectified.

Finally, on March 11th, 1791, the interest started to be paid, the first payment, covering a year and quarter, was issued at the Receipt Office of the Exchequer.

At the end of the process, per official lists published in 1792, there were 4,219 shares in the tontine, encompassing 3,498 nominees. In addition, 5,733 artificial shares were created with 4,812 'nominees' appointed by the 'Lords Commissioners of His Majesty's Treasury' to make the pool of lives 9,952, reasonably close to the target of 10,000 intended by the original statute. Later accounts showed that forty-eight shares were 'forfeited' by death of the nominee or failure to confirm a life in the period between the nomination deadline and the completion of the official list.

The regular calculations executed to arrive at the semi-annual dividend for the next ninety-seven years were based on the extant lives on both the lists combined.

Income Record

In 1811, twenty years after the first payment, the First-Class subscribers received £5/2/2¼, just short of pound more than the initial dividend. This is about a 25% increase. The full 1811 distribution was:

Class	*Age*	*Initial annual dividend*	*1811*
First class	Birth to 20	£4/3/0	£5/2/2¼,
Second class	20–30	£4/5/6	£5/4/11½
Third class	30–40	£4/8/6	£6/5/1¾
Fourth class	40–50	£4/13/6	£9/0/6¾
Firth class	50–60	£5/2/6	£12/13/2¾
Sixth class	Above 60	£5/12/0	£28/4/10

Sixty years after the creation of the Tontine, in 1850, the First Class paid £10/17/0¾ to 943 shareholders; the Second paid £35/10/4¼ to 59; and the Third paid £517/10/8½ to its four survivors. The other three classes had been declared 'extinct': the Sixth in 1824, the Fifth in 1834, and the Fourth in 1845.

For some, the Tontine worked its magic. This death notice recorded the last payments to a member of the Sixth Class, the oldest group: "A few days since, Mrs. Margaret Orton, aged 94, being the surviving nominee in the Sixth Class of the Government Tontine, anno 1789. The proprietor of the share has been for these five years past in the receipt of £890.8s per annum which originally cost £100. 5s."[26] The total pool for the Sixth Class was £890/8/0. The last survivor of the Fifth Class died in 1834.

The aftermarket for shares continued well into the nineteenth century. An 1804 auction notice from Exeter states £4/11/11 as the current income for shares in the First Class. Note this is two shillings higher than the prediction in the *Gazette and New Daily Advertiser* in 1790 mentioned above.

Another auction notice, from the *Hull Packet* of August 27th, 1845, reports the current income for a First Class share as £8/17/10½. This was the youngest class. It also states the number of nominees still living as of April 5th, 1845, as 1,139, slightly less than half of the nominees in that class, fifty-five years from the beginning of the tontine. Another auction, advertised in *The Times* of May 8th, 1849, seems to present an impossibility, stating the nominee's age to be 52. Perhaps it is a typo for 62. In any case, it reveals a current interest payment of £10/11/11¼.

An 1872 submission to the *Notes & Queries* magazine indicates a sense of disappointment in regard to fairly long lives of the youngest Class:

[26] *Coventry Herald*, July 23rd, 1824.

THE TONTINE OF 1780

> I have some little knowledge of the subject referred to having had two near relatives in the Tontine above-mentioned, and having in fact (some forty-five years ago) received for them their interest on stock in the tontine; for which purpose I had to grope my way along some dark passages to the office of the Clerk of the Pell (whatever that maybe) somewhere in the purlieus of Westminster Hall.

The author then describes a generic tontine, not the actual tontine with classes and caps that was created in 1789. He then continues:

> I will now simply state the facts as regarded my two female relatives. They were respectively aged about seventeen and twenty when their names were put into the tontine. The younger received the interest on her £100 tontine for about fifty-two years, and then died. At the time of her death she received about £7 or £8 only! The elder one lived about sixty-two years, that is, to the age of eighty-two. At the time of her death, I believe her interest had risen to more than £14/11. Any actuary can calculate how many persons out of one thousand would be living after the laps of sixty-two years. Your readers may draw their own conclusions.

The submission generated a response that attempted to show the tontine payouts were right where they should have been. The original writer responded with an apology as to exact figures, but still expresses his distrust, concluding with "[he] charges me with an ungenerous inuendo as to the management of the particular tontine referred to. In reply to which I will frankly say, that I should hesitate to place implicit faith in the financial operations of any government, whether Tory, Conservative, Whig, or Advanced Liberal."

The tone of the final two sentences of the first quote seems full of distrust and, even if based on faulty data, provides a hint as to why tontines slowly disappeared.

ADMINISTRATIVE COMPLICATIONS

Besides the payment process, administering the tontine involved the government printing and distributing blank forms for the nominee's parish Minister or Churchwarden to testify to the continued life of the nominee. The signatory could charge a small fee for filling these out. These had to be submitted before a dividend would be paid.

In August 1789, the *Public Advertiser* printed this text alerting readers to the comparative lack of fungibility of tontine shares due to possibilities of complications in keeping track of the tontine:

> … For supposing a tradesman purchases a share, or any number of shares according to his ability, upon his own or his to child's life, and should fail after the 10th of October 1790 and those shares be put up to public sale, they will never produce more than one third of the intrinsic value, if so much, because the purchaser must insure the life of the annuitant to secure his purchase money, besides incurring an immensity of trouble and difficulty in order to ascertain the existence of the annuitant every half year, and who, in order to procure employment may not confine his residence long to any one spot in England nor even to the Kingdom. These circumstances will operate greatly to the disadvantage of a sale to a stranger….

The Bedfordshire Archives holds a letter from a member of the Quaker community in Apsley Guise, Bedfordshire, to his son-in-law in London,[27] that illustrates the process. The writer instructs his son-in-law to arrange the signing of the enclosed Tontine Certificate confirming his wife's life. It was to be executed by their Parson and Churchwarden and then forwarded to an agent in London.

A similar 1794 letter in the Northamptonshire Archives[28] specifies how the certification of life was to be executed by an officer serving aboard the HMS Crescent based in Plymouth. In this case, it would involve a local Justice of the Peace, or, if none available, the Commander of the ship witnessed by a Lieutenant. It was then to be sent to James Martin, Esq., MP in London.

The writer then provides an outline of the standard text of the form. Besides being a Member of Parliament, James Martin was one of the senior bankers of the time, operating under the sign of the Grasshopper on Lombard Street. The officer, Peter Rye, ended up a Vice Admiral and died in 1851.

Multiply these examples by almost 3,500 subscriber nominees and it shows how complicated the administration of the Tontine was in comparison with the Consols. In addition, there were more than 4,800

[27] Bedfordshire Archives, HW 87/495.

[28] Northamptonshire Archive reference number Rye_x_7244_035.

'government' nominees that the Tontine Office had to keep track of as well.

Annual reports were distributed listing the deaths of both the contributor's nominees and the government's artificial nominees as well as a list of forfeits due to the failure to submit proof of the continued existence of a nominee. These reports also included a statement as to the interest to be paid that year and a summary of the numbers of extant lives.

The last 1789 Tontineer died on October 31st, 1887.

Conclusion

As in 1757 and 1765, the National Tontine of 1789 was a failure as well. It attracted only a little more than four percent of its targeted revenue. It is curious that in a financial environment that produced many successful private and municipal tontines, the national ones met with comparatively little interest.

One significant flaw was the tontine being sold to the first level subscribers essentially at face value rather than at a discount, as was the practice in the previous distribution of shares in the Consols. The market price provided a peg for the Consols. There was no obvious peg for the experiment with the tontine.

In England, once the lack of subscriptions showed the proposals to be failures in terms of revenue, there was still an understanding that the tontine should be preserved for subscribers who bought them. The government perceived itself under a contractual obligation to execute the tontine as best it could under the circumstances, as they did after the undersubscribed 1765 tontine. In 1789, this involved the creation of a pool of lives of non-participants to make sure the statistical outcome for the purchasers tracked the proposals even though there were fewer subscribers than anticipated. Whether this was executed fairly is questionable.

It is notable that the British Government adhered to the terms of the tontines for the persons who bought them in 1765 and 1789. This is in contrast to Louis XVI's repudiation of the French tontines on January 26th, 1770, when he arbitrarily converted the tontines into simpler life annuities. Although it was reported by the *Independent Chronicle* at the time that British investors were to be protected: "They write from Paris, that such British subjects as have received damage in their fortunes by the late reduction of Tontine annuities, are ordered to be made full restitution and, upon the whole, it was thought the loss would only fall upon the French King's natural subjects," the very act of repudiation was perceived as shocking. The capricious decree was widely noticed and abhorred in England, as shown by this text from *The Northampton Mercury* in August 1770:

> The fatal Stroke given to national Faith, Credit, and Honor, by the late violent Measure of stopping the Payment of the Interest arising on the public Funds, and taking away the Benefit of Survivorship in the Tontines, will be severely felt in any future one.

It is likely that the fatal flaw in 1789 was the Tontine being sold at face value to the initial subscribers. The custom was to offer the various perpetual annuities at the market prices for the year of issue. It was assumed there was no precedent for a tontine price, so the Tontine was bought by the pool of Monied Men at par. It had to rise in price for them to make a profit. This is also one of the main reasons for the conflict about when the interest was assumed to be paid.

Also, the sale of tontine shares was a more complicated transaction than the basic annuity. There was the process of naming, registering, and keeping track of the nominees. Since the nominee could not be changed, the shares were transferable, but by no means as easily as the basic Consols.

However, it should be noted that within four years of the issuing of the Tontine, England went through a severe depression that lasted from 1793 through the beginning of the nineteenth century. The National Tontine of 1789 shares paid their dividends all through that period and because they were detached from the fluctuations of the market, they held their value.

CHAPTER 9

Small-Sum, Short-Term Tontines

Prehistory: Societies for Survivors

As the Richmond Bridge Tontine was being marketed, on December 16th, 1774, this advertisement appeared in the *Public Advertiser*:

> Survivorship/Cock and Lion, St. Michael's Alley, Cornhill / The Society of Survivors, held at the above house, give this Notice, That all Persons willing to become members must pay in their Subscriptions on or before Monday evening... ...by subscribing Weekly, Monthly, or Quarterly any Sum from One Shilling to One Guinea per week... ...£1000 is already placed in the Bank of England.

And in the *Daily Advertiser* five days later, two other advertisements for 'survivorship' societies appear, one based in the King's Head in Charles Street and the other at the Angel and Crown in Cheapside. The King's Head group was also advertised in June 1774 and the one at the Cock and Lion in September 1774.

These appear to be variations on what were known as 'box clubs.' Box clubs usually served as a kind of informal health and funeral insurance for their working-class members. They were small and rarely extended beyond a neighborhood or trade-oriented group. They tended to have a kind of headquarters and lockbox in a tavern or coffee house. The three mentioned above were likely aimed at a more middle-class audience, all

K. McKeever, *The Role of Tontines, 1750–1800*, Palgrave Studies in the History of Finance, https://doi.org/10.1007/978-3-032-12849-2_9

based in the rough vicinity of Exchange Alley and were in venues that held auctions.

The Society of Survivors from the Cock and Lion successfully achieved a final distribution according to plan per this from the *Daily Advertiser* in February 17th, 1778:

> Cock and Lion, St. Michael's Alley, Cornhill/The Members of the advantageous Society of Survivors are requested to take notice, that the division of the capital Joint-stock of the said Society, amounting to near £5000 will be made at the above house.... Note, books are open for Admission of Members into a second Society, on the same plan....

Other similar groups did not fare as well. One was established at a tavern and auction venue known as the Red Cross in the Barbican. It was advertised as the second at that site. The first consisting of 822 members, claimed to be 250 more than any other society of this kind. The advertisement for the second specified that attorneys or Jews could not be members. A letter printed in the *Gazetteer and New Daily Advertiser* of January 24th, 1777, made claims in regard to the second group. The author was one of 'about three hundred' participants in the scheme. The first paragraph is basically a screed on such projects. It then continues:

The Society of about 300–400 members agreed to pay a set sum each week for a term of five years. The final accumulation was then to be divided among the survivors. After two years, a majority of members voted to dissolve the group. The capital of the Society was invested in three and a half percent annuities which proceeded to fall in price by twenty-four percent, precipitating the dissolution proposal.

> Since the above motion was made, the business of dissolution is at a stand by several out of thirteen being unwilling to deliver up the bonds, so that the trustees cannot sell out the stock and divide it, as the majority ordered.... Are not the bond holders and trustees obliged to comply with the general vote for dissolution? Are they in any danger of claims being made upon them (if they execute all the trust now) at the expiration of five years?

In the same paper on January 31st, 1778, this appeared:

> Last week was delivered into. the. Court of Chancery by an able attorney, who is retained by the five hundred poor men and women of the Society

> of Survivors, Barbican; a spirited honest answer to a most cruel Chancery bill, filed against them by the Cripplegate Clan when there is no doubt that in two or three terms the well known justice and equity of that Venerable Court will erect for these poor people the *banners* of triumph over the most cruel triumvirate malice that ever disgraced human nature or a court of justice.

Three years later the members were vindicated, per the *London Courant* of June 11th, 1782:

> Monday came on to be heard before Sir Thomas Sewell, Master of the Rolls, the long-depending suit in Chancery between Mr. William Banner of Cripplegate and the Society of Survivors at the Red-Cross, Barbican, when Sir Thomas decided the cause in favour of the 490 poor men, women, and children, who were members of the said society, and most of whom are now living.

These kinds of informal and local tontine clubs continued through at least the 1950s, often with a Christmas-focused annual payout date. A reference in *The Times* of December 23rd, 1955, stated there were at least '...50,000 clubs associated with public houses in England and Wales.'

Expanding the Idea

In the classic generation-skipping rhythm of the market, during which failures are forgotten, the concept behind these Societies reappeared in the 'small-sum, short-term' tontines that became something of a mania in the 1790s.

Although large-scale small-sum, short-term tontines first appeared a year or two earlier, the National Tontine of 1789 unleashed a flood of schemes aimed at a lower economic band than the traditional tontines. The traditional project tontines tended to be sold in shares of £100, although the Freemasons' Tontine share was £50 and the Covent Garden Tontine share was £250. The 1789 Tontine was sold in £100 shares. However, around 1785–90 a new style 'tontine' appeared whose contribution was small but continuous for the life of the scheme, which tended to be seven years.

The subscriber nominated a dependent life and contributed by the week or the month, although most allowed for outright purchase for a lump sum. The contribution was usually a shilling a week but could be as low as a sixpence a week or as high as a guinea a month. At the end of the term, the living subscribers would receive a dividend composed of their contribution, any interest earned, and the shared contributions of subscribers who died or defaulted, less the administrative fees charged by the projectors and managers.

There were dozens of tontines of this form, likely hundreds. They included the Commercial Society and Tontine Club (London, 1787), Banbury Tontine Society (1788), Bristol Universal Tontine Association, (1789), Sherborne Tontine Society (15 years, 1789), Tontine Society (Winchester, 1789), Newbury and Speenhamland Universal Tontine Society (1789), Gloucester Tontine Association (1789), Bath Universal Tontine Society, (1790), Bath Five Years Tontine Society (1790), Chelmsford Universal Tontine Society (5 years, 1790), Universal Tontine for the Counties of Worcester, Warwick, Etc. (1790), Dublin Tontine Company (1791), London and Middlesex Universal Tontine Society (1791), Boston Tontine Society (1791), Universal British Tontine Society (London, 1791), Royal Universal Tontine (Bristol, 1791), (Old) British Tontine (Bristol, 1791), Lichfield and Staffordshire Tontine Society (1791), New British Tontine (Bristol, 1792), Equitable and Universal Tontine (Bristol, 1792), General Western Tontine, (Trowbridge and Warminster, 1792), Chorley Tontine Society (1792), Rochester, Chatham, Brompton and Strood Tontine Association (1792), Cork Tontine Society (1793), etc.

These schemes raise some basic questions. How appropriate was the use of the word 'tontine' to describe these? Were they honest and realistic attempts to create savings plans for a broader portion of the community? Or were they always intended as scams?

The Oracle on July 7th, 1796, well after the fad had taken off, printed a complaint about their legality, implying that any tontine that did not have parliamentary authorization was illegal:

> The *qui tam* gentry do not mean to confine their speculations to the Faro Tables[1] and the Alley. They have taken a peep into the *Tontine* schemes, which they think a direct species of gambling, without the authority of an Act of Parliament. When Sir John BLACQUIERE first introduced into the Irish Parliament, during the Viceroyalty of Earl HARCOURT, this system of raising money on the benefit of survivorship, he was obliged, in order

[1] Faro was a card game popular for betting, especially among the upper classes. See *Faro and rouge et noir*, London: Debrett, 1793.

> to secure the subscribers, to have the sanction of an Act of Parliament; for without that authority it was *illegal gambling*. To the *Tontine* in this country, many respectable persons have affixed their names as *Committee-men*, and no doubt, will fulfil their engagements; but it is all a matter of honour. Law cannot bind them to what law does not sanction.

The references to Sir John Blacquiere and Earl Harcourt are to the administrators in Ireland who led the creation of the first of the three Irish Tontines in the 1770s, which were implemented with the authorization of the Irish Parliament. There is the additional implication that individuals with problems relating to the tontine they might be involved in would not be able to sue for redress. However, this warning comes during a period when the bulk of the transactions in the stock market were also technically illegal and unenforceable in court. 'Monied men' were used to this environment of honor. Lesser mortals might not have been as aware of it.

A letter with a critique of these sorts of tontines was published in the *Gazetteer and New Daily Advertiser* of October 15th, 1790:

> You seem to consider it as matter or wonder that any bankers should condescend to receive the cash of a *twelve-penny* tontine. For my own part, I think it much more wonderful that persons should be so infatuated as to subscribe at all to such bubbles. -- In the short term of seven years, money accumulates very little faster at *compound* than it does at *simple* interest; and as to any advantages which will be derived in this period from the mortality of the subscribers, it is certain, unless the ravages of an approaching war, or some pestilent disorder should lay waste the Community, that the survivors will find themselves much too numerous to congratulate each other at the last distribution of the stock.

After outlining some of the underlying math and its drear consequences, the author concludes with:

> I am sorry to see those schemes adopted and encouraged by persons, from whom a more enlightened conduct was to have been expected. -- While the public exigencies are provided for by lotteries and tontines, and even some of the representatives of the people become the directors and trustees of those twelve-penny gambling clubs it is no wonder that every designing projector should succeed in misleading the multitude, or that a contagion, maintained and cherished by such powerful and flagrant examples, should be so feebly refuted by the sober efforts of reason and argument.

A similarly harsh critique, entitled 'The Inutility of Tontines,' by J. J. G., was published in the *Monthly Magazine*, February 1798, and republished in the *Edinburgh Magazine* of March 1798.

While a large number of these schemes developed throughout the country, they ran into the market depressing effects of the Napoleonic Wars. Per the *London Packet*, August 23rd, 1797:

> The fall of stocks has been most sensibly felt by the Country Tontines, where the accumulation of compound interest has been sunk to nothing, by a sink of 50 per cent, below the original purchase of Government Securities.

The details of this are illustrated in the chart of Consolidated Annuity (Consol) purchases for the first City of London, Westminster, and Borough of Southwark Tontine as reported in 1798.[2] The columns consist of the date of the purchase, the amount purchased, the price paid, and the total cost of each purchase including the brokers' commissions. The original report showed 29 transactions. This chart has been reduced to show only the first purchase each year.

1791	July	20	100	@ 827/8	& Comm	£83/0/0
1792	Jan	17	200	@ 88¼	& Comm	£180/0/0
1793	(No purchases)					
1794	Feb	6	1000	@ 67¼	& Comm	£673/15/0
1795	Feb	4	1600	@ 627/8	& Comm	£1008/0/0
1796	Feb	1	2000	@ 67¼	& Comm	£1357/10/0
1797	Feb	6	2020/13/7	@ 543/8	& Comm	£1103/16/0
1798	Feb	9	3000	@ 49½	& Comm	£1488/15/0

The total involved a final par value of £37,828/5/4 costing £22,856/2/0. The market price of the Consols fluctuated between a high of 96 in February 1792 and a low of 47 in June of 1797.

William Fairman, in his *The stocks examined and compared*....,[3] also cautioned against the small-sum, short-term tontines. He wrote:

> Under this head, it may not be improper to caution the public against Tontines for a short term of years. The difference between simple and

[2] Digitized in Gale's Eighteenth Century Collection Online: *State of the City of London, Westminster, and borough of Southwark tontine at the end of the seven years*, London: 1799.

[3] London: Galabin et al., 1795.

> compound interest in the period of six or seven years, which is the usual term of these projects, is very inconsiderable, nor can much advantage be expected to accrue from survivorship, particularly as the nominees are generally young healthy lives and even this small profit is reduced, and sometimes over-balanced, by the charges of management. Experience has fully shewn the inutility of these speculations; for, on several which have lately expired, the division to the subscribers has been considerably less than the amount of their contributions.

The benchmark for these tontines could be envisioned as follows: if £100 worth of the three percent were purchased in July of 1791, it would have cost £82⅞. When sold in August 1798, it would have realized £49⅜, a loss of £33½. Over the seven years, the interest paid would have been £21, so the overall loss would have been £12/10/0, or roughly fifteen percent. Any scheme that paid better than a fifteen percent loss was doing better than the market itself.

That would have been rare. The common return was illustrated by a substantially anonymous snippet from the tantalizing 'news' as printed at the time from *Bell's Weekly Messenger* of August 20th, 1797:

> The subscribers to one of the Tontines lately expired and divided, are minus to the amount of forty shillings on every share, after lying out of their money for the short time of seven years and six months!

Perhaps the clearest expression of the failure of these forms of tontines is this 'obituary' for the Bath Five-Year Tontine, published in the *St. James Chronicle* of September 10th, 1795:

> *Bath, Sept. 9* The division of the fund of the Bath Five Years' Tontine, the subscription which was one guinea per month and half shares at half a guinea, took place on the 1st inst. There were 172 whole and 101 half shares: The number of deaths only *eight*. – By the failure of the original treasurers Cross and Co. and the loss by purchases in the funds, the division was only £46/17/6 on each whole share.

A subscriber would have spent £63/0/0 for a return of £46/17/6, a loss of roughly thirty-seven percent.

Some of these tontines were very large. In an advertisement[4] announcing a committee to review the situation of the Old British Tontine, started in Bristol in 1791, it was stated that the capital amounted to £118,992/16/11 in March 1794, with four years' payments still to come. That a five-year-old figure was used is an indication of the non-transparency of the management.

The context was not just related to the war. William Newmarch, in his *On the Loans Raised by Mr. Pitt During the First French War, 1793–1801*,[5] attributes the decline to a number of causes. There were weak harvests at the beginning of the decade, with 1792 being particularly bad. This had a strong inflationary effect. Bankruptcy rates increased with the number of failures in 1793 doubling from the previous year. In 1793, alone twenty-six country banks failed. Stabilization was only achieved through issuing an unusual tranche of Exchequer Bills. In the chart above, no purchases were made for the capital of the tontine in 1793 and the drop in the price of the Consols between February 1792 and February 1794 was more than thirty percent.

The Early Small-Sum, Short-Term Tontines Based in Bristol

Bristol served as the primary location for several of the purely financial Small-Sum, Short-Term Tontines of the late 1780s and 1790s, most notably, two early and large ones, the Bristol Tontine Association, 1788–1796, and the Universal Tontine, 1790–1796.

The Bristol and Universal schemes involved a contribution of a sixpence a week, or £1/6/0 a year per share. Over the seven year life of the first tontine, this would total slightly more than £9 per share.

An advertisement for the Universal Tontine listed 79 agents nationwide, from Truro to Deal and from the Channel Islands to Aberdeen. It also used information about the former one in its self-promotion, including a statement that the Bristol Tontine had 10,136 subscribers of whom 'near 100' defaulted in the first year.

An advertisement for the third tontine included this text:

[4] *Star and Evening Advertiser*, January 25th, 1799.

[5] London: Effingham, et al., 1855.

> Mr. L. B. Larwill refers the public to the whole of his conduct respecting the two former Tontines of which he had the honour to be Secretary. The first of which commenced the 16th of August, 1789, closed with nearly 14,000, shares and brought into the funds the first year nearly £19,000. The second commenced the 21st of December, 1791, closed with 18,926 shares, and brought into the funds the first year £25,7951, 13s. 6d.[6]

What has proven difficult to establish is the number of shares each subscriber owned. For example, an irregularly kept, anonymous, personal account book, likely from a merchant in Neath, Wales, notes Bristol Tontine payments on:

> August 11, 1795: Paid the Bristol Tontine per John Webber, due the 17th, £1/13/2
>
> November 16, 1795: Tontine paid John Webber for 5 shares, £1/13/2
>
> February15 1796: Bristol Tontine paid John Webber 1/4 year up to this day £1/13/2, expences 0/1/2

The sum paid each time corresponds to a sixpence a week for thirteen weeks multiplied by five shares. Presumably, John Webber's job was similar to a rent collector or an 'out-teller' at the Bank of England. He does not appear as an agent in any of the advertising for the Tontine.

An advertisement regarding the expiration of the 'Bristol Universal Tontine' included the following caveat:

> ...[B]ut it is necessary to remark that owing to the War with all of its dreadful Effects, which were not even suspected at the Beginning of the Tontine, the Price of Stock is now so much lower than it has been at any Time since its Commencement, that it is probable a Inconsiderable Loss will be sustained by every such Subscriber; for it is more than possible the Three per Cents. will not be worth Fifty-Five by February next; but if sold out by Sixty, even then our Loss by purchasing above that Price will amount to the enormous Sum of Twenty-five Thousand Pounds, notwithstanding every Attention has been paid by the Treasurers, Trustees, and Committee; and nearly the Whole of our purchases have been truly fortunate at the 'Times when made!'

[6] *Diary or Woodfall's Register*, April 5th, 1793.

The text goes on to encourage the subscribers to leave the money with the Tontine to await a better market price, although an offer is made to purchase the shares at current (depressed) market value if desired. The text is signed by L. B. Larwill, who served as the secretary to the Bristol Universal Tontine Association (aka Universal Tontine Society); the Universal Tontine; and the Equitable and Universal Tontine. The winding down of these large tontines had an effect on the prices. From the *London Chronicle*, Nov 17–20, 1798:

> The recent fall of stocks has been produced principally from the large sums of money sold out within the last two days by Tontine Societies the terms of which have lately expired. The Bristol Tontine alone is said to have no less than £500,000 stock, the whole of which sum was drawn out of the funds.

The *Times* reported the Bristol Tontine selling 'upwards of £300,000' worth.

One report tests the boundaries of speculative historical evidence. *The Times* of September 1st, 1797, includes a detailed report on the contents of two letters sent on August 17th to Esdaile & Co. Bankers, London, containing bills and notes that went missing. Three of the 'Bills not due' listed were drawn by L. B. Larwill on Dorset & Co., London, each for £6/16/0. Were these tontine payments?

City of London, Westminster, and Borough of Southwark Tontines

A comparatively successful example of this kind of tontine was the City of London, Westminster, and Borough of Southwark Tontine of May 2nd, 1791. It involved a contribution of one shilling a week for seven years, or a total of £18/4/0. This was actually the first of at least five related tontines that seem to have had overlapping lives. Keeping them straight can be very awkward, especially since the announcements of some of the later ones were merged into statements about the earlier ones. The first was started in 1791, the second started August 28, 1792, the third started July 14th, 1795, etc.

The first advertisement for the original one appeared on May 30th, 1791 in the *Diary or Weodfall's Register*. A progress report appeared in the *Review and Sunday Advertiser* of August 14th, 1791. It announced a series of three purchases of batches of stock, including one of four percent, one of three percent, and one of five percent. It indicated the management consisted of twenty-four gentlemen who appointed five trustees all unnamed. The bankers were Sir James Handerson, Brenchley, Harrison, Bloxam and Co, of the Borough (i.e., Southwark). The primary agent was William Wright, with sixteen others scattered throughout the metropolis. Another seventeen were listed in communities in the suburbs and Southeast England.

In 1798, the management published a one-page *State of the City of London, Westminster, and borough of Southwark tontine at the end of the seven years*, a portion of the chart is excerpted above at footnote 2. Additional key figures include:

> 1422 subscribers who contributed £18/4/0 for the life of the tontine.
>
> There were 10 who prepaid the seven-year contribution and were given one year's discount for a total of £156.
>
> There were 350 who either died or defaulted, but who contributed £1754/10/10
>
> With accumulated interest of £4953/2/5 less a deduction for 'Committees'[7] of £91/7/0, the total taken in was £32,652/14/3. This was used to purchase funds with a par value of £47,106/8/4

This summary does not record the two final steps in the winding down process, the sale of the accumulation and the division of the proceeds of that sale into a dividend per share figure. It does provide a current value for the Three Percent, Four Percent, and Five Percent Annuities, which when applied to the totals give a figure of roughly £26,000 to be split among the subscribers. If they succeeded in selling the capital at that price, the subscribers would just about get their investment back with no profit.

Note that if the figures in this statement are used in conjunction with the loss reported in the excerpt below, the projectors managed to sell the capital for £26,770 slightly better than the market prices in the Statement would indicate.

The projectors of the City of London, Westminster, and Borough of Southwark Tontine published a winding-up statement of the first tontine

[7] Possible typo for "Commissions?"

in November 1798. It tried to put the best light possible on their significant losses. It appeared in *The Sun* of March 19th, 1799. The trustees acknowledged a loss of £5,882/11/2, 'very near one-fifth of the capital "based on the difference of the purchase prices and the selling price of the underlying funds. "Yet the Trustees were able to pay more than the amount of the Subscription."

After decrying the effect of the depression of prices of the stocks (reprinted above), they then stated that a better economy would produce a better outcome and invited readers to join the tontine then in formation, which would have been the fourth. This advertisement is fairly candid in acknowledging the loss of value in the capital. Given that similar small-sum, short-term tontines did much worse, the candor may have been a subtle brag.

In April 1800, the second Society announced a dividend of £13/12/0. Regular subscribers would have paid £10/10/0 per share, or a profit of roughly three pounds or thirty percent per share over the seven years.

The advertisement for the Third Tontine printed in the *Star and Evening Advertiser* of March 25th, 1796, starts out with a statement of the funds involved:

£30,011/18/0	Three per Cents
£8888/2/0	Five per Cents
£100/0/0	Four per Cents

For a total of £39,000/0/0

The list of agents below the descriptive text stretches much further afield than the original one, from Swansea to Glasgow. The advertising for the fifth tontine included a notice in the distant *Aberdeen Journal.*

That notice also reported the dividends of the third tontine to be £15/6/0 per share on an investment of £9. The text ends with this statement "...for there is not any mode of getting small sums to interest, unless by joining a great number together." That encapsulates the attractiveness of the small-sum, short-term tontines in an environment before the creation of Savings Banks.

The Competition

A competing tontine started up in September 1790 called the London and Middlesex Universal Tontine Society. The lead promoter was Sir Herbert Mackworth, a banker who was involved in a number of these kinds of schemes. The agent was William Seymour, an attorney who was also the 'Steward' for the Duke of Norfolk.

It was a shilling-a-week Tontine with a seven-year term. The evidence of its existence is only found in promotional advertising. There are no references to a paying out. However, it is noticeable because of head-to-head competition with another tontine proposal in Boston. The Boston group advertised it only charged a one shilling admission fee besides the contribution to the capital and the London scheme charged two shillings. An advertisement in the *Stamford Mercury* of February 4th, 1791, devoted the whole of the bottom half of the text to defending the London and Middlesex Universal Tontine from that attack. The gist of the defense is that the Boston proposal was a shilling a year cheaper, but the London tontine did not charge any expenses and the Boston one did. It goes on to state the London tontine already had two to three thousand members:

> The Advantage of becoming a Member of an established Society, in Preference to One where Success may be doubtful, and where, as there is no Probability of ever being any considerable Number of Subscribers, the Expence attending the Business must greatly diminish the Stock, is too obvious to need pointing out to the discerning Public.

The London and Middlesex Universal Tontine had two iterations, the original one and a 'new' one a year or so later. No traces of either show up in the newspapers aside from the initial advertisements. The same is true for virtually all of the tontines of this type.

Yorkshire Tontine, 1790

The Yorkshire Tontine was another standard small-sum, short-term tontine. Its ultimate accumulation was ten times the capital of the first City of London, Westminster, and Southwark Tontine. However, it encountered far more critical opposition than any of its peers.

The subscribers paid a sixpence a week for seven years. This would amount to £9/1/0. There was an entrance fee charge of one shilling for the first share and a sixpence or any additional shares, but this was designated for administrative costs and did not count toward the accumulation of capital by the scheme. The final and only dividend would be paid after seven and a half years, with the last six months' interest on the corpus to be paid to the agent as his fee for the overall management.

The regular contribution to the Yorkshire Tontine was low enough for lower-middle-class participation. The term is short enough for each participant to have a reasonable hope of receiving the payout. And the payout, while relatively small, would still represent a profit. The Yorkshire Tontine was one of the few whose final distribution was accompanied by a public financial statement.

The mover and agent of the Yorkshire project was Frederick Atkinson, a Silk Mercer in York. He also appears a few years later advertising his taking over as the York agent for the Phoenix Fire Office, a London Insurance company.

The Trustees were a small group of the important political figures in York at the time. Sir William Mordaunt Milner, who had been Mayor of York and was elected Parliament the same year; Sir Thomas Turner Slingsby of Scriven, 8th Baronet; Henry Duncombe, MP; and Francis Ferrand Foljambe, an MP before and after the creation of the Tontine, but not in 1790.

There ended up being 2,395 subscribers ultimately holding 32,133 shares, an average of roughly 13.4 shares per subscriber. At no point in any of the advertising or other texts related to the tontine is a specific bank mentioned.

The first advertisements preserved online appeared in the *Leeds Intelligencer* in April 1790 and were quite detailed.

Among the items of interest is the geographical focus of the twenty-two agents. They are all from the north. There is no attempt to reach London or the south generally. Five of them were booksellers, one a postmaster.

In June, the first organizational meeting is called. A report of the July meeting published in the July 13th Issue of the *Leeds Intelligencer* indicates a Board of Directors was elected and a founding instrument was to be published. By August 31st, the Deed of Covenants was available.

The Tontine Scheme was then subject to anonymous attack via handbill. One, dated October 14th, 1790, has been preserved in the East

Riding Archives.[8] It is quite calm and detailed. Among other things, it points out that the likely profit to a subscriber is £1/7/10½ after seven and a half years, and that the Agent's Fee figures to be in the region of £5,890. There is a sarcastic line about the cost of visiting the agent once a week for seven years. At a penny a visit, it would total £1/10/1, which he avers would be more than any profit a subscriber could expect. The writer also attacks the promise of a shilling profit for each sixpence subscribed as unbelievable.

The proprietors responded in the October 26th issue of the *Leeds Intelligencer*, including this text:

> That there should exist Men so Depraved as to permit their envious and malicious Dispositions to induce them to oppose Schemes, planned with no other view than the beneficent Design of 'doing Good to Mankind' merely because they are at Enmity with the philanthropic Projectors of such schemes....
> The ill-timed and ill-natured Hand Bills which have been, within the last few Days, industriously distributed throughout this City, have given rise to the foregoing Observations, Hand Bills, which can answer no other purpose than to occasion Distrust in the Minds of of the timid and illiterate or to gratify the Spleen of Men who are ever on the watch to sow jealousy and Contention amongst those who have the Misfortune to live in the same Place with them...

The piece goes on to praise the good character and intentions of the Agent, the Trustees, and the thirty-one Directors who serve '*without the possibility of any emoluments or rewards.*' They are compared to: "those dark and anonymous Incendiaries, who prostitute their Abilities, and waste their time in disseminating their malevolent Strictures merely to gratify their their ill-founded Prejudices against those *who know and despise them*...," etc.

In the same issue, a meeting report provided some clarification of the rules. The Chair, Mr. Samuel Barlow, was a prominent York politician, later the Recorder of the City. Three of the twelve other members were Aldermen.

In November, the management of the Tontine issued another defensive statement stating, *inter alia*:

[8] Reference DDX1694/9/11.

> That we have always considered, and do now consider, this scheme to be strictly legal, and well calculated to answer many beneficial purposes.
>
> That it tends to promote industry and frugality, and to check extravagance and dissipation among the lower orders of the people.
>
> That by advancing the trifling, and almost imperceptible payments of sixpence weekly, it may accumulate to many poor persons such a fund, as, with care and management, may be of essential service to them and their families afterwards.
>
> That the deed of articles and covenants, which, as Directors, we have executed, forms in our judgment well established to afford to contributors every possible security.

It goes on to say:

> If the authors of those anonymous publications were sincere and honest in their intentions, and were really disposed to guard the public against the practice of fraud and imposition, their honour as well as their duty would lead them to support such intentions by the sanction of their names.... It has even been announced that the YORKSHIRE TONTINE *is given up*. The Contributors may be assured, that such an idea never was for a moment in contemplation....

The advertisement was signed by the thirty-one directors.

And, as with almost every tontine, a nudge aimed at late payers is published in the *Leeds Intelligencer* of December 14th, 1780.

An anonymous pamphlet called *Tontines calculated, and their Principles and Consequences explained, and exemplified, in the Yorkshire Tontine...* was published by Clarke and Son in London in 1791.

The text begins:

> It would be of little service to the Public to trouble them with a history of the origin and progress of Tontines. So long as they were planned on a large scale, and monied men were their principal supporters, the body of the people felt little interest in their consequences: the burthens fell on those who were well able to support them; and the world had only to laugh at their folly. But when this passion descends to the laborious part of mankind, and this phrensy seizes on those who cannot afford to sport with their losses, the public should then catch the alarm, and endeavour to stop the progress of the infatuation. The Yorkshire Tontine was among the

> foremost that was expressly calculated for the lower orders of the people, and every art employed to spread the delusion.

The author goes on to acknowledge the success of the tontine in attracting subscribers and then details the broader ‘phrenzy’ that has developed for similar schemes throughout the country. He then provides a detailed analysis of the offering, including how the interest is to be calculated and the realistic levels of survivorship with reference to Dr. Richard Price's *Observations on Reversionary Payments.* He or she predicts, at best, a final payment of £11/0/11½ on a subscription costing £9/3/0. This is compared to the same sum put out to interest for the same period, which would result in £10/11/9¼. He particularly decries the involvement of subscribers who could not really afford to participate.

The Yorkshire Tontine does not appear in the news again until 1798, when the time for the payout approaches. A statement of accounts appeared on February 26th, 1798 showing a corpus of £365,000 and announcing a dividend of only £7/17/10.

The Yorkshire Tontine ultimately had 2,395 subscribers. Many took multiple subscriptions, so the total number of subscriptions was 46,353. At the end of the seven years, 14,420 subscriptions had lapsed, either through death or abandonment. The number of subscriptions left is reported at 32,133, although the math indicates it should be 31,933.

A detailed record of the final accounts and the dividend appeared in the *Leeds Intelligencer* of April 30th, 1798.

The Yorkshire Tontine was never going to pay a huge dividend, but it also fell victim to the fall in the Funds caused by the Napoleonic Wars. The pool of varied Annuities that were the corpus of the investments fell in value by twenty-eight percent. Subscribers had paid a total of at least £9/1/0 and received only £7/17/10, a loss of roughly 12.8%, slightly better than the benchmark figure of fifteen percent worked out above.

Arguably, since the loss per shareholder was less than half the loss of the value of the pool of Annuities, the Tontine served to protect the funds of the shareholders in a falling market. However, severely critical lines appeared in S. W. Nicoll's *An account of the York Saving Bank:*[9]

> The Yorkshire Tontine had some years before, proved eminently unsuccessful —in that scheme, after exaggerated descriptions of gain, impossible

[9] York: Alexander, 1817.

> to be realized, a very serious loss was at last experienced. ...the deficiency in the Yorkshire Tontine, seems to have been nearly £100,000.

Stuffing the cash into a mattress would have been better....

Cui Bono? The Agent!

By setting his agent's fee as the interest on the corpus for the last six months, the sum allotted to Mr. Atkinson was large. Even with a falling market, the Annuities paid their interest at par, so he received £2/10 (a half year's interest) for £97,529/7/5 held in the five percent, or roughly £2,438. For the four percent he received £2/0/0 interest on £199,419/7/3 worth of shares, or roughly £3,988. The two pools of three percent (Consolidated and Reduced) totaled roughly £66,709, generating £1,000 as a half year's interest. Mr. Atkinson's total fee was almost £7,500 or £1,000 a year. By basing his fee on the par interest payments, he was insulated from the fall in the market.

One last echo appears in the February 8th, 1812, issue of the *York Herald*. A donation of a quarter of the unclaimed dividends was given to the York County Hospital. Unfortunately, the reproduction has been marked up in a way that makes the number illegible, although it seems to be £9/2/3.

The Wirksworth Tontine, 1791

The ledger of an unrecorded local tontine[10] can serve as an example of the less visible ones. It is from Wirksworth, in the lead mining country in Derbyshire. The monthly payment per share was two shillings, sixpence, or colloquially, half a crown. The handwriting is not always clear. Leaves seven and eight of the ledger give the appearance of being the original first pages. There is not an overall heading, but the page numbering starts at page seven with number one.

Column one is labeled '? of certificate,' i.e., number. Column two is labeled 'Members Name and Occupation.' Column three is labeled 'Places of their Abode.' Column four is labeled 'Time of Admission' (1791 for the first, and for the rest). Column five is labeled 'Nominees Name and Occupation.' Column Six is labeled 'Places of their

[10] In the author's collection.

Abode.' Column seven is labeled 'Age.' Column eight is labeled 'No. of Shares.' Column nine is labeled 'First Month's Subscription' (recorded in Pounds/Shillings/Pence). The rest of the columns record additional monthly payments for a period of twelve months.

A sample entry reads: "14 / Thomas Harlow (no occupation given)/ Hulland Do ('Do' is short for ditto, meaning the same county as listed above. All the primary listings are from Wirksworth and surrounding small communities) / ditto (as to year, ie., 1791) / Charles Harlow/ Hulland Do / 1 Share/2 Shillings Sixpence."

There are a total of 261 shareholders recorded in the primary list. The accounts for the second year show 276 local members. Of them, only thirty-three subscribers named a nominee.

There are references to agents in the nearby communities of Alfreton (twenty-two members), Derby (nineteen members), and Bakewell (five members), with names under them as well.

The income accounts extend through five years and the accounts start showing deaths, exclusions, and payments in larger sums to cover the entire year. Later pages show miscellaneous account information through 1797. On page 73 is a record of all payments made to the treasurer totaling £2,167/18/ including interest from £1,200 invested in three percent consols and interest payments from a three percent mortgage granted to a member of the Gells family, the local gentry. There is also a single column of miscellaneous small administrative expenses.

Unfortunately, there is no record in the ledger of a final accounting or distribution of benefits.

On the verso of the last leaf of the ledger is the heading 'The Names of the Committee as under in the Wirksworth Tontine':

Mr. Charles Potter	1793 May ….
Mr. Joseph Collinson	
Mr. James Frost	
Mr. John Dalley	1793 June ….
Mr. Matthew Dalley	
Mr. Henry Jackson	

Mr. Robert Blackwall	1793 July ....
The Rev. Mr. Hurd	
Mr. Edward Jackson	

Mr. Ralph Toplis	1793 August ...
Mr. William Harding	
Mr. William Fox	

No other documentation of this small-sum, short-term tontine has been uncovered. The ledger shows it in a healthy state at the end of the period it covers.

Conclusion

A general critique of the small-sum, short-term tontines can be found in Thomas Fry's *A New System of Finance*.[11] He alludes to six tontines of this type and gives the following analysis:

> I knew of six of these plans, two in London, two in Bristol, and two in Yorkshire. There might be more, but the evil will appear sufficiently extensive if there were not. The agent of one of the societies in Bristol boasted, by public advertisement, that its subscribers amounted to more than 120,000, but taking the average of the six societies to be 80,000 each, the whole of the subscribers to these plans would be 480,000 persons. These paid 2s per annum for management which in seven years would produce £336,000. But to this sum must be added six months interest of the whole capital produced by the subscriptions, because the managers did not divide till six months after the expiration of the term, on the pretence of settling their books. The produce of 480,000 subscriptions, at £9/16/0 each is £4,704,000, the half year's interest on which, at 5 per cent. is £117,600, making, with the money received by the projectors for the articles of management, the enormous sum of £453,600.
> I need not dwell on this statement. It is accurate, and no words can add to its eloquence.

[11] London: Sold by J. S. Jordan and C. Chappel, 1797.

Fry's text is over-generalized and under-detailed. His declaration of a five percent interest rate benefitting the managers is undercut by details of the Yorkshire fees described above. Only a portion of their capital paid five percent. However, the general point of extraordinary profits for the projectors is valid.

The notice below, from *The Observer* of July 21st, 1799, illustrates the dilatory cashing out process Fry claims was purely for the benefit of the management:

> ROYAL UNIVERSAL TONTINE – It having been expected by many of the subscribers, and some of the Agents that the Capital Stock of the Royal Universal Tontine would have been divided at Midsummer, it may not be improper to inform the Claimants at large, that the necessary arrangements for the payment of Dividends arising from the Shares purchased in this Tontine cannot be made before Michaelmas next. [ie, September 29th] [text omitted] ...the Society's property will continue in the Funds till the 24th of next Month, when the Three per Cent. Consols open for transfer; soon after which the Treasurers will proceed to sell out.... Bath, June 29th, 1799.

The implication of this is that the projectors would be taking the interest from Midsummer's day through the sale date, roughly sometime after July 24th. This would amount to at least a month's worth of interest.

This illustrates, on a small scale, the shenanigans possible with this kind of tontine as described by Fry. The misadventures of additional small-sum, short-term tontines are explored in the next chapter, 'Tontine Failures.' It is likely that these contributed to the poor reputation of tontines that developed in the nineteenth century.

The deficiencies of these small tontines were not entirely ignored by Parliament. *The Times* reported on May 10th during the debate surrounding the Friendly Society Bill: "It is to be hoped that the *Friendly Society Bill* will comprehend all the Tontine Speculations, and prevent that money now lodged in the Stocks from being taken out, until the time of the Tontine expires, and then that each party shall receive his dividend from the Bank. This will prevent any tricks from being Played; for as matters stand now, the persons in whose names the money is vested may sell out, and dispose of the whole property as they please." That is to say the trustees could abscond with the capital with no legal claim on them by the tontineers.

Perhaps the final word should be this notice from the *Northampton Mercury* of September 1796, in regard to the small-sum, short-term tontines which ends on a curiously optimistic note:

> The Tontines that are now become due, and in course of payment, the seven years being expired, have all failed, owing to the great difference of the Stocks, which were at 79 when they were bought in; but this is the exact moment to renew them, and in the next century and probably something may be got without any very remarkable mortality.

CHAPTER 10

Tontine Failures

The shaky reputation of tontines can be traced to a number of sources. The failure of numerous small-sum, short-term tontines certainly would have contributed. Other factors included a growing distaste for basing your good fortune directly on the deaths of your fellow investors.

However, other kinds of tontines also failed. They were as fragile as any other corporate structure. A mis-estimation of the income relied on for dividend payments could cause a fatal default or bankruptcy. Actuarial estimates could prove wrong, especially based on the crude knowledge of the period although the data gathered through tontines is rightfully credited with improving actuarial knowledge over time. Finally, there is simple chicanery, sometimes taking the form of what became known under different circumstances as a 'Ponzi scheme.'

The Coal Tontine Proposal of 1774

This much advertised proposal seems to have been an intentional swindle. The advertising for it began in September 1774. Here is an example from the *St. James Chronicle* of September 15th, 1774:

> BRITISH TONTINE, or COAL COMPANY.
> THE Society forming for the benevolent and patriotic Purpose of reducing the Price of Coals, GIVE NOTICE, That of the Capital of £150,000 to be employed therein, £100,000 is still wanting, which it is proposed to

K. McKeever, *The Role of Tontines, 1750–1800*, Palgrave Studies in the History of Finance, https://doi.org/10.1007/978-3-032-12849-2_10

> raise by Annuities commencing with an Interest rate of Six per Cent. increasing by Survivorship. The Annuitants will be divided into twelve different Classes, the Survivor to each of which Classes, after 41 Lives at most, or probably, not half so many, will enjoy for his £200 (the Price of each single Share,) £500. a Year for Life, with very great prior Advantages, with Security equal to any public Security, and without sinking the Principal.

The end involved a bankruptcy hearing reported in *The London Chronicle* in August 1776.[1] A summary of the cases included "the schemer of a coal tontine, advertised in all the public papers during the last year, [text omitted] it appearing that he had sold places in the said tontine, as those of Accountant-general, Clerk, &c. and had made use of the name of an eminent banker as concerned in the scheme, the better to enable him to impose on the subscribers." The villain was remanded rather than discharged.

The 'English Tontine' of 1775

The 'English Tontine' of 1775, was a private proposal, and should not be confused with the Government's National Tontine of 1789, although many writers use the term 'English Tontine' to label the 1789 one.

The July 24th, 1775, issues of the *Gazetteer and New Daily Advertiser* and the *Public Advertiser* printed the first advertisements for English Tontine Annuities. The capital was to be secured on 'Freehold landed estates in England, Wales and Ireland' with no further details of the location of the properties. The scheme was heavily advertised over the next few months.

A more detailed description of the financial aspects of the proposal was published in an undated pamphlet entitled 'The New Impression of the English Tontine' which made small changes to the original proposal. The interest rate was increased to five percent and the number of each class was reduced from 500 subscribers to 400. It promised the first interest payment would occur on June 21st, 1776.

The proposal was off-puttingly complex, far more so than a simple tontine. It encompassed six age classes and ten groups defined by subscription amount. The subscriptions were priced in guineas, although

[1] August 3rd–6th, 1776.

the accounting was in pounds. The added shilling for each guinea went to the administration of the tontine, essentially a five percent surcharge.

The bankers were Sayre, Coote Purdon and Company, and the subscriptions were to be received by Frederick Bull, a Tea Merchant, at his 'Compting-house' in Cheapside. Bull was at one point an Alderman and then Lord Mayor of London in 1774 and served as an MP around this time. Stephen Sayre, the banker, was elected one of the two Sheriffs the same year Bull was Lord Mayor. Sayre was American born and in order for him to be eligible to vote and hold office, he had to be a Freeman of London and member of a Livery Company. He purchased his Freedom for £0/46/8 on June 8th, 1773. The Livery company he joined was the Company of Framework Knitters, which seems to have been a convenience for all sorts of non-knitters. Bartholomew Coote Purdon, the other partner in the bank, was from minor Irish landed gentry.

A list of nine names, including Bull and two other members of Parliament, was included in the brochure alleging they had already subscribed enough to qualify themselves as eligible for trusteeship for the tontine and that they had agreed to act as such. The following text is from one of the later advertisements in the Public Advertiser, December 2nd, 1775:

> The written and signed opinions of the Counsellors Duane and Dayrell, as to the eligibility and sufficiency of the estates proposed as securities for the loans at present required, any one that pleases may peruse. -- The title deeds of which estates the moment the money is ready to be paid in, will be signed over to those particular subscribers, and in their proper names, whose several subscriptions compose these loans, and deposited afterwards wherever the trustees to this concern (consisting of the principal subscribers) think proper: by which means the subscribers will ACTUALLY and INDIVIDUALLY become annuitants upon such estates and be secured by freehold landed securities on the one hand; and by the collateral security of the Treasurers (who oblige themselves in the receipts given for the subscription money, for the regular payment of the interest, &c.) on the other hand consequently no security, (not even of a public nature) can exceed the security to the English Tontine Undertaking; as it will always consist, to wit, of the very best of real securities, second of unexceptional personal security.
>
> Sundry other important securities are likewise already before Council, for the purpose of future loans, and the security of future subscribers; and when approved, the Council's written and signed opinions thereupon, as at present, will be submitted to public inspection.

> Subscribers disposed to borrow any part of the money hereby raised, and which will be lett out at five per cent. per annum, with an exemption from the return of the principal, will be preferred to such applicants as are not subscribers, provided the securities are equally good; not but that the most respectful attention will be paid to applications for this money, from such noblemen, gentlemen, and others, as are not subscribers; especially if their estates are situate either in Middlesex or Yorkshire....

Later advertising compared the English Tontine favorably to the first of the Irish Tontines. There are at least fifty advertisements up through mid-January 1776, primarily in the London papers, but also nationally. The tontine then disappears from the public record.

The banking partnership between Sayre and Coote Purdon was announced as dissolved six months later, in *The London Gazette* of June 18th, 1776. The notice indicated that Coote Purdon would be covering any debts. By the fall of 1776, Sayre and Coote Purdon were in bankruptcy proceedings. Both of them had their real estate auctioned off soon after. This report appeared in *The Morning Chronicle* in January 1977 after the bankruptcy hearings:

> Saturday, being the third and last meeting under the commission of bankruptcy against Mess. Sayre and Purdon, late of Oxford-street, bankers. Mr. Sayre appeared, as he had done at the two former meetings, and then finished his examination, to the entire satisfaction of all the creditors who were present. The senior commissioner declared that he sat in that capacity five-and-twenty years, and that he never experienced an instance of so clear, candid, and satisfactory a state of accompts as Mr. Sayre had given in; in which the other gentlemen in the commission entirely concurred. Mr. Sayre seemed impelled, as he stated facts, to the necessity of Shewing that Mr. Coote Purdon had been too deeply involved in debt, from the very commencement of their co-partnership, to be extricated; it appeared that his necessities had drawn a very large sum out of the house; that his slate had been long subject to heavy annuities, unknown even to his own family. Mr. Sayre scarcely mentioned his unhappy commitment to the Tower....

At the end of the report, it was stated that "Mr. Coote Purdon not having surrendered to the commission, it is now generally believed that he put an end to his life the 25th of October last." Coote Purdon was presumed a suicide by drowning in the Thames, per an advertisement in *The London Gazette* of November 30th, 1776, and other contemporary papers. However, in June 1777 it was reported the suicide was faked and he was living 'abroad.'

The reference to Sayre being committed 'to the Tower' had to do with an accusation made against him in October 1775. He was arrested and charged with High Treason (plotting to kidnap George III) and sent to the Tower of London. It is generally now perceived as a totally false charge. The ensuing legal action involved a Writ of Habeas Corpus being granted by Lord Mansfield and Sayre was ultimately acquitted. Sayre had to pay a bail of £500 in the process, and Coote Purdon put up £250.

Stephen Sayre and Frederick Bull were both involved in the politics of the time, associates of John Wilkes and supporters of a Bill of Rights. Sayre was also a staunch pro-American, which proved a problem. Sayre was born in Southampton, New York, attended Princeton, and developed a trading business, possibly through contacts with Francis Lewis, a signer of the Declaration of Independence. Sayre moved to London for the first time in 1762. His career seems to have been as a classic trans-Atlantic merchant, travelling between America, England, and the Caribbean. The private London bank Sayre created in partnership with Bartholomew Coote Purdon was short-lived, first appearing in the newspapers in March of 1774 and dissolving in 1776.

Presumably, the looming insolvency and the treason accusation both contributed to the evaporation of the proposed tontine. However, a report in the *Middlesex Journal* on October 24th, 1775, included this line:

> The money subscribed to the Tontine Scheme is certainly thought to have been transmitted to Holland, and from thence to America, for the use of the Provincials.

Sayre went to Paris in February 1777 and started his irregular service with the diplomatic corps of the United States that continued through the Revolutionary War. In 1800, a US Congressional report[2] was published that included Sayre's claims for compensation for his services during the Revolution. He stated:

[2] United States. Congress (6th, 1st session) 1799–1800, *Report of the Committee of Claims, to whom was referred, on the 8th of January last, the petition of Stephen Sayre*. 4th March, 1800, Philadelphia.

That he was one of the sheriffs of the city of London, and that he zealously promoted the opposition made to the then anti-American administration.

That becoming by such conduct very obnoxious to the ministry, he was on the 23d of October 1775, committed to the tower; and that the failure of his bank; and the loss of a very considerable part of his property was owing to that circumstance.

Sayre never made any claim or statement to the effect that the tontine accumulation was used to support the Revolution.

Postscript: In 1784, Sayre exchanged letters with George Washington in which Sayre proposed a tontine as the means to finance the work needed to make the Potomac River navigable as far inland as possible. The Potomac Company, which was chartered the next year, did not include a tontine.[3]

Uxbridge Tontine, 1785

Uxbridge was at that time an important market town to the west of London.

The World, which repeatedly pressed for higher interest rates for proposed tontines, published on June 15th, 1789 a statement as to the current dividends of the different tontines:

RICHMOND BRIDGE Tontines were 4 per cent. – KEW BRIDGE 5. – COVENT GARDEN Theatre 6l. 10s. besides the freedom, which was a saleable *bonus*. – LORD CORK's scheme 5l. 10s.

The Uxbridge scheme failed. –

Development

A proposal was presented to Parliament for paving the streets of the town and rebuilding the market building. Uxbridge was a market and meal-milling town, the major conduit for agricultural goods, especially flour, coming into London from the West Country. The growth in traffic and business had become a strain on the community. In the spring of 1785

[3] https://founders.archives.gov/documents/Washington/04-02-02-0085.

Parliament passed an Act, *25 George III, Chapter16,* authorizing a project involving demolition, market reconstruction, street widening, paving, and lighting.

The Act uses the local trustee format to organize the project, similar to the turnpike trusts. There were twenty-nine trustees named, but able to act with a quorum of five. Clause Eighteen specified the source of funding: "...intended to be defrayed by a voluntary Subscription amongst several of the Inhabitants of said Town, and other persons...." It did not specify a tontine.

Implementation

On April 29th, 1785, an advertisement appeared in *The Morning Chronicle* announcing the tontine, with a target of raising £30,000 at five percent per annum "to accumulate without any deduction till each Share amounts to £50 a year, when every subscriber whose Nominee be then living, will be entitled to the principal sum of £1,000 New Navy Stock." The printed proposal was to be had at the bankers; Mildred,[4] Masterman, and Walker, White-hart-court, Lombard Street, and locally of Mr. Daniel Norton in Uxbridge. Norton was one of the trustees.

Similar notices appeared elsewhere, including the *St. James Chronicle* and the *Oxford Journal*. Also in May, the *Public Advertiser* published two small snippets boosting the scheme, one on the cliched premise that the town got the benefit at no cost to the citizenry, the other pressing for an additional one-half percent on the interest rate. The comment below, from the *Public Advertiser* of May 13th, expresses the common notion that tontines provided amenities to communities without any cost to them:

> The town of Uxbridge is soon to be paved, and the money to pay for it is to be raised by a Tontine -- and with what consequence to the town?-- Why, that at no great distance of time, the natural period of a few years, the whole money will revert to, and invest itself in the town -- of course then the town will be paved for nothing!

[4] Note that Daniel Mildred, of Mildred, Masterman, and Company was also one of the replacement trustees of the Society for Annuities Encreasing to the Survivors, described in Chapter 4.

In September, another boosting article[5] noted the participation of Dr. Richard Price in the planning of the tontine:

> The Uxbridge tontine is a scheme undertaken on the suggestion and calculation of Dr. Price. The object is to pave the town of Uxbridge; and the scheme is so well laid, that notwithstanding the terms are as usual in a tontine, an increase by survivorship, such will be the emolument to the towns-people, that the pavement will be executed for nothing.

The article continues as a push for a national tontine:

> Such being the success of this and other schemes of the same kind, is it not wonderful that Government neglect to avail themselves of this publick propensity, and thus turn into temporary annuities the different funds in perpetuity.

Dr. Richard Price was a prominent philosopher, mathematician, and an important early demographer and actuary. In regard to tontines, it is worth noting that Price's mortality tables based on the records of Northampton were very influential and used by actuaries for the next 100 years. However, a close scrutiny by Finlaison in 1819 showed Price overestimated mortality. Price set birth life expectancy at twenty four years, while the later critique indicated it should have been around thirty.

A National Tontine was tried four years later, in 1789. It was undersubscribed, and the government had to scramble to work out an alternative scheme to take in the income it needed.

Collapse

Self-dealing on the part of the Tontine 'projectors' caused the scheme to collapse. Reasons for the failure were detailed the following year in a letter to the *St. James Chronicle* of October 19th, 1786:

> The Schemers of the Town of Uxbridge will be great gainers by their Tontine, in not performing their Engagement to the Subscribers. When their Stock was raised near Twenty per Cent. they artfully dissolved the Tontine, and returned the Subscriptions with Five per Cent. Interest.

[5] *The Morning Chronicle,* September 16th, 1785.

By that Strategem they will gain near One Thousand Pounds.

Query: Have not the subscribers a Right to call the five Trustees to account?

Perhaps Parliament will take this Matter into Consideration, and prevent Abuses on the Publick for the future.

A certain amount of wrangling appeared in the papers in the Autumn of 1785, including a suggestion that each subscriber's share be returned with the profit specifically associated with it. It was followed by a note aimed at the bankers, asking them to provide restitution.[6] The paper published an apology on December 1st acknowledging the bankers were not responsible and pointing the finger at the Trustees.

The Morning Herald of December 7th, 1785, published this notice:

UXBRIDGE TONTINE.

THE Subscribers to the Uxbridge Tontine are desired to send their address to Mr. George Clark, of Uxbridge.

By order of the Trustees,

GEO. CLARK, Sec.

This seems to represent the first step in winding down the scheme. George Clark, the Secretary to the Trustees, was an Uxbridge solicitor. Finally, on December 15th, 1785, *The Morning Chronicle* has the last word:

The Uxbridge Tontine, after all comes to nothing. The rise in the price of the Funds has made it impossible to complete the plan; even if the subscription, which in no class was the case, had been full.

According to Redford and Riches, *The history of the ancient town and borough of Uxbridge,* published in 1818, a new marketplace was ultimately built in 1788 after demolition of the old one and adjacent buildings in 1785. The book does not mention a tontine.

The UK National Archives has an entry for an 'Uxbridge Universal Tontine' of 1791, for five years. This is an unrelated small-sum, short-term tontine.

[6] *The Morning Chronicle,* September 16th, 1785.

Coda

The 1823 case of *Nockels v Crosby*, 3 Barnewall & Cresswell 814, involved a very similar situation of abandonment by the projectors of the proposed British Metropolitan Tontine before implementation occurred. The court decided that the investors had to be repaid in full, without any deduction for expenses.

The 'Old' British Tontine (1791) and the New British Tontine (1792)

These were extremely ambitious small-sum, short-term tontines. Typically, a tontine of this type has an opening date, a date for closing to new subscribers and an expiry date. For both of these, which had interlocking management, the term of the tontine was a span of seven years. Subscribers paid £0/6/6 per quarter. Later subscribers paid an additional one time 'fine' of up to three shillings just before closing. An advertisement for the first, shortly before its closing date of June 24th, 1792, stated: "Between thirty and forty thousand shares [have been] already purchased by above twenty thousand persons." This seems much larger than any other contemporary tontine. The tontine had agents all over the country, which was divided into informal districts for administrative purposes.

At the end of the term for the first one, the selling up of the capital, as well as the capital of competing schemes, involved a sum so large it made news although the figures varied. From the *London Chronicle*, November 17th–20th, 1798:

> The recent fall of stocks has been produced principally from the large sums of money sold out within the last two days by Tontine Societies the terms of which have lately expired. The Bristol Tontine alone is said to have no less than £500,000 stock, the whole of which sum was drawn out of the funds.

Other papers gave the figure as £300,000 which seems to be more accurate in regard to the 'Old' British Tontine based in Bristol. Part of the problem is that a couple of other tontines cashed out at roughly the same time, depressing the already weakened market.

However, when an interim dividend of £8/8/0 was declared, unhappiness ensued. The basic subscription involved a contribution of slightly more than nine pounds, so the result was a loss.

A meeting of subscribers in Exeter in December 1798 was reported in *The Sun*[7] in London. Relying on the '21st rule of the printed Articles,' it was stated that distribution of dividends should have taken place on or before October 12th, 1798. Letters between some subscribers and the Tontine Office were also presented. The situation was that "the Persons concerned in the Distribution of the Stock of the Society, declined fixing any stated period for the Payment of the Shares or giving any satisfactory Account of the Proceeds of the Society." A postscript in one of the letters from the Office in Bristol was quoted as reading: "It is neither threats nor insinuations that can remove impossibilities, and you may as well advertise for a Meeting to inforce the winds to blow in a particular direction, as to inforce the Observance of Rules that cannot possibly be fulfilled in any respect." Whew.

Another meeting, ten months later, also in Exeter, was reported in the *Salisbury and Winchester Journal*, October 21st, 1799. The report noted that payment had been 'procrastinated beyond any other Tontine which has hitherto entered into.' The committee felt the secretary, a Mr. Greenwood, who had laid the blame on agents not submitting their records to him, had thus forfeited £100 for 'not furnishing the subscribers with accounts of defalcations by Agents,' as required by Article Seven. They further felt he had "also forfeited his Bond for £2,000 by not investing all of the money in the names of the Treasurers, but in other personal names" which had been his practice for the last four years. The Eight Guineas interim dividend was compared very unfavorably with the £11/3/6 dividend paid by the Royal Universal Tontine Society which had started nine months after the British Tontine. A case had been submitted to a 'counsel of the first eminence' who felt a lawsuit might be successful and it lay with the committee to decide to move forward. The report of the meeting was to be published in London, Liverpool, Manchester, Birmingham, York, Cambridge, Salisbury, Bristol, Bath, Sherborne, and Exeter.

[7] Dec 24th, 1798.

A report[8] of a similar committee meeting for the Liverpool District provides more details:

> The Shares are in number about 28,000, and each Share, supposing all the Nominees to have lived, has contributed £9/2/0. besides contingent Expenses, Which at Simple Interest only makes the Fund of the Tontine amount to upwards of £282,000. From this Fund only Eight Guineas a Share has yet been paid, which, on the whole number, amount to little more than £235,000 leaving, on this mode of calculation (which is merely returning to each surviving Life its own, without allowing for accumulated Interest, and for Survivorship), a deficiency of £47,000.

It goes on to indicate the additional income that is not specified: the accumulated interest from the capital, the various fines paid, and the accumulation from forfeited and lapsed shares. Liverpool also called for action to 'compel redress.'

Litigation followed for both the Old British Tontine and the new one. Both involved cases in the Court of the Exchequer or Chancery. The suit challenging the management of the first tontine was *Durbin v Esdaile,* and the one against the New Tontine was titled *Hance v Esdaile*. The simultaneous notices posted in the Hampshire/Portsmouth *Telegraph* of September 26th, 1803, were solicitations for claimants based on having held shares March 25th, 1798, for the British Tontine, and March 25th, 1799, for the New British Tontine. In both cases, the claims were to be lodged with the attorney for the plaintiffs in London.

Sir James Esdaile, a leading banker, was the lead treasurer for both tontines. Durbin was one of the trustees of the first. Hance was an agent for the New British Tontine in Southwark.

An announcement from the office of the plaintiffs' solicitor in regard to the New British Tontine in *The Times* of April 7th, 1807, indicated that a sum upwards of £90,000 was to be divided among the 5,697 shares ".... substantiated in the Law-suit." This would provide roughly £15/15/0 for each shareholder, less costs.

A number of advertisements in regard to the Durbin case appeared over the years, up through *The Times* of August 1st, 1835! In *The London Gazette* of July 20th, 1841, there is a notice, under the heading of 'Durbin versus Esdaile' stating that the Accountant-General of the Court

[8] *The Sun* (London) Nov 2nd, 1799:

of the Exchequer will issue to properly accredited claimants a sum of £1/15/5 per share. Echoes of *Jarndyce v Jarndyce*.

Tracking these tontines through the contemporary press is made difficult by the awkward similarity of the names of the different projects.

Universal British Tontine Society, 1791

This small-sum, short-term tontine seems to have had a complete life cycle. The Universal British Tontine Society trustees included Rowland Stephenson who was also a trustee of the Covent Garden Theatre Life Tontine. The advertising compared the potential savings to the riskiness of lotteries and specified the hope that the investment become a 'sufficient sum for parents to put out their children to respectable trades,' i.e., pay the fees for an apprenticeship.

The tontine involved subscriber payments of seven shillings a quarter to be 'laid out in the public funds.' An advertisement of March 16th, 1792, claimed there were a core of 792 shares on the lives of 45 persons, i.e., an average of 17.6 shares per life. Seventy-two more investors held six shares apiece, and 'a much greater number' holding three shares each. Note that the price of three shares would amount to a Guinea a quarter. Subscriptions closed June 23rd, 1792, with payout scheduled for 'the week before Christmas 1798.'

In *The Oracle* of December 8th, 1798, a report is published saying the trustees are authorized to sell the corpus (held by Stephenson's bank) of £58,500 in Four Percent Annuities. There is no indication whether this figure represents the par value of the Bank Annuity Certificates or the current market value. At the point of the closing of the Tontine to new subscribers, in June 1792, the Four Percents were floating around par, i.e., £100. The price of Four Percents dropped to roughly £67 by December 1798, a loss of thirty-three percent. This would have been partially counterbalanced by seven years' worth of annuity dividends. However, there are no further public statements as to the payout per share.

Astley's Liverpool Theatre Proposal, 1795

Philip Astley, a London circus impresario, was notified that his regular touring venue in Liverpool, the Theatre Royal, was no longer going to let him perform there. Astley advertised a tontine of £5,000 to construct a new amphitheater. The shares were to cost £50 with a bonus of free admission to the shareholder. However, Astley ultimately continued to perform at the Theatre Royal in Liverpool in subsequent years, so it is unlikely the proposal was ever fulfilled.

The New Tontine, 1799

An advertisement for 'The New Tontine' was printed in *The Oracle* of August 14th, 1799. The 250 shares were to cost £100 each. The survivors were to share £10,000 in 1808. An additional £1,000 was to be shared per annum after that. Both sums were presumably the result of accrued interest and reductions through nominee deaths. The total capital of £25,000 was to be the property of the single surviving life. The security was to be an unspecified 'freehold landed estate.'

While this was a short-term tontine, it was not a small-sum proposal. However, it was likely an intentional swindle. A lawsuit was brought against the projector in the Court of Common Pleas which came to trial in 1802. A printed summary of the resulting trial, printed in *The Morning Post*, London, July 22nd, 1802, gives the details.

> Common Pleas, July 21 PROSSER v. COOPER.
>
> This was an action to recover a sum of £100 paid to the defendant in 1799, on a tontine scheme advertised by him... ... It was stated in the proposals that the distribution was to take place in 1808. Ten thousand pounds were then to be divided among the surviving subscribers, who were also to enjoy an annuity of £1000 a year, together with a dividend of a further sum of £25,000 in a short time after, all stated to be secured on landed estates; but no mention was made of the place where these estates were situated. The proposal also stated that from the number of persons who had given in their names, the subscription was expected to be very soon filled, and therefore it called upon those who may be disposed to lay out their money in such an advantageous way to apply immediately.
>
> ...In the proposals it had been said, that subscriptions would be received in many of the most respectable banks. Mr. Hobbes said, he had given his consent to receive subscriptions at the bank to which he belonged, if any other respectable bank came forward in the business. No subscription had, however, been paid into the bank of Messrs. Hobbes and Co. nor into any other of the banks referred to, neither had any of them seen Mr. Cooper in the way of business after; he had never called to make any enquiry about the state of the subscription. Mr. Nichols, of Fleet-street, was mentioned

> in the original proposals, as secondary, with his own consent but he soon after withdrew his name, and declined all concern. Several letters, written in the course of last year, were read; in these letters the plaintiff demanded an account of the state of the fund, and the defendant sent in answer, that the subscription was not yet filled, but that now we had more favorable times, and he expected to be filled without delay, when he would give the plaintiff immediate information.
>
> … A notice served on the defendant's attorney, to produce a list of the lands mentioned in the proposal, and the circumstances in which these lands are, was also read; but the defendant's Counsel thought it improper to make any further resistance. Verdict for the plaintiff £115.

This is another example of income from land being proposed as the capital of a tontine. Once again, no details of the lands involved were forthcoming.

Failures at Early Stages

Tontines were often proposed but never gelled beyond the initial stages. In the early nineteenth century, both Waterloo Bridge and Regent's Canal were proposed with tontine funding, but both shifted to a corporate form pretty quickly.

A huge tontine was advertised in the *Chester Chronicle* of September 11th, 1789 consisting of 'One thousand shares of one hundred pounds each….' The projectors listed included well-known bankers around the country, including Lockart[9] of Pall Mall, in London, Fector in Dover, and Thomas Parron in Chester. The notice seems to be the only appearance of this proposal.

Conclusion

The array of tontines described above should be seen as a sample rather than an exhaustive list. There were many tontines proposed, some successful, but there were many, many more about which it has proven impossible to trace more information.

[9] Typo? for Lockhart.

CHAPTER 11

The Breadth of Tontines

Eventually, the tontine became a relatively standard means of entrepreneurial investment and development.[1] There were three main strands in the evolution of Georgian tontines: general government borrowing and revenue; construction projects, both government and private; and long-term or intergenerational financial instruments.

Revenue

Revenue was the reason for the invention of the tontine and its use in France was regularly scrutinized by governments in the United Kingdom. There were a number of variations. The British national government revenue tontines included the Million Act, 1692; the Irish Tontines of 1773, 1775, and 1777; and the British Tontines of 1757, 1765, and 1789. There were local revenue tontines as well, such as the City of Dublin Tontine issued in 1776.

Local Government tontines could have general revenue purposes, but were more often related to projects. The early one in Chester was described in Chapter 2. Others included market buildings in Gloucester (1784) and Plymouth (1804); four tontines in Boston in 1792, 1799,

[1] Query: the last outbreak of the plague in UK was in the 1660s. Did the population grow more relaxed about gamble-able lifespans after no plagues for a generation or two?

K. McKeever, *The Role of Tontines, 1750–1800*, Palgrave Studies in the History of Finance, https://doi.org/10.1007/978-3-032-12849-2_11

1805, and 1815 for paving and a bridge; the London/Middlesex Gaol (1789); the Forehoe, Norfolk, Poorhouse (1776); and the Uxbridge market and paving project described in Chapter 10.

Projects

Other construction projects financed by tontines developed in the provinces and arrived in London with the use of a tontine to finance the Richmond Bridge in 1774 described in Chapter 3. Besides the ones described in earlier chapters, the more prominent private large project-related tontines included a Birmingham Hotel (1772); Freemason's Hall in London (1775); a Tontine Inn in Paisley, Scotland (1780); St. Stephen's Warehouses, Bristol (1785+); the Glasgow Coffee House (1781); the Cork Coffee House (1793); a school in Gainsborough (1794); Glasgow Assembly Rooms (1796), Glasgow Tontine Society, which financed a hotel (1816); Kew Bridge (1784); Shoreham Bridge in Sussex (1780–2); and libraries in Liverpool (1789–99) and Birmingham (1799).

Other projects included Assembly rooms such as the ones in Beccles, Essex (1786) and Armagh (1794). Theatres financed by tontines included ones in Bath (1807–1872); Swansea (1805); Chicester (1792); and Plymouth (within a hotel project) (1811). A market ('Shambles') in Hull (technically, Kingston-upon-Hull) was built using a tontine. The statute authorizing civic improvements in Hull specifically indicated the use of a tontine: *50 George III, C 41, (1810)*, Clause 38. Tontine housing projects were created in Swansea; Swanage; Brunswick Square, Bristol (1786); Leith; Pery Square, Limerick; Cirencester (1802); Cambray Street in Cheltenham (1809); and Colquitt Street, in Liverpool. Another Hull Improvement Act of 1795 (*35 Geo III, C 46*) created a framework for a tontine-financed new street and terrace of residences in Parliament Street in Hull. The parish church in Wanstead, Essex, was repaired via a tontine limited to £4000 authorized by Parliament in 1789. A summary of municipal projects financed via tontines can be found in David Green's essay *Tontines, annuities and civic improvements in Georgian Britain*.[2]

Many coffee houses, hotels, and inns financed through tontines were built in the late eighteenth and early nineteenth centuries. However, the

[2] 46 *Urban History*, Volume 649–694, November 2019.

use of the word 'tontine' in the name was no guarantee that a tontine was used in the financing. Some places simply used the word to indicate a level of quality for a new inn rather than its financing. An example is the Tontine Hotel in Kirkbymoorside in Yorkshire offered for sale in 1849. The details in the advertisement imply it was recently built, it was offered by a single owner, and there is no hint of a tontine in the construction of the hotel. It is likely that the Stourport Tontine Inn was also not financed via a tontine.

There were establishments with tontine in their name in Alloa (Ramsay's Tontine Tavern, later converted into a prison), Ardrossan, Ashton-under-Lyne, Balfron, Brede, Broseley, Birmingham, Buildwas, Clackmannan, Cleveland, Coalbrookdale, Colchester, Cork, Cupar, Edinburgh (Fortune's Tavern), Glasgow, Glossop, Greenock, Guildford (White Hart Inn Tontine), Helensburgh, Ironbridge (aka Madeley Wood), Kirbymoorside in York, Macclesfield, Melverley, Newport on the Isle of Wight, Northampton, Paisley, Peebles, Perth, Stourport, Sheffield, Thurgoland, Weymouth, Whitchurch, and Whitehaven. Many of these are traceable because they served as venues for local meetings and bankruptcy proceedings. The meeting rooms could accommodate the gathering of creditors involved in the bankruptcy commission hearings. Notices of these kinds of meetings were common, especially for the Tontine Inns in Sheffield, Paisley, and Madeley.

Examples of proposals that never got off the ground included Chorley, Dawlish, Newcastle, and a church in Petersham, upriver from Richmond in 1777. A tontine was authorized by the statute enabling 'better paving, cleansing, and lighting the town of Cambridge' in 1794 and another act for the paving of Piccadilly and nearby areas of St. George Parish in 1813 but neither seem to have been created. The bridge in London that ultimately became Waterloo Bridge was initially proposed as a patent iron bridge financed by a tontine.

Some unsourced tontine location references remain mysterious. Hanley, in Stoke, has a Tontine Square and Tontine Street. An advertisement for a municipal shambles to be constructed in the early 1830s made reference to the location of the project being 'erected on the Tontine premises,' perhaps an earlier inn.

Investment

Another variation was the large-sum financial tontine: The first was 'Siprut's Tontine' formally the 'Society for Annuities Encreasing to Survivors' (May 22, 1769). Later ones were based in Doncaster (1788), Bath (1789), Ipswich (1790), and Bristol. These tontines provided a means for investment at the local level. The securities market was awkward for non-London-based investors. Dividends were expected to be picked up personally, or else a power-of-attorney form had to be filled out (for a fee.) A locally-based tontine meant nearby payment source, or that the Trustees or Directors handled the receipt of dividends in London and the local holders simply picked up their share at the local office, upon presentation of the evidence the nominee was still living.

Another form of large-sum tontine involved rich people cashing in on their landed estates, including the Earl of Cork's Tontine (1789) and Mr. O'Hara's Tontine (1792). The dividends of this sort of tontine were paid by the income from the encumbered properties. The property would revert to the landowner or his heirs at the conclusion of the tontine. It was not the prize for the longest liver. A later one of these was Mr. Drew's Jamaica Tontine (1805) based on sugar plantation properties in Jamaica. It failed almost immediately. More of these estate-based tontines were advertised than seem to have come to fruition.

The next step in the evolution of tontines was the numerous small-sum, short-term schemes, the 'penny stocks' of their day. These tended to involve quite small regular contributions to a capital fund. The payments were designed to be continued through the life of the tontine, usually seven years with the accumulation distributed to the members at the end of the term. The first seems to have been the Bristol Tontine Association in 1788 of a shilling a week. There were quite a number of these and the most visible are listed in Chapter 9. Very few proved profitable.

Another variation were the 'military' tontines related to colonial service in India, with two based in Calcutta and one in Bombay. The Calcutta Tontine of 1788 was open to 'Subaltern Officers and Assistant Surgeons on the Bengal Establishment' via payment of one gold Mohur a month according to *The Calcutta Chronicle* of September 11th, 1788. These also existed in France. The French even publicized a tontine specifically for foreign soldiers serving under the French flag.

What follows are details of some of the more visible projects.

The Royal Hotel, Birmingham, 1770–03

This was another early project. Per the *Birmingham Daily Post,* April 3rd, 1869:

> The Royal Hotel... ...was a first-class house, offering every accommodation for families of distinction, and has been patronised by crowned heads. It was built in 1772, under the direction and plans of the late Dr. Ash, (MD.) Originally it was intended for an infirmary, but prior to its completion was purchased by a Tontine Company for an hotel; a large assembly room was built in addition, and the balls and other entertainments then held at No. 11, Old Square, and No. 85, Bull Street, were removed to the Hotel.

There were fifty shares of £60 each held by thirty-five subscribers, fifteen held two shares. The initial interest was intended to be four percent. The capital was insufficient for the purpose, the project struggled, and although the hotel opened in June, 1773, it did not pay a dividend until 1813! The formal enrollment of the Tontine agreement did not take place until 1781. Sometime after 1838 the five remaining shareholders arranged for legal approval to end the tontine agreement and vested shared ownership in themselves.[3]

City of Dublin Corporation Tontine, 1776

This municipal revenue project was first advertised in the *Daily Advertiser* of October 18th, 1775. It was likely inspired by the First Irish Tontine of 1773 and was relatively complicated, as shown by this later report:

> The Tontine debt was created about the year 1775, when the corporation had occasion to borrow a sum of £60,000. Of this a sum of £30,000 was raised upon single lives in three classes, £10,000 in each, at 5 per cent. Being unable to raise more at this rate, the corporation offered to give double lives at the same rate, and thus raised £15,300 in one class, and £7,700 in another. In these latter classes the persons advancing the money were allowed to nominate two lives instead of one. Thus a sum of £53,000 in all was raised. The annual amount of the annuities paid on this account by the corporation is £2,563/2/9. None of the classes have as yet fallen

[3] A detailed history can be found in [Liddell (A.)] A Birmingham Tontine, the Royal Hotel. [Signed: A. L.] In *Central Literary Magazine,* Vol. 12. PP. 14–22 (1895).

> in by the expiration of the lives nominated, but the first class of single lives is now reduced to four or five, and may soon be expected to expire.[4]

A tontine offered on two lives was very rare. While it is not stated here, this tontine had a cap on dividends so that no shareholder received more than £100 per year. This meant that as it was winding down, the corporation's annual budget allotment for dividends started shrinking. This effectively counteracted the negative aspect of the Boston and Middlesex Tontines mentioned above. Outstanding Dublin City Bonds could be used to pay for these tontine shares at par.

The WorldCat website has a record for "City of Dublin Tontine: regulations adopted on the 11th day of July 1774 for the management of the tontine scheme, printed by Richard Taylor, London, [1774?]." Unfortunately it is listed as not held by any WorldCat library!

The Corporation appointed a London agent for the Tontine, a merchant house with strong Irish connections, Allen, Marlar & Company. In a letter from Bath to an unknown correspondent in December 1775, William Melmoth complained:

> It seems somewhat extraordinary that Messrs Marlar being appointed by the Corporation of Dublin to receive subscriptions to their Tontine shd *[should]* not be furnished with forms of all the instruments necessary for that purpose. I am fully satisfied however that in completing my subscription you will take all the proper measures requisite for my security.... ... When you shall have settled the matters concerning the Tontine subscription you will be pleased to give me notice.[5]

A committee report[6] in the Dublin Assembly Roll for 1830 confirmed that the 'principal sum' was reduced with deaths, rather than remaining the same as in a standard tontine. The annual payment was limited to the amount of the subscription, so a subscriber for £100 would never receive more than £100 a year no matter how small the pool became. The excess principal sum seemingly reverted to the Corporation as the shareholder

[4] Appendix to the First Report of the Commissioners: *Report on the City of Dublin, Part two,* London: Clowes and Sons for His Majesties Stationery Office, 1836, p. 246.

[5] Collection of the author.

[6] The report is transcribed in the *Calendar of Ancient Records of Dublin* (CARD) edited by Lady Gilbert, Volume XVIII pp. 434–452 (Dublin: Dollard, Ltd., 1922). The report includes a list of subscribers alive at that time.

pool shrank, and there was no concluding large distribution to a final life or lives. At the same time, the interest paid did increase, but the formula is opaque.

From an earlier report in 1786:

> Ten nominees dead in first class: dividend increase of £0/11/1 per annum
> Three nominees dead in the second class; dividend increase of £0/6/4
> Six nominees dead in the third class: dividend increase of £0/11/1
> No double deaths yet in either class of the two-life nominees, although in some cases one nominee has died

In 1815 and again in the 1820s, the Dublin Assembly was informed that payments of the Tontine dividends had become a mess. In 1815, it was resolved by debiting the City Treasurer, John Carleton, for the overcharge he had reported to the Assembly. In 1828, it turned out that the London agent (where ninety-seven percent of the payments were made), William Conningham, had *sua sponte* handed the records to the James Esdaile bank and they made payments based on some sort of ledger without consulting the underlying papers. Esdaile wanted out and recommended John Boyd, Treasurer of the Board of Chancery. Ultimately, in 1830, Henry Schultes was appointed agent and given instructions on straightening things out.[7]

The UK Parliamentary Papers, 1847; *Report from the Surveying Officers on the Dublin Improvement Bill* at page 29, shows forty-two annuitants alive seventy-three years after the creation of the tontine.

The Forehoe Tontine, 1777

A tontine was authorized by Parliament in 1776 to build a workhouse to serve twenty-three of the twenty-four adjacent parishes of the Forehoe Hundred to the east of Norwich in Norfolk. It involved 110 shares of £100 paying five percent. In 1827, there were fifty survivors. In 1845, the tontine was reported to have roughly thirty survivors. In 1813, there was an aftermarket auction notice indicating the interest was at that point £6/18/0. There was one survivor reported in 1867. Some of the original

[7] *Calendar of Ancient Records of Dublin*, (CARD) Vol XVII pp. 70–71; and Vol XVIII, primarily p. 304 et seq.

investors had connections to subscribers in the Ipswich Universal Tontine detailed in Chapter 5.

The institution expanded a bit during the nineteenth century and later served as a hospital. The primary building still exists and has been converted to residential use.

The Beccles Tontines, 1777 and 1820

The Beccles Assembly Rooms were constructed via a tontine in 1777 and the Town records indicate these first Tontine accounts were not closed until 1871. A second was created in 1820 in order to renovate the building. The last nominee of this second Tontine lived for 103 years, dying in 1921!

As reported in the *Solicitor's Journal*:

> With the recent death of a Miss Matilda Sayer, of King's Lynn, says the *New Statesman,* vanishes one of the curiosities of English municipal finance. In 1820, the Becoles Corporation borrowed for the repair of the town hall £500 by means of fifty tontine bonds of £10 each, bearing interest at the rate of 5 per cent. [text omitted] In the case of the Beccles transaction each subscriber nominated a child to receive the annuities. By 1897 the number of survivors was reduced to five. between whom was shared the 5 per cent. on the £500. In 1910 Miss Sayer was the sole survivor, and when she died a few months ago she had reached the age of 103, and for ten years, therefore, had received the whole of the interest. Now the whole transaction is completed, but it has not proved a good bargain for the corporation, and the town hall has no doubt required further repairs meantime.[8]

Resentment of the ongoing cost of the tontine can be found in this 1889 report of a debate in the Beccles Town Council over the length of a contract with the local Waterworks in the *Ipswich Journal* of April 19th. In warning against a long water supply contract, it was stated:

> Inquiry had shown they could supply themselves at less than half the present cost; and if anything more advantageous should turn up within

[8] 65 *Solicitor's Journal* 584, May, 28th, 1921.

> the next 21 years, the ratepayers would blame them as they now did their forefathers for entering into such arrangements as the tontine bonds.

The Beccles example shows how the longevity of a tontine can prove a problem for local funding. The usual tool for borrowing in municipal government was the bond, which could be redeemed. If standard Life Annuities were used, the amount paid out each year shrinks as the pool of investors dies off. A tontine involves a commitment to make the same payment for many years to a smaller and smaller group.

The Clerkenwell Sessions House, 1779

A local courthouse was constructed in Clerkenwell from 1779 through 1782. Years later, in a public meeting in 1862 reviewing the proposal that resulted in the Westminster Chambers Mutual Tontine Association, it was reported:

> In reply to questions as to what advantages a tontine presented, Mr. Burchell (the under sheriff for Middlesex) said his father and uncle united with a class of twenty persons, who each laid down £100 for the building of the present Clerkenwell Sessions House. The interest was small at first, for the magistrates would not allow more than 4 per cent., but it went on increasing year by year, until at length the whole property of £100 per annum, fell into the hands of his uncle, who happened to be the oldest surviving member, he having lived to the age of 92. It might be an objection, looking at the question from a commercial point of view, that the interest was not larger at first, but considering it under the mutual point of view he did not think that was any objection at all.[9]

As described, this was a very small Tontine. The courthouse project was created by statute (*18 George III, cap. 67, 1778*) which authorized borrowing the necessary money, £11,000, from the surplus of the coal-tax-supported London Orphans' Fund, something of municipal slush fund at the time, with a proviso that an additional £4,000 could be raised if necessary. The Tontine may have been completion money under that clause. However, no advertisements as to a tontine appeared in the

[9] *The Standard*, Dec 10th, 1862.

press. James Burchell was one of the directors of the Mutual Tontine Association.

The Sessions House opened in 1782 and its beauty was appreciated in the press at the time. The building has since been restored and is now an elegant multi-use and reception hall.

The Ironbridge Tontine Inn, 1784

The statute *(16 George III, C 17)* authorizing a bridge over the Severn between Benthall and Madeley Wood makes no reference to a tontine. It specifies 100 shares of £50 each and that each of the shareholders thereby became a trustee. The bridge that was ultimately constructed between 1777 and 1781 is noted as the first major bridge made of iron, and the evolution of the communities around Madeley Wood into the town of Ironbridge was the result. However, the local hotel, built in 1784, after the construction of the bridge, was based on a tontine.

The Tontine Minute book[10] held by the Shropshire Archives details the business of the organization without providing full details on the subscribers and the costs. It starts in mid-April 1784 at the White Hart Inn. The participants in the initial meeting were Rev. Edward Harries, Richard and William Reynolds, Joseph Rathbone, John Wilkinson, Edward Blakeway, John Parry, Joseph Roden, Thomas Addenbrooke (Secretary), and Abraham and Samuel Darby. The latter two were the designers and builders of the bridge. Wilkinson was another ironmonger and proponent of innovative uses of iron. The overlap of this group and the trustees of the bridge itself are significant. By July, the committee met at the Tontine Inn.

The first London listing of a bankruptcy meeting scheduled at the Inn was in September 1784. The Madeley Wood establishment seems to be the first to use the name, with the one in Sheffield appearing the next year. It then appears regularly as a venue for such meetings. The hotel has gone through the usual ups-and-downs for a building of its age and purpose, but it still stands, elegantly restored, serving as a small hotel and restaurant, a key element of the tourist attraction centered on the bridge itself.

[10] Shropshire Archives, *Books of Acts of the Tontine subscribers*. System reference X245/6, Document Reference 245/6.

The Shropshire Archives records indicate a number of legacy share transfers, but no auction advertisements seem to exist.

While the community around the bridge is now known as Ironbridge, it was known as the parish of Madeley or Madeley Wood at the time. Iron Bridge started being used as a landmark name at the end of the eighteenth century, but it did not become a single-word place name until the 1820s. The famous and innovative bridge itself ended up the property of the Rathbone family, Quakers from Liverpool. When it was handed over to the Shropshire County Council in 1950, a Major Rathbone did the honors.

The Sheffield Tontine, 1785

The Sheffield Tontine Inn was the primary hotel in the city for many years. It was a classic coaching inn, serving as the terminus for the stage to London and other cities. An old handbill describing the Inn was reprinted in 1874:

> The above inn is in the most central and convenient situation. On the ground floor are 7 or 8 rooms of different dimensions for entertaining company; up one pair of stairs is a room 50ft. by 23ft. for public occasions, and there are upwards of 30 separate lodging rooms.[11]

The origins were described in an 1849 report:

> The Tontine Hotel was erected in 1785, by subscription among fifty gentlemen, the present Duke of Norfolk (then Earl of Surrey[12]) being one of the chief promoters of the scheme. The amount originally subscribed was £5000, or £100 for each proprietor; but this being found inadequate, a further sum of £1000 was raised among the proprietors.

[11] *Sheffield Independent,* August 22nd, 1874.

[12] In 1785, the then Earl of Surrey was a subscriber to the Covent Garden Theatre Life Tontine. He was also instrumental in the creation of the Shoreham Bridge in Sussex via a tontine in 1781. This involved fifty shares (36 subscribers) of £100 each. See *The Whitehall Evening Post,* June 20th–22nd, 1789. He led the ceremonies at the opening of the bridge. The Howards had property everywhere in England....

That description is taken from a report of an arbitration in th*e Sheffield Independent* of August 11th, 1849. After an existence of roughly sixty-five years, a renewal of the city center was proposed by the Duke of Norfolk, the primary landowner. It involved tearing down the Tontine Inn to create a new market. The remaining tontineers resisted the purchase offer and the dispute over the compensation was resolved through a public arbitration. The Tontine stood on land whose lease would expire in 1883, so the interest involved would be the anticipated value between 1849 and 1883. At that point, there were seventeen subscribers left. They asked for £10,500 and were awarded £7,720.

In *The Making of Sheffield, 1865–1914*, the author transcribes material from a manuscript volume called 'The Tontine Inn Book 1850.' It details both the creation of the tontine and its dissolution. As part of the early chronicle, the names of the subscribers and their nominees are listed. Interest payments were not recorded regularly and varied related to both the rent paid by the lessee and the number of shares remaining. The text of the manuscript has a break of many years and starts again in 1838. In 1839, the dividend was £9/14/10 per share, in 1845 it reached £14/0/0, and in 1849, as the compensation situation was being worked out, the annual dividend was £19/14/0.

Over the next few years, the Tontine property became a target for two projects, the development of the Manchester, Sheffield and Midland Junction Railway and the Duke of Norfolk's market construction plan. The railway proposal involved a figure of £10,000, but it was abandoned in December of 1846.

The Duke's market plan was approved by Parliament and in July 1848 negotiations started as to a compensation price for the Tontine. That resulted in the Arbitration mentioned above. The post-arbitration wrangling over the award showed another weakness of the standard tontine form: A single tontineer had a veto over the various solutions offered. Ultimately, the award money was used to purchase a government annuity paying out over the original projected period of the Tontine. Once the income shifted to the Annuity, it was £16/11/0 per share in 1853, rising to £36/0/0 in 1861, with the final annuitant receiving £368/7/4 annually before she died in 1867.

The Various Tontines of Boston, Lincolnshire

The Corporation of Boston seems to have used tontine financing more than any other municipality. However, the first local tontine was a private one.

Boston Tontine Society, 1791, was advertised in the Stamford Mercury from January through March. The advertisements indicate this to be a small-sum, short-term financial tontine with payments of one shilling a week for seven years. Anyone over sixteen allowed—no age discounts or classes. It was presumably unrelated to the government tontines.

The municipal tontines were as follows:

Boston Paving Tontine, 1792–1874, was created under the parliamentary Boston Improvement Act of 1792 (*32 Geo III, C. LXXX*) and issued by the Paving Commissioners under authority of statute text reading "Commissioners may borrow money, and assign the rates as a security. Commissioners may grant annuities."

Aftermarket auction listings showed a slow rise in dividends. It was paying 'more than' five percent in 1814; six percent in 1830; £7/14/4 in 1844; and £9 in 1848.

Boston Bridge Tontine, 1799–1874, was less visible, with auction listings showing payments of eight percent in 1814 and 1815. The *Stamford Mercury* of December 11th, 1874, reported the last death:

> The claim of the representative of the late Mr. Goodbarn, the last of the Bridge Tontine annuitants, for a quarter's annuity due at the time of deceased's death was again brought forward and after some discussion, was allowed.

The advertising for **Boston Tontine, 1805–1873**, started in 1803. According to the *Lincolnshire Archives Report* in 1964 (p. 62), the Tontine was created to pay a portion of the cost of the construction of a new bridge. Other kinds of securities were issued as well to raise a total of £10,000. The object of the Tontine was to raise £4,000 in shares of £100 each at a rate of seven percent. 'Nearly One Half of the Money is already raised' was claimed in an advertisement posted by the Town Clerk on December 23rd, 1803. A much later description reads '...4000l., 280l. per annum...' The £280 means seven percent interest and the total sum to be divided each year among the living annuitants.

It paid eight percent in 1814 and £11/4/0 in 1844. Its last death, a Mrs. Ann Hopkins, was reported in the *Stamford Mercury* of May 16th, 1873.

The advertising for the **Boston Tontine of 1815** started in mid-1813. The object was to raise £10,000 in shares of £100 each at a rate of six percent. Later evidence indicates this was raised to seven percent in order to completely reach the goal of £10,000. One hundred shares were sold on the lives of sixty-eight nominees.

From auction and other listings, the dividend was £9/6/8 in 1844; £10/5/8 in 1849; £12/5/6 in 1861; £12/10/0 in 1862; and £140 in 1889, when there were five nominees still living. The *Stamford Mercury* of December 9th, 1904, reported the winding down:

> When the Town Bridge at Boston was erected the money was raised on the tontine system and by an indenture dated February 1st, 1815. one hundred shares of £100 each were issued, each shareholder being entitled to £7 each, per year. Thus since that date Boston has been paying £700 per year for the bridge, or a total of £62,300. On Monday last the last nominee under the tontine died, and the bridge is now free. The last nominee was Mrs. Mary Anne Maillard, of Camden House, Kenilworth, who passed away at the advanced age of 92 years. For the past ten years she has been the only recipient, her predecessor, Mrs. Elizabeth Roberts, dying on November 5th, 1894. Mrs. Maillard was nominated by her father, Mr. Francis Thirkill, when she was two years of age, but many years ago the interest was sold to the late Mr. S. H. Jebb, whose executors have been receiving the annuity. Mrs. Maillard's death was reported to the Corporation by Messrs. Jebb and Son at a meeting on Tuesday night.

A correspondent to the *London Standard* (January 8th, 1889) used these Boston tontines to show how expensive tontines drafted like these were for the original municipal borrowers in the long term. He was responding to an earlier article which reviewed the history of tontines provoked by the death of the last survivor of the famous 1791 LaFarge Tontine in France:

> Sir – Your article to-day upon Tontines concludes, 'The Tontine is to-day dead in England.'
>
> Permit me to state that one now exists in Boston, for which the Corporation are paying £700 per annum for the sum of £10,000, secured upon the lives of 63 persons, nominated by 100 subscribers of £100 each in 1815.

> It may be useful to point out how ruinous to borrowers such speculations in human longevity generally prove.
>
> In 1792, a Tontine was created by the Boston Corporation, which did not expire until 1874, when the last life ceased, at 90 years of age. In 1805 another Tontine was created by the same body – £4000, £280 per annum, -- which lasted until 1873, the last survivor dying at 87 years.
>
> In the current Tontine of 1815 five lives remain.as the youngest is only 76, and the others 80, 81, 82, and 82, it is a fair presumption that the Corporation will have to pay for this £10,000 several more sums of £700, in addition to the £51,800 they have already paid. [Additional text eliminated]
>
> [signed] Zachary Ingold.

This is a particularly clear statement of a kind of criticism that also appeared in comments on the Beccles and Middlesex tontines,

Middlesex House of Correction Tontines, 1788+

In 1786, the Justices of the Peace for Middlesex were authorized by an act of Parliament to build a new 'House of Correction' in Cold Bath Fields. It was financed by a tontine. In 1788, this advertisement appeared in The *Times* of April 29th:

> COUNTY of MIDDLESEX
> LIFE ANNUITES, with Benefit of SURVIVORSHIP.
>
> NOTICE is hereby given, That his Majesty's Justices of the Peace for the County of Middlesex, propose so raise a sum not exceeding THIRTY THOUSAND POUNDS, upon the credit of the County Rates, pursuant to an Act of Parliament passed in the 26th Year of his present Majesty's reign, Entitled, "An Act to enable the Justices of the Peace for the County of Middlesex, raise money in manner therein mentioned, for erecting A House of Correction within the said County." The fame to be raised by Tontine in four Classes,-viz. Upon lives not exceeding Twenty; above Twenty, and net exceeding Forty; above Forty, and not exceeding Sixty; and above Sixty, at 4l. 10s per centum, per ann; with benefit of Survivorship, in each respective class.

This original offering, based on *26 George III, c 55,* was supplemented in subsequent years (1791 £20,000, and 1795, £12,000 at five percent), so the total Tontine borrowing amounted to £62,000. An auction notice in 1819 cites an interest payment of 'upwards of 6 per cent.' The London Metropolitan Archives has extensive Tontine Account records through 1888.

The final form of the prison complex was quite large and it was the object of a contemporary coffee-table book:

> Plans, Elevations, and Sections, of the House of Correction for the County of Middlesex, erected in Cold Bath Fields, London; together with the Particulars of the several Materials to be contracted for, and manner of using the fame in building.
> N. B. This Work is engraved from the original designs, and published with the authority of the Magistrates, by Charles Middleton, Architect. Engraved on 53 plates, imperial folio, half bound, 2l. 12s. 6d.

Middlesex Debentures appear occasionally in the aftermarket auction advertisements, but the increased interest is rarely specified. A critique from 1836, along the same lines as the Ingold letter on the Boston Tontines reproduced above, is scathing:

> The history of this tontine affords a striking proof of the impolicy of this mode of raising a sum of money. The whole amount raised was 62,0001 and the borrowings took place at three different periods, each loan being divided among three classes of purchasers -- first class, those under 20 years of age; second, those above 20 and under 40 years of age; and third class, those above 40; The principle of a tontine is that the whole stipulated amount of interest shall continue to be paid, and be devisable among the class so long as a single member of it exists. On the extinction of the class, all payment, as far as such. class is concerned, ceases. The first loan was made in 1790, the second in 1792, and third and last in 1795. Each of these loans was contracted for among the three different classes before enumerated; and it is a singular fact, that no one of the nine classes, created by these borrowings, has yet died off, and the county has to pay to this day the same amount of interest as at first. For £62,000 money borrowed, the payments already made amount to £136,250.[13]

[13] *Jackson's Oxford Journal*, September 3rd, 1836.

Tontine interest rates seem to have been a bugbear of *The World*. It published interest rate nudges regularly, including this specific one about the Middlesex Gaol Tontine on May 6th 1788:

> The success, however, of the TONTINE cannot be expected, on the present terms. – When the rate of INTEREST is RAISED to Five per Cent. Subscriptions may be forthcoming. But, to be a fit bargain to the Annuitants, the Scheme should start, at Five and a Half in the *Younger Classes* – and at least Six in the ELDER.

This was followed on May 8th with: "The TONTINE SCHEME for the Middlesex Gaol, goes on very tardily—The INTEREST must be RAISED."

In any case, the subscription was filled, per *The World*, by May 22nd, 1788. The proprietor of *The World* was a shareholder in the Covent Garden Theatre Life Tontine of 1785.

The prison was closed in 1885. The site is now the location of the Mount Pleasant Mail Centre.

The Kew Bridge Tontine, 1784–89

The stone bridge over the Thames from Ealing to Kew was partially financed by a tontine. The project was started in 1784 and was the second bridge on the site. It was built entirely of stone and replaced the 1759 bridge which had stone arches near the banks of the Thames but was made of wood for the central part of the span. The tontine was created when it was realized by Robert Tunstall, the owner of the first bridge, that the replacement project needed more funding. The architect was James Paine, who also designed Richmond Bridge.

A search of the digitized newspapers of the period has not turned up any advertising for the Kew Bridge Life Annuities, or Tontine. However, a short description of the history of the project is found in a letter to the *Gentlemen's Magazine* of December, 1789. The tontine was something of an afterthought.

A First Class share certificate in the London Metropolitan Archives (LMA)[14] indicates the annual dividend for the £100 share to be £6, paid half-yearly. The future survivorship income increase is added as a separate clause: "*…[W]ith such additional Interest, which from Time to Time, as*

[14] London Metropolitan Archives ref. ACC/2103/001.

shall accrue by Survivorship...." Dividends were to be paid at the office of Castell, Powell, Sumner, and Company, 66 Lombard Street, bankers. The new stone bridge, which was built alongside the old one, opened on September 23rd, 1789.

The back of the certificate was used to record dividend payments, and the first half-year dividend of £3/1/0 was made in January 1786. The handwriting gets increasingly more difficult to read, but the last payment recorded on it seems to be in January 1856. However, the sum does not seem to be recorded. The last legible payment figure seems to be £21/6/8 in 1835.

In the *Public Advertiser* of August 13th, 1791, there is this comment, pressing for a way to eliminate the tolls on the bridge:

> Kew Bridge already pays a dividend of nine per cent. without the public being accommodated with a footway. These kinds of impositions should be abolished; the property bought up, and become throughout Great Britain county-work.

While the text indicates a nine percent dividend, the notations on the LMA share certificate indicate a total of £6/9/0 paid for 1791 or 6.45%. The percentage gap could be the result of different payment amounts given to different pools. Another newspaper report in 1789 indicated the interest rate to be only five percent originally.[15]

In 1795, the Bridge and all the surrounding land and buildings were put up for auction. The sale notice[16] serves as a progress report on the Tontine as well. The amount that had to be put aside for Tontine dividends was £1,100. Per a later sales offering, the £1,100 was divided irregularly, with £330 in the First (youngest) Class, £357/10/0 in the Second, and £412/10/0 in the Third Class, the oldest group. The £1,100 per annum implies there were originally roughly 180 shares of £100 each, or a total of £18,000 total, assuming all the shares were paying six percent in the beginning. Per the advertisement, at this point there were still 137 nominees alive—forty eight in the First Class, forty-seven in the Second, and forty four in the Third. The average would be a dividend of roughly £8 a year. The LMA share records payments amounting

[15] *Whitehall Evening Post,* June 13th–16th.

[16] *Morning Post,* July 11th, 1795.

to £6/12/0 for the First Class, which had the smallest income pool and presumably the lowest payment.

In 1824, the bridge and surrounding properties were once again for sale. The announcement[17] gives details on the state of the tontine. The average annual tolls for the previous seven years was £2,273. The total tontine payment each year was £1,100, divided into three Classes. At that point, the First Class had thirty-four survivors sharing £330 per year. The Second had twenty-three survivors sharing £357/10/0, and the Third had only three survivors sharing £412/10/0. The annual expenses for maintaining and managing the bridge came to £273. This left a net income of £900 per year. As the Tontines expired, and the Third-Class members were at that point 81, 84, and 85 years old, the funds assigned to pay the Tontine reverted to the owner of the bridge.

The tolls were abolished in 1873, and the bridge was demolished and replaced in 1898.

The Fulneck Tontine, 1784

Leaders of the Moravian Community in England created a tontine to provide annuities to its members in the early 1780s. A prospectus was circulated indicating subscriptions would be accepted starting in June 1783. When the Tontine was fully subscribed, a pamphlet was published containing an Abstract of the Deed and a list of the participants dated March 25th, 1784.[18]

The administration of the Tontine involved Proprietors, Trustees, Directors, and a Secretary. Given the sums of money involved, it was not aimed at the rich, but at the everyday members of the community.

The corpus of the Tontine was based on the rents of various pieces of real property owned (or held on very long-term leases) by the Proprietors and devised to the Trustees in Pudsey and Lower Wyke in Yorkshire; St. Luke Parish in Chelsea, Middlesex; and in Fetter Lane in the City of London.

Pudsey was the location of the primary English Moravian settlement, founded 1744. The description of the property in Chelsea includes a

[17] *The Times,* 3 Aug. 1824.

[18] Bedfordshire Archives, Ref A-22-5-076.

chapel. The Fetter Lane Society was a Moravian congregation founded in 1738 and it had its own chapel, later destroyed in the Blitz.

The initial intention was to raise capital to the value of £10,000, but the final total was only £6,000. The share price was only £5. The subscriptions seem to have been used to obtain rights in the property from the Proprietors, but they kept reversion rights in the property, like the Irish-based landed estates tontines a few years later. The property for the capital was declared to provide rental income of £600 'and upward.' The Annuity dividend paid each year totaled £347/11/0. Excess income was to revert to the Proprietors.

There were five Classes, divided by age, with the oldest in the First Class, whose annuity worked out to a seven percent dividend a year. The youngest class only received five percent.

There were 393 'lives' and 1,200 shares. One only subscribed in one's own name, thus no was nominating a much younger life. The children nominated in the Fifth Class appear in the shareholder list not as nominees but as shareholders.

As the lives decreased, no individual could receive an Annuity greater than £60 a year.

A limitation on the directors made the administration very local. They "...should live within Ten Miles of the Place where the Annuities should be paid..." On the other hand, subscribers lived all over Europe, Russia, Utrecht, and Lusatia (in Niesky and Hernhut, a Moravian Community in Lower Saxony, near the Polish border).

The Proprietors specified in the indenture were in the hierarchy of the Moravian Community, including the Rev. Benjamin Latrobe, the Rev. Abraham Taylor, James Hutton, Gent, John Wheeler, John Edmonds, Philip Hurlock, and John West.

Rev. Benjamin Latrobe was the formal leader of the Moravian Community in Great Britain. Based in London. Died 1786. He officially controlled the finances of the church in England. He was the father of the noted architect, Benjamin Latrobe, who designed the US Capital building in Washington DC. The Rev. Abraham Taylor is noted as having participated in a provincial synod in Fulneck in 1750. James Hutton (1715–1795) was among the founders of the Fetter Lane Society within the Moravian Community and with Latrobe, the most influential leader and contact with the upper levels of English Society. He moved in high circles, including royal ones, and is credited with helping to make the Moravian Community acceptable in England.

John Edmonds was one of the group, along with Latrobe and Hutton, who lobbied King George II to allow the Moravians to set up a mission to Labrador. Philip Hurlock, 1713–1801, was a surgeon and apothecary at St. Bart's Hospital. He was elected a member of the Royal Society in 1780.

The Moravian community in Zeist, Holland, created a tontine in 1767 in order to build *'een Zaal en Huis,'* a hall and house for themselves. It is conceivable the English Church was copying their Dutch peers in establishing their own tontine.

The Doncaster Tontine, 1788

This purely financial tontine was founded in September 1788 and was the closest one in content and style to the Ipswich Tontine of 1791. The capital was to be invested in government securities. The subscription price varied by age. There were fourteen classes defined by the age of the nominees, from one-year-olds to lives exceeding sixty-seven. The full price of £100 was only paid for shares whose nominees were between twenty and thirty-one. The youngest paid £85, the oldest £50. The classes were later adjusted, so that those subscriber whose nominees were under three years old paid £95, three to twenty paid the full £100, and twenty to thirty-one dropped to £95.

All shareholders received the same dividend, and the tontine was to be wound down when the division of the capital would yield £1,000 per survivor. However, if the funded capital for any class did not exceed £2,000, the whole capital of that class would go to the sole survivor. Multiple subscriptions were allowed. The primary bank was a Doncaster one, but later advertisements named others in London, York, Pontefract, and Lincoln.

An entry fee of £0/10/6 was included in the process, and the same sum would be charged for any transfer or succession of a share or shares. The annual salary of the Secretary was to be £0/3/6 per subscriber. Subscriptions were to close at the end of 1791, and any subscriptions initiated after the end of 1788 were subject to increasing penalties through to the closing date. The advertising stated a twenty-person list of directors, all from the midlands except for one London resident. It was headed by Sir George Cooke, the Seventh Baronet. The secretary was a Mr. H. Standish. There were 933 nominees.

In June 1860, the dissolution clause was triggered. Apparently, the age bands were treated as 'Classes,' so when the capital derived for group labeled by the court 'Class One' would, at £46,000, generate £1000 per tontineer, the shareholders petitioned the Chancery Court to start the distribution process. Unfortunately, the taxman interfered. The government claimed succession duty on the distribution. This resulted in the 1862 Chancery Court case of *Oldfield v Preston* (45 Eng. Reports 932). In short, the court decided the Tontine Deed amounted to a *bona fide* contract, and that the situation was not one of succession. No duty need to be paid.

Notwithstanding the legal headache on dissolution, the Doncaster Tontine worked as planned.

Manchester Area Tontines, 1790

At least three projects were proposed that used the structure of a small-sum, short-term tontine to construct housing in the New Winsor area in Salford in March 1790, on Hanover Street, Manchester in April 1790, and on Chapel Street, Salford in June 1790.

The New Winsor Tontine involved a payment of a sixpence a week for each share. The shares were defined by the separate lives nominated. As the houses were built and let, the rents were to be added to the corpus of the Tontine. After seven years, the finished properties were to be auctioned off and the overall proceeds divided among the subscribers. The division at the end depended on the continued lives of the nominees. If a subscriber died, the heirs or assigns could sustain the membership by keeping up the payments. The advertising indicated this was originally a small-scale proposal that was extended to the public only days before the subscription deadline was to be implemented.

The Hanover Street advertising first appeared a month after the New Winsor Tontine closed and involved the same basic model and some of the same agents. The first paragraph indicated it was developed in response to would-be subscribers having been shut out of the New Winsor scheme. Its deadline was July 24th. The Chapel Street offering appeared slightly later. It was a much less detailed advertisement, and the term was only five years.

The Hanover Street Tontine seems to have evolved well beyond its original framework. In August 1791, it was looking into borrowing money to cover construction costs. In September, they advertised for builders to submit proposals. However, in April 1803, the *Manchester Mercury* has a lengthy advertisement inserted by the Tontine for the auction of fourteen lots, most with houses. A similar auction took place in May 1815 offering some of the same lots, so the sale in 1803 did not succeed in selling all of the properties offered. In November 1806, there was an advertisement addressed to the proprietors announcing a meeting to select new trustees. If the scheme had been executed as originally advertised, the Tontine would have been wound up years earlier. It is possible that the general depression of the mid-1790s caused the cessation of the project for a period, and it was revived some years later.

The St. John's Street Tontine Building Society, Swansea, 1791

This scheme seems to have evolved from the concept of neighborhood 'Box Clubs' that developed in the 1700s. The Articles of Agreement preserved in the West Glamorgan Archives[19] specifies one hundred members subscribing through a monthly payment of twenty pence and half-penny, of which eighteen pence went to the fund, two pence for meeting expenses, and the ha'penny for the administrator. The subscription period was five years. This means a share ultimately cost £5/2/6. The meeting site was the Black Horse Inn. The funds and the documents of the organization were to be kept in a triply locked box in the possession of the landlord.

An unusual aspect of the group was that in case of a sale or transfer of a share, the new owner could specify a new nominee, as long as the age of the new nominee was within five years of the age of the original nominee.

The fund was intended to build five houses, the rental proceeds of which were to be shared by the members. Additional houses could be built if the accumulated funds could support it. As the membership dwindled, the scheme proposed two endings. As the membership became only ten, the houses were to be sold and the proceeds split among the survivors. However, they could agree to postpone division until the remaining shareholders equaled the number of houses built, at which

[19] West Glamorgan Archives, Reference Numbers. GB 216 RISW T, GB 216 RISW/SFS 5a-b.

point the houses would be divided by lot among the survivors. A volume on the history of Building Societies mentions this organization in its introductory chapter, as a kind of prototype of the formal societies that developed a little later.

The Chichester Theatre Tontine, 1792

This project involved raising £1000 to construct a theatre in Chichester. There were forty shares of £25 each, with three subscribers taking two shares and one subscriber, a banker, taking four. All except four were local. There is no indication of the interest paid. According to one source, His Grace the Duke of Richmond, whose seat (at Goodwood) is near Chichester, superintended the building, and generously furnished it, when completed, with some beautiful scenery, painted by first rate artists, for his private 'Theatre in Privy Garden.'

A later pamphlet history[20] of the origins of the theatre includes a transcription of the subscriber/nominee information and notes on after-market transfers. These include a sale in 1815 for £18/0/0, in 1818 for the same price, and in 1841 for £19/19/0. In 1828, three children inherited a share, and one of them bought the shares of the other two for £18/0/0. The building was auctioned off in 1850 and converted into a brewery.

Armagh Tontine Assembly Rooms, 1794

It is uncertain whether the financing of this building should be considered a tontine even though that is how it was referred to.[21] Instead of a large share price, the subscriptions to the 'tontine' were closer to the practice of the small-sum, short-term tontines of the period. Subscribers paid £0/5/5 per quarter. The capital accumulated this way amounted to £1,120. The fee seems to have been continued after the completion of the construction as a membership fee. It served as a classic assembly hall as well as having a news-room. In 1818, the local Savings Bank office was established in this building.

[20] Steer, Francis W, *The Chichester Theatre*, Chichester: City Council, 1957.

[21] Quinn, Kevin, The Armagh Tontine Assembly Rooms, 1794–1907, 4 *History Armagh* No. 1, pp. 5–9, (2017).

By 1820, the building had become quite dilapidated and was used for miscellaneous other purposes. In 1823, initial steps were taken for the subscribers' trustees to surrender the ownership to a new trust created to hold the property for the benefit of the community. This took place and by 1830 the building was refurbished and once again used as an assembly space. In 1907, another transfer took place, the old building was demolished, and the property became the city hall of Armagh, consciously designed to reflect the look of original tontine hall. It was severely damaged by a bomb during the 'Troubles' in September 1972 and demolished.

Gainsborough Grammar School, 1796

This was perhaps the smallest tontine created. It was designed to augment dwindling old charitable endowments and was used to build a proper schoolhouse and a house for the master. There were only forty shares at £10 each, paying five percent. After a sale of a share in 1832, it was noted thirty nominees were still alive. There were twenty-one still alive in 1845.

Birmingham Public Office, 1798

J. A. Langford's *A Century of Birmingham Life*[22] mentions a proposal in July 1798, to build a 'Public Office' on High Street on a tontine plan. The scheme was to pay five percent and subscriptions were to be £10 each, for an original target of £1,000, but the final cost was £1,600. It opened for business in May 1799. It initially served as a courthouse and municipal offices, but ended up as a debtors' prison. Its primary purpose was superseded almost immediately by a new Public Office Building on Moor Street which opened in 1807.

Tontines in Scotland

In 1772, a notice was published in a number of the London papers, including the *Daily Advertiser:*

[22] Volume 2, Birmingham: Osborne, 1868.

> Edinburgh, Aug 4. A project is now under consideration to raise for the common good of this city £20,000 sterling in 800 shares of £25 each, by way of Tontine, the interest of the whole sum to be shared equally among the survivors yearly, till the whole subscribers die out, and then the principal sum to fall into the town's revenue, and become part of the publick stock of the incorporation.

This came after the failed national tontines of 1757 and 1765, but before the successful Irish and Dublin tontines of the middle 1770s. There is no trace of it having been implemented.

Glasgow

There were at least three different major tontines in Glasgow. The original and most famous one was created to build what came to be known as the Tontine Coffee House at Trongate in 1781, with the building opening in 1784.[23]

> The old Tontine Hotel at the Trongate was built in 1781 by William Hamilton behind the existing frontage of the town hall with its pedimented windows and street-level arcade. The keystones of the arches of the arcade were carved with heads and grotesques known as the "Tontine Heads", preserved nearby at St. Nicholas's Garden.

An advertisement looking for a lessee gave this description in 1799:[24]

> TO BE LET, For a term of years, and entered to on the 28th May, 1799, or sooner as may be agreed upon, THE GLASGOW TONTINE 'TAVERN, HOTEL, and COFFEE ROOM. It is proposed that the premises shall be let either altogether or separately, in the Following parts.
>
> The Buildings fronting the Exchange, containing a large and convenient Coffeeroom, an Assembly-room, a Dining-room sufficiently large for a hundred persons, seven Dining-parlours, ten Bed-chambers, with many Closets and Servants-rooms, a Billiard-room capable of containing three Tables, a Tap-room, and an excellent Kitchen, Scullery, and Servants-hall,

[23] There is a detailed description of its development in *The Regality Club*, Vol. 2, (1889), entry by C D Donald, p. 65 through 87.

[24] *Star and Evening Advertiser*, March 21st, 1799.

with a range of dry and spacious Cellars under the Buildings, and many other conveniences too long to be enumerated in an advertisement.

A Large and well laid out house, fronting a handsome Back Court connected with the front Buildings, and which contains 26 apartments, besides Dressing-rooms, Servant's. rooms, Cellars, and many other conveniences.

The Coffeeroom is supported by a subscription, which for the last year amounted to about eleven hundred pounds.

The Coffee House complex was the center of commercial and social life for the merchant community of Glasgow. It functioned as an exchange, an informal and formal meeting place, a library, a tavern, and a hotel. No dividends were paid in the first eleven years of the tontine's existence. A text from 1820 reported:

The dividends were paid on each share as follows:- The first dividend was paid in 1793. From 1793 to 1802, inclusive, the dividend amounted to 3£: 15 per annum. From 1803 to 1808, both inclusive, to £5. During the years 1809-10-and 11, there were no dividends, owing to the erection of additional buildings. In 1812-13; the dividend was £5. In 1814-15 and 16, £10. In 1817-18 and 19, £20.[25]

The reading room, in particular, became important as the place where all the latest information could be found and as a social environment. It was supported well into the latter part of the nineteenth century by subscription membership separate from the Tontine subscription. The importance of the Tontine to the commercial and social life of the city made it the most visible institution with tontine in its name in the United Kingdom.

The second Tontine project resulted in the Glasgow Assembly and Concert Rooms created in 1796.

The building was financed on the Tontine principle, with 274 shares of £20 each taken out by a number of Glasgow citizens. Their aim was to provide the city with a meeting place for dancing, music, reading and other

[25] Cleland, James, *The rise and progress of the City of Glasgow...*, Glasgow: Young, Gallie & co., 1820.

cultural pursuits. Designed by the brothers Robert and James Adam, it was begun in 1796 and two wings were added in 1807.[26]

In 1847, the space was rebuilt with a theatre and was renamed the Athenaeum. The MacLennan Arch in Glasgow Green was originally part of the façade of the Assembly Room.

As the number of tontineers dwindled, the management of the Athenaeum contrived to purchase subscriber shares when they could. By 1882, they held one of the two outstanding shares and reached an agreement with the other shareholder for a division of the property. On the death of the Athenaeum's nominee, they ended up with one fourth of the full ownership of the property, thus preventing a sale of the property out from under the organization.[27]

Also in 1796, three tontines on relatively new tenements were all promoted by a single entrepreneur, Robert Smith. A single advertisement in *The Times*[28] in London offered one in George's Square, one in Brunswick Street, and one in 'Hutcheson's Street.' The buildings forming the capital were said to be 'new' and already tenanted. Each one was to have its own management committee, elected by the subscribers. For all of them, the shares were only twenty pounds.

The Hutcheson Street Tontine was created on three residential buildings with one hundred and forty-five shares. In 1833, it was paying a dividend of ten percent, but since the share price was low, that meant only £2 a year. The winding up starting in 1886 involved a lawsuit in which the son of the single surviving nominee, and thus sole owner of the properties, had to fight off claims from the estates of the nominee's sisters and a legacy tax bill.

The third major tontine in Glasgow was the Glasgow Tontine Society, founded in 1816. It owned the George Hotel on George Square, and that fact was used in share sale advertisements to differentiate it from the Coffee House Tontine.

The site of the hotel is now the Glasgow City Chambers, the municipal building. The City Chambers were built in 1889, so the capital of the Glasgow Tontine Society of 1816 went to buy another site/building as

[26] https://www.theglasgowstory.com/image/?inum=TGSA01084&t=2

[27] *Glasgow Herald*, September 30th, 1882.

[28] August 10th, 1796.

a hotel nearby. The formal winding up did not take place until 1939, although it is likely the winding up of a successor organization, not the original tontine.

The 1781 and 1816 Tontine Societies are often confused, and some writers were careful to designate the year to differentiate the organizations. This 1855 aftermarket auction offered shares in all three:

> One Share and one-half Share in 'the Exchange Tontine Buildings of Glasgow.'
>
> Two Shares in 'the Glasgow Tontine Society and Concert Rooms Tontine.'
>
> Ten Shares in 'the Glasgow Tontine Society, established in 1816.'
>
> The Shares form part of a Trust Estate.....[29]

The Renfrewshire Tontine, 1783 (1801)

A classic stagecoach inn on Gauze Street in Paisley, Scotland, was constructed around 1783 via the patronage of the Earl of Abercorn. Besides hotel rooms, the assembly room was large enough for the space to serve as a theatre as well. The building became the object of a tontine in 1801. The capital was £10,000 at only £25 a share. It was reported to have been fully subscribed in two days. After about fifty years as a significant venue, both as a hotel and as an assembly space, it became dilapidated and essentially abandoned by the 1880s. The building was torn down in 1969.

Fortune's Tontine Tavern, Edinburgh, 1795

Fortune's Tontine has a number of unusual aspects. It was created as a Tontine after the building had been an active business for twenty years. The Tontine was seemingly the first with a minimum age requirement for the subscribers, in this case, sixty years. The original single survivor takes all scheme was eliminated by an agreement of the surviving tontineers

[29] *Glasgow Herald*, October 25th, 1855.

after only twenty-five years. The details are given in a volume of essays on Edinburgh history published in 1908.[30]

The property that was subject to the Tontine was number 15 Princes Street. Starting in 1796, the house was known as Fortune's Tontine Tavern and Coffee House. One of the title deeds states that:

> Matthew Fortune, Vintner in Edinburgh, in the year 1795, made a proposal for purchasing the property in question 'in order to convert the same into a Tavern and for raising the value therefor by way of Tontine, that the said property was purchased for the above purpose and after several meetings the following agreement was entered into, viz. that the value of the said property should be estimated at Five thousand pounds Sterling, that the said sum should be divided into Fifty shares of one hundred pounds each, that each subscriber should name a person of sixty years of age or upwards and the subscriber whose nominee should be the longest liver of the persons so named should become the sole proprietor of the said subjects, the rents thereof in the meantime being divided annually among the subscribers whose nominees were in life.'

The tontine was not fully subscribed on those terms, so "it was agreed to accept subscriptions for half or quarter shares of £50 or £25, a nominee to be fixed on by every two or every four of such subscribers. In the end about ninety subscribers were obtained and the transaction was duly carried through." The subscribers drew heavily from the Scots aristocracy, including "the Duke of Hamilton, and the Duke of Buccleuch; the Earls of Eglinton, Cassilis, Dalhousie, Breadalbane, Hyndford and Hopetoun; Henry Dundas, afterwards Lord Melville; Robert Dundas, the Lord Advocate; Dr. Baird, Principal of Edinburgh University, and a number of well-known landed proprietors, lawyers, and Edinburgh merchants."

In 1820, when only nine nominees survived, "the shareholders, represented by these nominees, agreed that at the termination of the Tontine the property should be divided among them or their representatives in proportion to their respective holdings, instead of falling entirely to the shareholder whose nominee was the last survivor." Apparently, the death of the last of the nominees did not occur till about 1830, for it was only

[30] Cowan, William, The buildings at the east end of Princes Street, in *The Book of the Old Edinburgh Club for the year 1908*, Edinburgh: Printed by T & A Constable, 1908, p. 143 et seq.

Another snippet of gossip in the *General Evening Post* of March 2nd, 1790, proposes the same idea: "It is reported that all the London Bankers are about to enter into an association for the purpose of proposing to the public a Tontine properly secured in Freeholds in England."

While nothing came of this, it appeared at a time when two tontines based on landed estates were being developed based on property in Ireland.

Earl of Cork's Tontine, August 1789

The prospectus for the scheme was a twelve page pamphlet bearing the title *An Abstract of the deed for securing the payment of the Earl of Cork's tontine; bearing date the twentieth of November, 1789.*

The Abstract noted the underlying Indenture was written into the records of the Registry Office in Dublin in March 1790 and enrolled in the Court of Common Pleas in London in 1789. It stated the amount to be raised was £45,000. The properties to be encumbered were in four counties and the city of Cork in Ireland and in the English counties of Devon and Cornwall. The share price was £100 and there were four classes.

The shares in this tontine showed up regularly in the aftermarket auctions including in 1829 and 1831. The last dividend payment notice appeared in *The Times* of October 19th, 1840.

Mr. O'Hara's Tontine, 1792

Many newspapers of the same period had advertisements for an unnamed tontine offered through Boldero, Adey, Lushington, and Boldero bankers. The only description was that the tontine was to be 'secured on a large Freehold Estate.' These turned out to be for a scheme known as Mr. O'Hara's Tontine. The proposal ultimately encompassed 330 shares in three classes of £100 for a total income of £33,000 and a total interest to be paid of £1,815 a year. The property serving as the security had a 'yearly Value of £3,240/17/4 English Money.' Note that in the understanding of the period, this means the property generated that much in yearly rents. It does not mean that would be its sale value. There were four classes and the dividends started at six and one half percent.

The Tontine filled quickly and notice of regular dividend payments were relatively common. As with all tontines, "…the Subscribers may

in 1831 that the Tontine was finally wound up, and the shares in th property allocated as had been agreed upon.

Fortune himself died in 1799 or 1800, and the business was carried or by his widow and son. In 1837, two 1/29 shares were offered at auction. Presumably, these were straightforward, non-tontine shares that existed as a result of the tontine dissolution process. They were offered with an upset price of £500 for the pair.

Leith, the port community for Edinburgh was the site of a couple of small tontines for the construction of residential buildings. The most visible records are occasional shares offered via auctions, such as the one advertised in the *Caledonian Mercury* of January 23rd, 1815, and the two in North Leith in the *Mercury* of May 9th, 1822. There is one reference to a Tontine Coffeeroom in Leith, in the Mercury of December 31st, 1825. It was presumably part of the first Leith Tontine.

Tontines Based on Landed Estates

The successful versions of these sorts of tontines seem to be related to the absentee landlord tradition in Ireland. The two most visible ones were Mr. O'Hara's Tontine of 1792 and the Earl of Cork's Tontine of 1789.

Early Proposals

In 1774, advertisements appeared for a proposed tontine based on estates in England, Wales, and Ireland without any indication as to ownership of the properties involved. It is described in more detail in Chapter 10, Tontine Failures.

Another early hint as to the possibility of this kind of tontine appeared in 1784, speculating that a tontine would be created by a person accused of enriching himself while in a government position. The idea was that the tontine would be used to repay the government for the funds that were embezzled and spent on buying the properties. Sir Richard Rigby, MP, had come under scrutiny for having profited enormously from his long years in public office. From June 1768 through March 1783, he was the Paymaster of the Forces, i.e., the Army. That meant he had access to large sums as balances in the payment process and it was clear he used these to his own advantage. By 1784, he had just about ceased his public life. The notion of a tontine based on his real property income seems to come from nowhere and in this case did not develop.

receive their Dividends on producing their Debentures and proper Certificates of the Lives of their Nominees."

Like the Earl of Cork's Tontine, aftermarket auction of Mr. O'Hara's Tontine occurred sporadically. The papers of the O'Hara family included a reconveyance of the property back to the O'Hara family at the end of the Tontine, in 1884.[31]

A short history of the O'Hara family and their finances can be found in Thomas Bartlett's *The O'Haras of Annaghmore c. 1600—c. 1800: Survival and Revival*,[32] but it does not go into details about the Tontine.

A Rare Legal Case

There was also a legal case involving rights within O'Hara's Tontine reported in 30 *Law Times* 1 (1857). The case was called *Re O'Hara's Tontine and the Trustee Relief Act*. It involved a widow who was originally the nominee of her father but became the owner on her father's death. The tontine share was then handed over to a third party with a view, "as it was said on one side, that he might by means of it pay himself the debt due to him; on the other, that it was intended in liquidation of that debt." The third party received the interest and the wife received £0/10/0 a year for her cooperation in providing a certificate of life. When 'W,' the person who held the share, died, the original nominee/shareholder sued for the return of the tontine share.

It was held "that this was an interest in land, and the wife never having levied a fine, nor the husband and wife transferred their interest in the annuity, and she having survived her husband, she was now entitled to the arrears of the annuity which had accrued since the death of 'W'."

By defining the tontine share as an interest in land, any transfer would have to be more formal than the simple surrender of the tontine's debenture and allowing the dividends to be collected by a third party.

[31] National Library of Ireland, Collection List 66, O'Hara Papers, page 56 et seq.

[32] 9 *Irish Economic and Social History* 34–53 (1982).

A Later Irish Attempt

In 1818, the London bankers Morland, Ransom & Co issued a two-page proposal for a scheme to sell annuities 'to increase by survivorship' secured on: '…Estates in Ireland producing more than £20,000 per annum.' There was no statement of ownership other than '…property of a Nobleman of the highest respectability' with 'unquestionable title.' There were to be ten sub-groups divided into five classes with the age of nominees to be five to eight in the First Class and eighteen to twenty-one in the Fifth Class. Older nominees were seemingly excluded. The initial dividend was to be four percent. The objective was to raise £150,000 although the value of the property only secured the money necessary for the interest payments. Any surpluses and the property were to revert to the grantor.

The project does not seem to have gotten beyond the proposal stage. The word tontine does not appear, perhaps a reflection of a change in attitude toward them.

An Abortive Proposal, 1801

The *Morning Post* and *The Morning Chronicle* printed the following advertisement fourteen times in January and February 1801:

> LIFE ANNUITIES. PROPOSALS for raising FORTY-EIGHT THOUSAND POUNDS by way of Tontine, or Securities for Life Annuities, increasing by survivorship, to be divided into four distinct classes, and to be secured (under the direction of eminent Counsel) upon Estates in the county of Sussex of the net annual value of £6270, may be had of, and particulars respecting the same obtained from Joseph Ward, Esq. No. 15, Newman-street, Oxford-street; and Messrs. Maberley and Daniel, corner of King's Road, Bedford-row.

Joseph Ward was a solicitor and was unlikely to have been the principal behind the proposals. Maberley and Daniel were also solicitors. This project does not seem to have come to fruition.

Mr. Drew's Tontine, 1805

In 1805, a prospectus was distributed seeking £20,000 to create a tontine on an estate in Jamaica. It was known as Mr. Drew's Tontine, and it failed. The property involved was claimed to be near 2,000 acres recently planted in 'guinea grass,' a species introduced from Africa, about a mile from Spanish Town and close to Kingston and its market. The suggestion was it would be used for fodder crops and for fattening cattle.

The initial proposal was quite candid about what the investment income would be used for. Except for £2,500 to be applied to pay off a mortgage, the rest of the money would be spent on the purchase of enslaved people. Their value was also to serve as security for the dividend payments. Investor/nominees included Princess Charlotte, the daughter of the Prince of Wales, and J. M. W. Turner, the artist.

This Tontine has also attracted the attention of social historians because it involved the slave agriculture of the Caribbean. Some of the earliest tontines involved slave-owners as projectors or subscribers, but this one was directly dependent on the profits produced by slave labor.

The trustees placed an advertisement in the July 5th, 1809, *Morning Post* for a meeting of the shareholders "to consider whether the Penn and Estate, and live and dead Stock, now upon and belonging to the same, should, or should not be Sold; and also, whether to proceed in the Chancery Suit commenced in Jamaica against Mr. Drew, or to compromise the same." The case, entitled *Harrison v. Haggitt* (Haggitt was one of the original trustees), dragged out through 1836. The Tontine solicitors' papers are held by the University of London Archives. In the meantime, an aftermarket for the shares still existed, as ten shares were offered for sale by a bankrupt in the *Law Advertiser* in June 1825.

The Library Tontines

The Liverpool Library as an organization was founded in 1758, and, as it expanded, a tontine was created to finance a new building in 1786–87. Seventy-five shares raised £1,800. A nominee list was published in 1789. It was subsumed into the Lyceum in 1802. The library operation of the Lyceum ceased in 1842 with books being given to the Liverpool Free Library. The tontine owning the property continued through 1865, when the tontine expired with the reduction of the shareholders to a final three. In 1866, the property was sold for £7,680.

In Birmingham, a Library Tontine was proposed in 1789, but not executed until 1798. The project was so underfunded and clumsily managed that the first dividend was not paid until 1813. The winding down was still in court in 1899, with advertisements for claimants continuing through 1904.[33] A transcription of the 1799 Tontine Deed in the form of an indenture among 158 parties is printed in Charles Parish's *History of the Birmingham Library* published by the Library Association in 1966. The book also reproduces a list of the 181 nominees.

A Comic Coda: The Truro Assembly Rooms Tontine, 1797

The records in the Kresen Kernow (Cornwall Archives) in regard to the Truro Assembly Rooms[34] show a strange process. The rooms were constructed in 1787 using a tontine, but it seems the organizers neglected to ask for or create a list of nominees, so no lives were nominated. The surviving original subscribers and heirs thereof regrouped in 1810 and at that point designated nominees. An Eliza Sandys, a granddaughter of one of the original group, John James, was the last surviving nominee in 1889 and a Chancery case in 1892 was needed to settle title. The façade of the building has been preserved.

Variations

The breadth of tontines meant there were variations in the elements and clauses of the tontines.

Purpose: While civic improvement could be a shared purpose, generally there were two intentions, one for the projector and another for the investors. The projectors were interested in the ultimate product, usually a profit-making institution, such as an inn or theatre. A local government might support the construction of a bridge or a municipal building. The subscribers might be more interested in the sustained income provided by the dividends and the pension-like late life enhanced payments for themselves, their heirs or their legatees.

[33] *The Times*, March 15th, 1904.

[34] Kreson Kernow, i.e., Cornwall Centre, Old Assembly Rooms: *Deed of Limitation*, Ref DCT, 200, (1810), and *Abstract of Title, Old Assembly Rooms*, DCT 202, (1892).

Projectors: The managers varied according to the nature of the project. The Freemasons' Tontine was created among the members of the London masonic community. The Richmond Bridge started out a general civic proposal. The core members of the commission that actually executed the project were a combination of local worthies and politicians on the national level.

In some cases, the projectors were the local government. The mix with private actors could be complicated. The Cleveland Tontine, for example, was developed in conjunction with a new turnpike, anticipating a need generated by the traffic.

For project tontines, the source of income tended to be fees charged by the institution created: bridge tolls, theatre rents, chapel pew rents, or real estate income, etc. The financial tontines were based on buying and holding the standard form of government securities, known as Consolidated Annuities or 'Consols.'

Structure: Most tontine involved the creation of a trust deed as the primary legal framework, thus avoiding a more complex and expensive formal corporate structure and procedure. For many tontines, the only formal procedure was enrolling the Trust Document with the Court of Chancery. However, as trustees died or resigned, adding the new trustees could get complicated.

Others were the result of a formal commission if created by statute: Some statutes specifically mentioned a tontine. Other projects, without a specific mandate beyond the authorization to borrow money to execute the project, simply chose a tontine.

The governance of most tontines centered on the Trustees. Subscriber meetings tended to be only to select new trustees.

Defining the pool of nominees was one of the ways of insuring fairness. The French models were structured this way, usually with classes of nominees within a ten-year range. The National Tontine of 1789 followed this model. Other ways of ensuring fairness was having smaller batches of nominees within a wider age range, down to the above or below the age of thirty, as in the Covent Garden tontine. The Ipswich tontine pioneered the notion of subscriber price discounts based on ages of nominees.

Virtually, all tontines insisted the nominees remain the same no matter who owned the share. The notable exception was the St John's Street in Swansea where a share transfer could involve naming a new nominee, as long as the new one was within five years of age of the original nominee.

As the slowness of the mortality premise became more apparent, variations were introduced to speed up the process. Terms were created for less than the full lives of nominees, often for twenty-one or fourteen years followed by distribution. Other tontines, especially the later ones, insisted on a minimum age for nominees. These tended to be sixty or above.

One 1861 real estate-based company issued both standard shares and a class of shares held within a tontine. Sixty years later the dividends for the remaining tontine shares were considerably higher than the regular shares.

For the traditional tontines, the subscription amounts tended to be in £100 units, like the Consols of the period, but as tontines became more widespread, it varied from £20 to £250.

The final distribution or 'winner' structure also varied. The earlier ones had a single winner or a small number sharing the distribution. Some of the larger financial tontines had larger pools, usually when the capital accumulation would allow the distribution of a set sum to the remaining tontineers. For the Ipswich Tontine, it was the pool of nominees shrinking to the point where they would each get £1,000.

Tontine Curiosities

A commercial sailing ship, the brig *Tontine,* was active in the first part of the nineteenth century. It served as a cartel during the war of 1812. At that time, the term 'cartel' meant a ship that was protected by both sides in a conflict to allow for some level of communication between the combatants. According to the *Encyclopaedia Perthensis,* Volume V, 1796+: "… a ship commissioned in time of war to exchange the prisoners of two hostile powers; also to carry any proposal from the one to the other. The officer who commands her must carry no cargo, ammunition, or implements of war, except a single gun for signals." Cartels carried papers showing their status to show to naval officers or privateers who might attack it. As a cartel, the *Tontine* sailed between Liverpool and New York. Later, in 1818 she is noted by one writer as a ship of 'established reputation' appropriate for a group of would-be emigrants to use for a trip to the United States.

In 1827, she carried goods to the Mediterranean for the relief of battered Greeks in their rebellion against Turkey in the 1820s. It was reported that the Greek Government sold the cargo for roughly twenty percent of its value in order to generate cash. Papers at the University of Villanova Library show the *Tontine* was an active trader to southern Europe and the Caribbean.

In 1800, the *New Register of Shipping*[35] lists a sloop *Tontine* based in Scotland. In the 1820s, there was also an American schooner named the *Tontine* working the southern and Gulf coasts. In August 1859, an American clipper ship also named the *Tontine* was wrecked in a storm in English Channel.

Tontine, a mare owned by the Duke of Grafton, won the 1825 One Thousand Guineas horse race by a walkover.[36] It was the only classic won in a walkover. She was third in the Oaks that year.

A Birmingham 'Jacobin Club,' also known as the Twelve Apostles, met regularly at John Freeth's Coffee House. The members sat for a group portrait by John Eckstein in 1792. The painting was owned in a tontine by the sitters. The last living member, James Bissett became the ultimate owner. It is now held by the Birmingham Museum and Art Gallery.[37]

In the late 1800s, a stadium in Renton, Scotland, home to the Renton Football Club, was known as Tontine Park. The underlying real estate was part of a municipal park created in the 1860s(?) by a combination of an aristocratic gift supplemented by a local tontine, although details have proven difficult to find. The football pavilion was not itself the tontine. It was built in the early 1880s. The training stands burned down in 1906, but games were played at the Park until at least 1923. Renton was one of the most successful teams at the national level in the early years of the Football Association.

'Tontine Silver' is the name given to miscellaneous pieces of plate that have been engraved with a series of names and usually death dates and the age at death.[38] The name is traditional among silver connoisseurs although there are seemingly no records connecting the pieces with known tontines. On the whole, they have the air of *memento mori.* While a couple of these pieces are in museums, most seem to be in private hands. Objects of this sort offered at recent auctions include a London

[35] Published by the Society of Merchants, Ship-Owners, and Under-writers, 2nd Edition.

[36] *Cambridge Chronicle and Journal,* April 22nd, 1825.

[37] See: https://dams.birminghammuseums.org.uk/assetbank-birminghammuseums/action/viewAsset?id=25826&index=0&total=4&view=viewSearchItem

[38] Glynn, Gale, Some tontines commemorated on English plate, 8 *Silver Society Journal,* 445–461, 1996.

desk 'standish' hallmarked for 1819; a chamber candlestick, York, 1793; a salver, London, 1740; a quart mug, London, 1762; an inkstand, London, 1789; and a teapot, London, 1784.

One piece of regimental silver from the Argyll and Sutherland Highlanders with a tontine element survives in their museum. Its history is described in Keltie's 1887 *History of the Scottish Highlands, Highland clans and Highland regiments…*:

> The officers' mess of the 1st Argyll and Sutherland Highlanders has quite a little museum of precious and artistic curiosities. One of the most valuable and interesting of these is a tontine snuff-box of silver gilt, casket-shape, eight inches long, six inches wide, and three inches deep. This very handsome box originated in one purchased by the officers who were in the regiment in the year 1810, on the condition that it could be claimed by the last survivor if replaced by a similar box. It was claimed in 1841 by Colonel Anderson, and the new one then presented not having been claimed in 1870 by Colonel Bertie Gordon, the last survivor of those whose names were inscribed on it, became the property of the officers then serving in the regiment, whose names are inscribed on the inner lids.

An early stagecoach line between Leeds and London, started in 1785, was named the Tontine. It made an overnight stop at the Tontine Inn in Sheffield, and that is the likely source of its name.

Tontine was also the name of a French card game. It rules were published in English by Abbe Bellecour, in *The academy of play; containing, a full description of, and the laws of play….*, Dublin: Printed by James Potts, 1768, at page 185. To oversimplify: each player starts with a set stake of chips. Everyone puts three chips into a central pool. As cards are exposed, the players in turn must either draw chips from the pot, if their card is high, or pass chips to a neighbor if low. The participants who have lost all their chips are 'dead.' The winner is the one who ends up with all the chips.

The Tontine Group is an Australian maker of bedcovers and pillows. Dupont window shade material from the 1950s was trademarked 'Tontine.'

CHAPTER 12

The Nineteenth Century

Tontine proposals continued into the nineteenth century. The actual raw number of new tontine proposals might not have been lower, but they were a smaller and smaller fraction of new financial proposals. A couple have been mentioned in earlier chapters because of their similarity to eighteenth-century schemes.

The market for life annuities and similar products was significantly altered by the Life Annuities Act of 1808 (*48 Geo III, C 142*). The Act was created in part to reduce the overall government debt by making the annuities initially purchasable only through an exchange for Three Percent Consols. The participants had to be at least thirty-five years old, and the interest payments were capped at age seventy-five. The proof of continued existence required of the participants echoed the documentation necessary for tontine payments. While there was no increase in dividends over time, the combination of simplicity and government security undercut the potential market for new tontine products.

Another cause of the decline is that as the century progressed, the repeal of portions of the Bubble Act in 1825 allowed 'common law' companies to exist, and they were simpler to create and maintain than a tontine. Another likely reason for the decline is that the competition for speculative funds was fierce, especially once the railway mania took off in the 1830s. The modern enterprises promised tontine-style profits in perpetuity if the project succeeded without the penalty of the need for

K. McKeever, *The Role of Tontines, 1750–1800*, Palgrave Studies in the History of Finance, https://doi.org/10.1007/978-3-032-12849-2_12

the deaths of fellow investors and the end date precipitated by the death of all the nominees.

Tontines supporting local civic development and construction projects continued regularly in the early part of the century. The purely financial ones declined earlier.

Following are some of the more prominent nineteenth-century schemes.

Cleveland Tontine Inn, 1804

This building in Northallerton still stands as a small hotel and restaurant on the western edge of the North York Moors National Park. The unusual aspect of this Tontine is that it was created simultaneously with the securing of finance for the 'turnpiking' of the Thirsk to Yarm Road.

The printed agreement and subscriber list[1] has three columns of names: one for the Cleveland area, one for Stockton area, and one for Sunderland, Shields, etc. Each name is accompanied by a figure for the Turnpike Share and/or the Tontine Share. Only the local list has more Tontine Subscribers than Turnpike Subscribers, and on the whole, the Tontine subscriptions are for smaller amounts. The Inn served as a classic coaching and mail route stop for many years, but was made redundant by the development of the regional railways in the late 1840s, which bypassed the area. The Inn was refurbished in the early 2000s.

In 1806, additional outbuildings were needed, so the Tontine was enlarged by selling twenty more shares at £25 each.[2]

The idea of a turnpike trust-related tontine was not new. The terms in the report which appeared in the May 1st, 1790, *Northampton Mercury* are a clear and concise description of the standard tontine model:

> A Tontine of a novel Nature is offered to the Public by the Trustees of a Turnpike in Wiltshire.— At a Meeting last Month, the Trustees resolved that £1200 should be railed by Way of a Tontine, for the Purpose of erecting an Inn, for the better Accommodation on the Road; and also for purchasing a convenient Spot of Ground for erecting; such Inn.— The Trustees also propose there shall be 48 Shares, at £25 each, to be subscribed by Persons of any Age.— A Dividend to be paid on each Share

[1] A copy is in the author's collection.

[2] *York Herald*, August 30th, 1806.

of every Subscriber, or Persons named, in Proportion to the Rent of the said Inn.— When a Subscriber dies, the Dividend of such Life so dying, or Interest of the Money subscribed, to be paid to the Survivors, in Addition to their Dividends; and the Inn to become the Property of the last Survivor.—Should this Scheme meet with the Approbation of the Public, we may shortly expect other Places to adopt the fame Method, and thus afford to Travellers comfortable Accommodations, which, in many Parts of England as well as Scotland, are not now to be met with.

There is no record of this notice resulting in a firm project.

St Peter's, Wallsend, 1807

A new parish church in Wallsend authorized in 1807 was the result of a statute that included the right to use a tontine to a maximum of £3,294 at five percent interest. It had four Classes: under twenty years of age, twenty to forty, forty to sixty, and over sixty. The youngest paid £60, the next £51, and the others £42. William Richardson, a later historian, noted the breadth of subscribers:

> Among those whose lives were entered in this novel competition, we find persons of every rank: labourers, sons of labourers, schoolmasters, innkeepers, merchants, ladies and gentlemen. There was one knight, Sir Wm. Scott (afterwards Lord Stowell), who was nominated by the Rev. Wm. Haigh of Wooler, and there was a baronet, Sir Matthew White Ridley.[3]

The tontine was wound up in 1875 through a process of buying out the last two nominees. It is still the local Parish Church, St. Peters.

Folkestone, 1849

Folkestone was a relatively small municipality until it was reached by a railway in 1843. As it started to grow in importance as a seaport, a major urban renovation was developed by Sidney Smirke and executed by the Folkestone Tontine Building Company, registered April 24th, 1849. The core was a new main street, known as Tontine Street, designed to become the new town center, essentially replacing or superseding the old

[3] Richardson, William, *History of the parish of Wallsend, Newcastle-upon-Tyne,* Northumberland Press, 1923.

medieval High Street, and to provide for modern commercial buildings. The project covered an ancient stream which had developed into an open sewer in the worst section of town and constructed new buildings along it. It was transformational.

The funding target was £50,000 in shares of £100 each. The core elements were that the nominees had to be less than fifteen years old and at the death of each nominee, the subscriber or his heirs were to receive back the amount subscribed. When the number of surviving nominees reached twenty, the survivors would split the property proportionately per shares owned. An optimistic and detailed presentation of the scheme, within a description of tontine building companies generally, can be found on pages 68–77 of William Stone's *A Practical Treatise on Benefit Building Societies….*, Maxwell: London, 1851.

The Tontine certainly succeeded in its plans for civic transformation. Tontine Street became the new main thoroughfare. However, the company itself seems to have failed. Per Cornelius Walford, "The famous Tontine; scheme for enlarging and improving the Town of Folkestone, unfortunately proved a failure."[4]

The Folkestone scheme was one of a wave of such tontine supported building programs that were created elsewhere, including Croydon, failure in court, 1857, and housing in Harrow, 1856, in distress 1860. Later schemes included the Sutton Freehold Tontine (1857) and others in Putney, 1857, and Hornsby, 1858, twenty-one year term.

Islay Tontine Life Association, 1849

This proposal involved a company purchasing the island estate of Islay, a large island to the west of Glasgow. The intention was to raise £600,000 in shares with a price of £50 and pay the subscribers with the rents of the estate. The unusual aspect of this scheme was that the tontineers were also buying a life insurance policy, so they or their heirs were protected against an early death. While the backers did purchase the estate, it was on the market again a year later. Contemporary reports indicated the tontine had not attracted a sufficient number of subscribers.

[4] *The Insurance Guide and Handbook*, 2nd Ed., London: Layton, 1867, at p. 12.

The failure is reviewed in more detail in Andrew McDiarmid's 'Hardly a Kent name absent,' Raising Capital in Scotland via Tontine, 1775–1850, 43 *Journal of Scottish Historical Studies* 1-53 at pp. 48 and 49 (2023).

Westminster Chambers Mutual Tontine Association, 1862

In *The Daily News* of April, 24th, 1861, a notice appeared announcing that the directors of the Mutual Life Assurance Company were going to create a separate business called the Mutual Annuity Endowment and Tontine Association:

> Various descriptions of Tontines will be opened. Classes of subscribers will be formed according to age, and the yearly proceeds of the investments will be divided *pro rata*. When a subscriber dies, his interest will cease, and the amount to be divided among the remaining members of his class will be proportionably increased. Thus, supposing 100 persons, each of the age of 20, subscribe £100. a-piece, with the condition that the principal shall ultimately be distributed among the 10 latest survivors, the income would be paid to each in half yearly dividends, and those who lived the longest would be constantly receiving an increasing amount. At first, the return would be about 4 or 4½ per cent., but it would at last be 40 or 45 per cent., and the 10 individuals who had survived their 90 co-subscribers would then each receive £1,000.

At this point, the proposal seems to be a classic tontine, independent of any insurance element. The notice referenced insurance schemes of this sort in France and Spain.

However, what developed was not a free-standing tontine. Instead, the tontine concept was grafted onto a construction proposal under the title of the Westminster Chambers Mutual Tontine Association. The next year the following scheme was advertised heavily in the national press. An example from the *Bath Chronicle* of October 9th, 1862, gives some details. A large office building was to be built "opposite the Westminster Palace Hotel, and in the immediate vicinity of the Houses of Parliament, courts of law, and new Government offices." Investors were to pay £100 a share for 1800 shares in the project. The shares were essentially in a tontine:

...Each subscriber will be placed in a class with other subscribers of his own age. For example, if a person of the age of 31 subscribes £100, and 19 others of that age also subscribe, then the income from 20 shares of the entire property will be annually divided among them or such of them as may be surviving at the end of each year, until only two of them (that is, 10 per cent, of the original number) are left, when the income of the 20 shares will be made over to these two and to their representatives in perpetuity, and the class will be extinguished.

...The Direction is composed of 10 members of the Board of the Mutual Life Assurance Society.

The building consisted of seven structures close to the Parliament buildings with more than two hundred units. However, the tontine aspect of this joint-stock company seems to have been a matter of choice among the original subscribers. From the *Builder,* of July 11th, 1853:

The shareholders have the option of subscribing to the undertaking in the way of *ordinary shares* bearing a dividend to the net profits in the usual way, or on the *tontine principle* by which subscribers of similar or nearly similar age are arranged in classes, and a ratable proportion of the net profits is allotted to each class. As any of the class die off, the income of the survivors, therefore, steadily increases; and it has been arranged that when any class is reduced to one-tenth of its original subscribers the property belonging to that class is to be then absolutely divided among and vested in each remaining one-tenth.

The building was a success, with the last company report in *The Times* of January 26th, 1928:

Westminster Chambers Association—Dividend of 6¾ %, being £0/13/6 on each Investment share and £6/15/0 on each Tontine share, for the half-year ended December 31, 1927, making 12¾ %, or £0/25/6 on each Investment and £12/16/0 on each Tontine share for the year, less tax. Warrants to be payable on February 28.

The Tontine shares paid a dividend almost exactly ten times what the regular share paid.

Ending the Tontine

A virtually simultaneous meeting notice in *The Times* of January 24th, 1928, proposed the dissolution of the last batch of Tontine shares:

> That each of the 49 Tontine Shares of £100 each. forming Sections R, V. W. Z. and Cc. of the Tontine Class, be converted into ten Ordinary or Investment Shares of £10 each in the Company, and that such Shares be issued equally between the surviving proprietors of each section. any odd shares which cannot be divided to be sold at the price agreed between the surviving proprietors of each section. and the proceeds of sale to be divided equally between the surviving proprietors of each section or otherwise in accordance with the terms of the Agreements which have been respectively arrived at between them and submitted to and approved by the Board.

The proportion of ordinary to tontine subscribers is unknown. This is likely the last successful major project involving a tontine.

Alexandra Palace and Muswell Hill Estate Tontine, 1871

This proposal envisioned financing the construction of a private pleasure-grounds and exhibition hall on a fifteen-year Tontine plan, with share-holders paying one Guinea a share.[5] Besides participating in the division of the proceeds of the property at the end of fifteen years, tontineers were to have entrance privileges of different sorts depending on how many shares they subscribed to.

The Tontine did not take off, and it was announced that as of November 15th, 1871, subscribers would have their contributions returned.[6] Ultimately, 'Ally-Pally' did get built and opened in 1873. A somewhat polemical pamphlet on the failure of the Alexandra Palace scheme was published in 1872: Robert Hill's *Pauperism and crime: a true cause and a true antidote*.

[5] For an extra shilling a share, the subscribers could also receive life insurance.

[6] 7 *Pall Mall Budget,* 36, November 17th, 1871.

Tontine Park, Renton, 1873

Although 'Tontine Park' appears as a name in 1863, records show that in June 1873, a thirteen-acre municipal park incorporating a football pitch and pavilion was opened in Renton, Dumbarton, Scotland. This took place just as football as an organized sport was taking off. Renton FC, which no longer exists, was a significant team at the time, winning the Scottish Cup several times in the 1880s, and beating West Bromwich Albion for a 'World Champion' title in national championship in 1888.

The park was funded in two parts. Three local industrialists underwrote a portion, and the rest was the result of a subscription by the local townspeople. Given the name of the park, that subscription was likely in the form of a tontine, although details have not been traced.

Variations in the Basic Scheme: Minimum Ages and Terms

It is likely that the occasional news stories of deaths of long-lived tontine beneficiaries had a double-sided effect. On the one hand, the participant had a large income from being a long-lived survivor. However, it cannot have been ignored that the age of said survivor was extraordinarily high, and that few were likely to live that long. The projectors scrambled for means of making tontines more attractive which included a shorter life for the proposed tontine either via a minimum age for nominees or to have the tontine end after a certain relatively short period.

An early example of a minimum age was the tontine financing Fortune's Tavern in Edinburgh in 1795 described in Chapter 11. The idea became more common in the nineteenth century.

The Monmouthshire Tontine, proposed in 1845, consisted of three hundred and fifty shares of £25 each with no interest rate specified. It was based on an estate and hotel in Tredegar. The projectors found their original age specification did not work. From an advertisement dated well after the initial ones: "Seventy-three Years, on the last Birth-day, was originally fixed as the required Age of Nominees, but in consequence of many parties who had applied for shares, having subsequently abandoned their intention from the difficulty of finding eligible lives known to themselves of so advanced an age as 73, it has been determined to reduce the required age, to 69 years last birth-day...." In the last advertisement found for this tontine, the price per share was halved and the number of shares was doubled.

A second one was proposed at almost exactly the same time. The two schemes shared a trustee, Christopher Shapland, Esq., of Sneed Park, near Bristol. He is more visible as a member of the board of directors of two of Brunel's railways in the southwest.

The Glamorganshire Tontine, 1845, had available 6,500 shares at £10 each, paying four percent interest. The income-producing property was a twenty-one-year lease including a large brewery located at the proposed junction of two railways. The advertisements for it included this sentence: "In order that the Tontine may terminate at an early period, no Life is to be nominated who is under sixty-five years of age."

Perhaps to avoid the problem of the Monmouthshire proposal, while a subscriber could nominate someone of their own choice, the projectors offered a list of three hundred eligible names to select from if desired. This may have also been to get around the bother of having to affirm the continued existence of nominees. Seventeen years after the creation of the Tontine, the October 18th, 1862, issue of the *Cardiff and Merthyr Guardian* published an unannotated list of one hundred and ninety-six nominee names and their ages at the start of the tontine. It was substantially male—only eight are female. They are all upper class. It is likely the remaining lives from the list were prepared by the projectors.

In regard to this Tontine, the *Leeds Intelligencer* reported on derivative schemes: "We have heard of subsidiary tontines, in connection with the above, being proposed, in which each of the subscribing parties retains an interest in the concern so long as either of the lives nominated shall be in existence—certainly a good plan for individuals nominating other persons." This was reprinted in other newspapers of the time, so was likely written by the projectors as aid to sales.

The Southampton Tontine of May 1845 was an attempt to raise £19,500 for property producing rental income of £1,000 a year on shares of £10 each. Nominees had to be seventy or above.

In September 1845, a similar age-restricted tontine was proposed in regard to property in the Bath area. The age minimum was seventy. A trustee, Edward Jay, was also a trustee in the Monmouthshire Tontine.

The Bournemouth and Christchurch Tontine Life Association was proposed in October 1849. It involved a group of disparate properties as the core of the tontine with a capital of £10,500, in 1,000 Shares of Ten

Guineas each. As per the *Salisbury and Winchester Journal*, the properties included:

> First—The Belle Vue Hotel, together with the Library and Reading Room, at Bournemouth.
>
> Second—No. 14, Villa, Bournemouth.
>
> Third—Ten shares in the Baths at Bournemouth.
>
> Fourth—The Masonic Hall, Christchurch.
>
> Fifth—Six houses and a Chapel, at Spicer Street and Bargates, in Christchurch.

All the nominees had to be at least sixty-five.

Another example was the proposed City of London Tontine in 1853, 3,600 shares, £10 each, entrance fee five shillings; Capital was a warehouse, tontineers must be at least fifty years old, four percent interest, distribution when pool shrinks to thirty.

An Irish Land Tontine proposed in 1854 specified nominees of seventy years or more. It does not seem to have advanced beyond discussions.

The Oxford Tontine, 1855: proposed raising £8,700 through two hundred and ninety shares of £30 each 'on Lives not less than Sixty-five years of age....' No interest rate was stated in the advertisement. It was based on a thirty-five acre freehold on which it was proposed to build a single large residence. Five months later two adjacent advertisements appear, one stating thirty shares remained available and the other offering the land as a possible market garden site on a seven-year lease.

Also in 1855, the Trenalt Tontine based on an estate in Trewen, Cornwall was proposed with a limit of '...not less than 70 years of age.'

In 1880, a tontine was widely discussed as a means to fund the completion of a new Opera House on the Embankment in London. The construction, started in 1875, had stalled for a lack of funds. The *Pall Mall Gazette* of January 24th, 1880, reported that: "The novelty of the Operatic Tontine consists in its being limited to nominees or to actual subscribers of or above the age of sixty." Nothing came of the proposal and the site ultimately became the Metropolitan Police headquarters, Scotland Yard.

The Rosebank Tontine proposal of 1850 was perhaps the most extreme example of an age limited tontine. Rosebank was an estate near Dumfries of twenty-seven and a half 'imperial acres' with a dwelling house, office houses, extensive gardens, and an orchard. The tontine was initially advertised in January 1850 and there were to be no nominees younger than eighty years old! By March the project was abandoned. A notice in *The Glasgow Herald* stated:

> A SUFFICIENT Number of Shareholders not being likely to come forward to ensure a Sale of the above Property by Tontine, as lately Advertised, the scheme is dropped, and the Property will be offered for Sale, by Public Roup,[7] in the Coffee House, Dumfries .... [text omitted] ...The Proprietor being now resident in London, and finding the Management of the above Property inconvenient, will offer the same at such a Price as will yield a fair per-Centage, and ensure competition and a Sale.

Term-Limited Variations

Another way of speeding up investment returns was to impose a limit on the life of the tontine itself. An example of this was the Norfolk Crescent, in Bath started in 1809. It involved nine residences with the survivorship period winding down after twenty-one years. The buildings still exist.

Others included Cheltenham, Cambray Street, 1809, twelve residences, tontine for a period of twenty-one years; ditto, four houses, 1815 (across the street from the originals), for a period of fourteen years; although there is an alternate 1821 report of fifty shares of one hundred five guineas each, dividends based on rents from two residences, to be sold in 1834 and proceeds divided among survivors; Lochlands Tontine, a civic improvement scheme in Aberdeen, started at some point before 1819. Its term expired in 1830 and it was converted into a joint-stock company. A late attempt in the west country was the Bristol Tontine of 1838 consisting of nine hundred shares at £20 each, expiring in twenty-one years.

[7] A 'roup' is a Scottish term for an auction.

Caveat

The information provided through newspapers and other printed sources advertising tontine proposals need to be taken with large sackfuls of salt. It is likely that most of them never got off the ground, especially when no trace beyond the initial proposal can be found. An example of this was the Worthing Tontine of 1838, based on a sea bathing establishment, consisting of 1,000 shares at ten guineas each. It shows up occasionally in stock price lists of the period.

Note, however, the details of the property proposed to be the basis of this scheme were exposed as shaky if not outright fraudulent in a letter addressed to the Trustees (many titled) and printed in the *Brighton Patriot* of May 29th, 1838, which included this text:

> With several of you I am personally acquainted, and from the high and honourable character that I have entertain of you, and know you to bear, not only here but in this county, I feel assured that you would never have allowed your names to have been introduced in the advertisement to the public had you been aware of the real character and value of the property in question.

The last stock listing showing a share price for the Worthing Tontine was in *The Standard* of February 15th, 1839, showing a price of fifty-one shillings, up from thirty-six shillings, sixpence the previous week.

Tontines Elements in Life Insurance Schemes

In the 1840s, at least one British insurance company experimented with incorporation of tontine clauses into life insurance contracts. In the latter part of the nineteenth century, these became a dominant feature of the United States industry but were eliminated in the early 1900s by regulators because of what amounted to looting by the US companies.

In January 1846, the first advertisements for the Tontine Life Assurance Company appeared in a number of London newspapers. The tontine annuity scheme that was offered seems to be independent of any life policy, simply a Six Percent Annuity sold in shares of £100, with the survivors' dividends increasing as the initial pool shrinks. The payouts were to be capped at £1000, and the capital was to revert to the company at the extinction of the class. However, by October 1849 winding-up notices for the company started to appear. The process dragged on for several years.

A Selection of Other Nineteenth-Century Examples

Sussex Estates, 1801, proposal via Joseph Ward, Esq., and Maberly & Daniel, Solicitors; series of advertisements aiming for £48,000 based on estates with an annual income of £670. Four classes, no price given.

Cirencester, residences, 1802, which still exist.

Greenock, Scotland, 1802, an Inn; three hundred and forty seven nominees, £25 a share, £10,000 capital; a premature winding up was proposed and approved in 1880, creating the Greenock Improvement Trust. A winding-up notice for the trust appeared in the Glasgow Herald of April 14th, 1893. It is still an active hotel.

Royal Theatre, Bath, 1804, one hundred subscribers at £200 each at six percent. Steps were taken to provide a pool of nominees, similar to the completion process for the National Tontine of 1789, although it is not clear if that became necessary.[8] Destroyed by fire, 1862.

Liverpool, Colquitt Street project, 1805, one hundred shares at £100 each.

The Swansea Tontine Society, 1805, built a theatre in Swansea which opened in 1807. Shares were £10 and the project accumulated capital of roughly £3000. It served as an active theatre through most of the nineteenth century, but the Society was dissolved with the capital split among the four remaining shareholders in 1891. The building was torn down in 1899. The records of the Tontine are held by the West Glamorgan Archive Service.

George Hotel, Northampton, 1806, fifty-seven Subscribers to upgrade the existing building; reached a final five in 1887.

Peebles, Scotland, 1807, an inn, which is still an active hotel.

[8] *Bath Chronicle*, January 2nd, 1806.

Sunderland Bridge, 1807: An iron bridge over the Wearmouth was constructed in 1796. In 1805, it needed repair. In 1807, a tontine was proposed to absorb the costs, with the interest paid out of the tolls. The Tontine did not fill, so the funding shifted to a lottery.

Kingston-upon-Hull, 1806: A tontine to create a new city market complex, known as the 'New Shambles Tontine,' was reported subscribed in three days in 1806 and opened in 1807. The city wound it down in October 1828.

Plymouth, Tontine Hotel, Theatre, and Ballroom: Cornerstone laid, 1811, shares £100 at five percent, supplemented with municipal corporation funds. The mayor, Lockyer, was the Projector.

Salisbury National School Tontine, aka St. Martin's, ±1811, paying five percent. Advertisement for selecting new trustees, *Salisbury and Winchester Journal*, December 22nd, 1823.

Glasgow Tontine Society, 1816, financing the George Hotel and nearby buildings; likely converted to a straight company at some point, as its winding up was advertised in *The Times* of May 1st, 1939.

Tontine Tavern, Cupar, opened 1816.

Tontine Patent Iron Bridge across the Thames, from Ratcliffe to Rotherhithe, proposed but never built, 1816.

Regent's Canal Tontine proposed as a tontine in 1817, but it never took off. A standard company was used to construct the canal.

European Museum, St. James Square, operating fund tontine proposed 1819.

Hestercombe Estate, 1822, near Taunton, a tontine was proposed to purchase the property, but it was not sold out of the original family until 1872.

Queensborough and Sheerness Bridge, aka Sheppy Swale Bridge, tontine proposed, 1825, 2,000 shares, £12 each.

Ascot Racecourse Grandstand, 1839, involved one hundred subscribers at £100 a share. After a rocky start it opened in time for the 1839 races. Five survivors in 1858.

Westbourne-Terrace Tontine, 1846, 3,700 shares, £100 each; capital consisted of an already started housing project to consist of 'seventy-three first-class mansions' on property with a ninety-nine-year lease started in 1830. Ultimate single winner takes all until expiry of the lease.

St Austell Tontine, Cornwall, 1848, fifty shares, £20 each, based on miscellaneous properties.

Prince's Park Tontine Company, Liverpool, (1854) voluntarily wound up 1874, paying £36 per £100 share after twenty years of no interest payments.

Irish Land Tontine, 1854, based on eight estates acquired via the Encumbered Estates Court in Ireland with a target of £180,000 raised by 1,800 shares of £100 each. Nominees to be seventy or older.

Isle of Wight—East Cowes Park Tontine, 1855.

Harrow Freehold Land Tontine, 1856.

Dundee Tontine Association, 1856, ceased 1862.

Australian Tontine Society, 1866. Contrary to its name, this was a London-based scheme based on an 'agricultural and coal estate' in Hexham, near Newcastle, New South Wales. It was to have a term of only seven years and the nominees had to be at least seventy years old. It was to consist of four hundred shares of £100 each.

The list above shows a trend of increasing failure as the century progressed. While it focusses on tontines and their particular vulnerabilities, the history of general corporate formation during this period is equally full of failure.

The Growth of Alternative Savings Systems

The beginning of the nineteenth century saw a shift in the meaning of a 'tontine.' On July 27th, 1805, the *Lancaster Gazette* included a short notice reading:

> A new Tontine - not for the benefit of survivorship — has just started up in Birmingham. It may be called a dead club, or funeral association, when every member, from the small deposit of a single penny per week, will have the unspeakable satisfaction of being decently put under the sod. — The

secretary of this social set is said to be an apothecary and the two stewards, an undertaker and a sexton.

This seems to be the first appearance of another kind of scheme that used the word 'tontine.' It was widely prevalent in the nineteenth century, especially in the Midlands. Hundreds of funeral societies developed and used the word tontine in their name. Abuses of trust occurred and regulation were first implemented in 1855 culminating in the Friendly Societies Act of 1875. This form of 'tontine' was a distortion of the original concept and does not really fall into the subject matter of this text.

Benefit Societies and Savings Banks

However, this new kind of association was an aspect of a movement that did have an impact on the market for tontines among the middle classes. Benefit Societies had slowly developed as a grassroots solution to times of financial stress.[9] In their earliest form they were 'box clubs,' mutual support groups literally formed around a safe box holding participant contributions and maintained by one of the members. Many of these centered on a local public house, others were formed within particular trades. The benefits could involve support during unemployment, sickness, or providing a funeral benefit. These clubs or societies evolved independently during the eighteenth century. Most were informal, although Huguenot immigrants formed a 'London Benefit Society' in Bishopsgate in 1666 that lasted two hundred years.

By 1793, benefit societies had achieved sufficient visibility and impact for a Parliamentary Act to be enacted to register them. One report indicated there were 600 in London in 1796. The most visible were the ones we now see as the major fraternal organizations, like the Freemasons and Odd Fellows. In the nineteenth century, many small ones were organized around a range of nuclei—neighborhoods, trades, factory staff, parishes, pubs, etc. In some cases, they continued well into the twentieth century. Financially, they operated around the same level as the small-sum, short-term tontines.

[9] See: Cordery, Simon, *British Friendly Societies 1750–1914*, Palgrave Macmillan, 2003 and Ismay, Penelope, *Trust among Strangers: Friendly Societies in Modern Britain*, Cambridge University Press, 2018.

The 'Friendly Society' impulse tends to be traced to the social aspects of traditional guilds. However, the number of local societies with 'tontine' in their name would indicate an understanding that the regular contributions to cover medical and unemployment benefits and funeral costs, as well as some sort of annual members' bonus, reflect aspects of a the small-sum, short-term tontines.

It is unclear how some of these groups picked tontine to be part of their names. It is likely the naming was through a loose conceptual connection to the death benefit to pay for a funeral or the accumulative nature of the group's capital.

Savings Banks

The movement that led to the opening of the first savings banks arose on the continent in the late 1700s. In England, *The Times* published a letter on November 24th, 1815, outlining a plan to create savings banks for 'servants and other laboring classes' following models from Scotland. The next month they printed a plea for the creation of such banks buried in a story noting civil unrest in Paris. It noted the existence of such banks in Edinburgh, Bath, and Southampton.

Although there was an earlier savings bank, the Ruthwell Savings Bank in Edinburgh founded in 1810, the first one to have a broad impact was the Edinburgh 'Saving's Bank' which was an offshoot of a charitable organization, the Society for the Suppression of Begging. Other communities followed: the Ettrick Forest Savings Bank was created in Selkirk followed by ones in Brechin and Fordoun. A meeting in Exeter on November 22nd, 1815, chaired by the local Member of Parliament, examined a proposal for a 'Provident Institution or Saving's Bank.'

An article on savings banks was reprinted in several newspapers throughout England in late 1815. The version in the *Cambridge Chronicle* of December 15th, 1815, was given a classically academic footnote reading:

> We are by no means pleased with this innovation in our language. If a bank for savings is to be called, not a Saving Bank, but a Savings Bank then a warehouse for shoes, and a manufactory for pins, ought to be called Shoes warehouse, and a Pins manufactory.

In any case, the concept was spreading quickly, and in 1817 parliament passed an Act to encourage the establishment of banks for savings in England. This provided a framework for the banks to invest their capital in 'The Fund for the Banks for Savings' run by the Commissioners for the Reduction of the National Debt paying an annual interest of £4/11/3 per £100. This was better than the standard Consols. While the system was tweaked over time, this stabilizing act ensured the continued existence of a savings system for the not-so-rich.[10]

Conclusion

Tontines clearly continued into the Victorian era, but many never got beyond the proposal stage. The most successful seem to have been the ones financing local and coherent projects which did not need a huge amount of capital.

The evolution of company law slowly made the process of creating a modern corporation simpler. The share market reached a broader public, although the modern 'company' had not yet fully developed. More than 600 companies were created in a boom-and-bust period in the early 1820s. At roughly the same time, the Bubble Act of 1720, which technically restricted company creation, was repealed in 1825. A more formal set of rules did not exist until the Joint Stock Companies Registration Act of 1844.

Also at the same time, the railway building mania started around 1830 with the initial burst continuing through 1850. At the lower end of the market, Benefit Societies and Savings Banks competed in the realm of savings systems for the less rich.

All of these factors eventually eroded the demand for tontines. Their niche had disappeared.

[10] See: Home, H. Oliver, *A History of Savings Banks*, London: Oxford University Press, 1947.

CHAPTER 13

Tontine Aftermarket

The idea of buying an aging tontine share may seem a little strange. Tontines had a 'shelf life,' albeit a fairly long one. If purchased soon after issuance, they were simply another interest-bearing security paying a reasonable dividend. Bought many years after their creation they tended to be riskier but paid a dividend higher than equivalent funds and still held out the promise of a large profit if the share was one of the 'winners.'

The eighteenth-century evolution of the stock market had resulted in an efficient and well-understood process. The stock shares and annuities were represented by pre-printed small single sheets that acted as receipts of the transactions as recorded in the books of the companies and institutions involved. The 'ready money' transactions were simple, and the artificial transactions that drove the market prices, while perhaps opaque to the non-participant, and accompanied by professional jargon, functioned reasonably well.

The attempted introductions of tontines into the range of government securities were failures, unattractive to the market players in part due to the awkward nature of the record keeping in regard to the nominee connected to each share. Once a tontine had been established, the shares were transferable although, of course, the nominee had to remain the same. A buyer of a tontine share took on the responsibility of maintaining communication with the nominee to ensure the certificate of continued existence was filled out each year or six months.

K. McKeever, *The Role of Tontines, 1750–1800*, Palgrave Studies in the History of Finance, https://doi.org/10.1007/978-3-032-12849-2_13

The excerpted text of the 1793 letter below, from a Scottish merchant in London, G. F. Kinloch to Charles Buchan, Esq., (Manager of the Bank of Scotland branch in Ayr) is an example of the difficulty in maintaining contact with a nominated 'life' after the transfer of ownership of a share in a tontine. Kinloch had evidently taken a tontine share as collateral on a loan to a Scots lawyer, judge, and one-time provost of Ayr.

> We rec'd for some years an Irish Tontine in the principal sum of £100 for the late Provost David Fergusson who died considerably in our debt on the life of his Daughter Mrs. Stevenson, but no certificate of her life has been transmitted to us since the Provost's death. We shall be obliged to you therefore to procure us a certificate signed by your Minister agreeable to the enclosed form as after the expiration of three years from the last receipt there may be some risk of its being forfeited. We hope you will excuse and believe us very much at your service in any similar election....

The three years mentioned in the letter refer to the process whereby the tontine managers would declare a share abandoned after three years of not receiving a testament as to the continued life of the nominee. The failure to notify was the functional equivalent of a death because it was perceived as unfair to the other participants if their increase in the dividend were held up by the neglect of the shareholder in certifying the life of their nominee.

Private tontines were subject to the same process, whereby the shareholder had to provide a certificate attesting to the life of the nominee. While in many cases any transfer was an inter-familial situation, such as a legacy, the share being sold to a third party likely created a more complicated situation. The public venue for these transfers were often auctions, although private sales must have taken place.

Why Buy an Aged Tontine Share?

Once a tontine share was paying above the standard annuity rates of the time, the aftermarket buyers would receive that higher interest rate. This would be tempered by the negative chance of the death of the nominee and the positive possibility of participating in the final distribution. The factors for arriving at a price were (1) the purchaser's estimate of the nominee's health and likelihood of survival, (2) an assessment of the complications of administration, and (3) the current rate of interest on the original share price. For example, a £100 share that generated four percent interest when issued might be paying seven percent twenty years later due to the tontine effect of other nominees dying off, and a thirty year-old nominee might be expected to live another twenty years.

Examples

A share of the Ipswich Universal Tontine of 1790 went up for auction in 1846. The purchaser paid £290 for one of the 179 remaining shares which were paying £11/11/6 per share with a par value of £100, slightly more than a rate of eleven and a half percent. However, the interest rate on the inflated purchase price was roughly four percent with a 68 of 179 or thirty-seven percent chance of holding one of the £1,000 shares at the final distribution. The distribution point was fourteen years in the future, but that would not have been known at the time.

However, a few months earlier that premium was not replicated in another tontine share sale result also reported in the *Law Times*. "One share of £100. in the Plymouth Corporation Tontine, established 1811, capital stock £30,000. raised in fifteen classes—£95." This one sold at a slight discount. It is unknown what the Plymouth Tontine was paying at this point.

In a footnote in James Denholm's 1798 *The history of the city of Glasgow and suburbs*, there is a very rare assessment of the aftermarket price of a share in the Glasgow Tontine Coffee House.

> This Tontine was divided into 107 shares at £50 each. [text omitted] It is impossible to say exactly how these shares sell at present, as that depends entirely upon the age, constitution, and mode of life of the nominee. At an average, however, £100 is thought a good price for a share, provided the nominee is not engaged in a hazardous employment, or resides out of the country. The Tontine Coffee Room and Hotel draw at present of rent to the subscribers about £700 per annum.

A 1957 pamphlet history of the origins of the Chichester Theatre in 1792 includes a transcription of the subscriber/nominee information and notes on aftermarket transfers. The shares were issued at £25, but one was sold in 1815 for £18 and another in 1818 for the same price. In 1841, a share sold for £19/19/0. In 1828, three children inherited a share, and one of them bought the shares of the other two for £18/0/0.

A website devoted to a short history of the Freemasons' Hall Tontine reports this:

> However, some shares in the tontine were actually sold. One 1793 document from the Freemasons' Tontine archives advertises the sale by auction of two shares. One share was on the life of a "healthy gentleman aged 33 years, or thereabouts", the other share on the life of a male, 23. Perhaps, surprisingly, the share staked on the life of the older man sold for £55, which was £5 more than that of the younger man.

Unfortunately, there was no regular reporting of actual prices paid in aftermarket auctions at the time.

One other substantial record of a tontine valuation exists. The Sheffield Tontine Inn was created in 1785 on land leased from the Duke of Norfolk at £20 a year for ninety-nine years. There were fifty subscribers at £100 a share, later increased to £120 as additional funds were needed for completion. The business was to become the property of the last living nominee.

A plan for a New Market in Sheffield was developed in 1848 that proposed to tear down the Inn and build the market on that site. The rent being paid by the current Hotel lease was £350 a year, but no figure was reported as to the current interest payment to the remaining seventeen shareholders. Their demand, in light of an additional thirty-four years to run on the lease, was £10,500, which was thought too high by the Duke and developers of the market proposal. Everyone agreed to submit the compensation amount to arbitration.

An extensive report of the arbitration proceedings was printed in the *Sheffield Independent* of August 11th, 1849. The evidence given included the financial history of the Inn properties, the estimates by professional valuers relating to speculative alternate uses of the property, and comparative values of neighboring property. Ultimately, the arbitrator decided to award the tontineers £7,720, or roughly £450 per share for shares that still had leasehold rights for another thirty-four years.

A third example is a bit more convoluted. It involved a situation where tontine shares were accepted as part of a restitution deal for a clerk who had embezzled funds.

The Chief Clerk of the London Office of the Irish Tontines, William Carr, who had an office at Boldero's Bank but was not their employee, was discovered to have been embezzling from the Irish Tontine payment process. Rogerson Cotter, the London agent of the Irish Tontine office, admitted that Carr was kept in his job after the discovery because he had skills no one else in the office could match. Cotter further testified:

> What did you do, in order to obtain the repayment of the £2,200. which you state Mr. Carr to have had out of the money received from Messrs. Boldero and Co. ?
>
> -- Mr. Carr, at the distance of some days, sent à message that he would, as far as he was able, bring back what money was at that time remaining in his possession. After some messages backwards and forwards, that he would bring back what money he had, and deposit Notes, and some other little securities which were not indeed worth a farthing, he endeavoured to compromise the matter. Carr paid £400. into the hands of Field, a Clerk in Messrs. Boldero's bouse, which was afterwards given to me on account of the money which Carr had in his hands.
>
> What other sums of money did you receive from Carr, or from his friends, on account of the money he had in his hands?
>
> -- I received £200. more.
>
> What did you receive besides in Bills, Notes, or Money?
>
> -- Carr then offered to give up what salary was due to him; and the salary that was stopped in consequence of that was 150; it was the salary due at Christmas 1810 and Midsummer 1811; Carr, in the half year from Midsummer 1810 to Christmas 1810, had paid up £126/8/3; he assigned over to me, four Tontine Debentures, two in O'Harra's Tontine and two in the Exchequer, which four I agreed to take at £400.; I paid into Boldero's £1,922.; I paid in the whole of the money in a month or two after to Messrs. Boldero; there was a policy upon his own (Carr's) life; I do not know what that was worth.

Thus, as part of the restitution in 1812, the clerk surrendered two shares in O'Hara's Tontine (1792) and two shares in the National Tontine of 1789. He was credited with par value (£100) for each. It is possible they would have brought more if openly auctioned.

Some civic tontines did not thrive as financial investments. In 1835, a Leamington Spa newspaper, quoting the *Birmingham Advertiser*, reported on an estate sale in Birmingham in which "[T]en tontine shares in the Birmingham Library were sold for £16/10/0 the lot." The par value of those shares was five pounds each. Other lots in the same sale seem to have brought in standard market prices.

One very successful aftermarket purchase was by a Mr. Webb in Bristol. In 1860, he was one of the 'winners' of the Brunswick Square Tontine, ending up with two of the five houses distributed in its dissolution. They were worth around £1,000–1,200 each. He had purchased the shares three years earlier for £190.

An estate auction advertisement in 1816 hints at a person's deliberate accumulation of a range of tontine shares: In *The Times* of April 12th, the auctioneer Mr. Adamson announced a sale at the Auction Mart at the behest of the executors of Mrs. Ann Wilcox, deceased. The seven lots offered were:

(1) One exchequer tontine annuity, during the life of a lady aged 50, the last half-yearly dividend of £3/12/6.
(2) One 'ditto' during the life of a lady aged 66, the last half-yearly dividend of £5/7/2.
(3) One 'ditto' during the life of a lady aged 66, the last half-yearly dividend of £5/7/2.
(4) One 'ditto' during the life of a lady aged 75, the last half-yearly dividend of £9/15/5.
(5) One share of the Earl of Cork's Tontine, during the life of a lady aged 48, the last half-yearly dividend of £3/6/0.
(6) One 'ditto' during the life of a lady aged 63, the last half-yearly dividend of £4/12/0.
(7) One Irish Tontine, during the life of a lady aged 44, last half-yearly dividend of £4/16/10.

The annual income from these lots amounts to slightly over seventy-three pounds a year. The first four lots are likely different Classes of the 1789 British Tontine.

A selection of tontine aftermarket offers:

Year of creation	*Name of tontine*	*Par share*	*Dividend rate*	*Date of auction*	*Report of dividend*
1769	Siprut's Tontine	£100	0.0400	1794	£4
	1st Class, 1st Century			1796	
	2nd Class, 1st Century			1801	£4/11/0
1773	First Irish Tontine	£100	0.0600	1826	£9/13/10
				1835	£17/0/0
				1843	£30/10/10
1774	Richmond Bridge	£100	0.0400	1777	£4/1/2
				1794	£4/15/10
				1796	£4/15/0
				1802	£11/14/0
				1833	£14/0/0
1777	Third Irish Tontine	£100	0.0750		£18/18/6
				1826	£9/14/0
	Irish Tontine, Date Unknown	£100		1792	£6/9/0
				1814	£8/10/0
1781	Glasgow Tontine Coffeehouse	£50	0.3750	1803	£5
				1820	£20
1784	Kew Bridge	£100	0.0600	1795	£9/8/0
				1805	£6/0/0
				1819	£9
1784	Gloucester Market Tontine	£4000 total	0.0500	1805	5%
				1843	£12/10/0
1785	Covent Garden	£250	0.06 and 0.064	1792	£16/0/0
				1794	£16/13/0
				1794	£17/0/0
				1804	£17/10/0

(continued)

(continued)

Year of creation	*Name of tontine*	*Par share*	*Dividend rate*	*Date of auction*	*Report of dividend*
1787	St. Mary's Church, Wanstead			1811	£5/0/0
				1831	£8/7/0
1789	Earl of Cork's Tontine	£100	0.0550	1802	£5/16/0
				1811	6%
				1816	£6/12/0
				1818	£6/10
				1829	£7/7/6
				1831	£7/0/6
				1831	£7/8/6
1790	Ipswich Univ Tontine	£100		1816	5%
				1841	£9/3/0
1792	Mr. O'Hara's Tontine	£100	0.0650	1811	£7
				1818	£7/7/0
1792	Chichester Theatre T	£25		1815	£18
				1818	£18
				1841	£19/19/0
1792	Boston Paving Tontine	£100		1814	5% +
				1830	6%
				1844	£7/14/4

This chart addresses two primary issues: it attempts to describe the relative value of various eighteenth-century, project-oriented tontines established at auctions in the years after issue and it tracks the rise in dividends over time. For many of the tontines, the public record of the dividend is only found in the auction descriptions when shares were sold.

As to dividends, there were many more auction listings than are shown here, but these are the ones whose information included an estimate of the current income derived from the Tontine. Many of the advertisements specify only the original interest rate.

This sampling shows the increase in dividends was real, although slow. Probably disappointingly slow as illustrated by the Irish complaint reviewed in Chapter 7. Arguably, given the long and relatively flat initial part of the increase in dividends for the typical tontine, buying a share just as the dividends started to increase significantly was a smart strategy.

Some of the Tontines continued for decades. Last payment advertisements included:

City of Dublin Tontine (1775)	*March 18th, 1845,* Morning Chronicle
Earl of Cork's Tontine (1789)	October 19th, 1840, *Times*
Mr. O'Hara's Tontine (1792)	October 31st, 1874; *Money Market Review*

The winding-up dates for others included the 1775 Freemasons' Tontine ending in 1863, the 1775 Richmond Bridge Tontine in 1859, the 1781 Shoreham Bridge Tontine in 1846, and the 1791 Ipswich Universal Tontine in 1860. The 1789 National Tontine's last survivor died in 1887, ninety-eight years after the original statute.

In the nineteenth century, the disappointingly slow increase in dividends was addressed by tontine proposals that had terms. Some proposals included final distribution to be made after only fourteen or twenty-one years. Others limited the minimum age of the nominees, so participants had to be sixty years old, or older, at the outset, thus achieving the same shortening effect.

The active market during this period for older tontine shares confirms they were not a freakish aberration, but simply another part of the spectrum of the securities market of the time, a commonplace part of the financial world of Georgian and Victorian Britain.

CHAPTER 14

Conclusion

Tontines, now regarded with suspicion and perhaps a little humor, were simply another part of the financial landscape of Georgian England. They were conceptually simple and teased extraordinary returns to a fortunate few.

Tontines were not exotic. In the 1790s, Tom Paine used the idea of a tontine to imagine a more effective way to use taxes and ultimately provide individual pensions.[1] He stated that "every person in England, male and female, pays on an average in taxes, two pounds eight shillings and six-pence" a year from the day he or she is born. At the end of fifty years that would total £128/15/0 and at sixty, £154/10/0. He then proposes "converting, therefore, his (or her) individual tax into a tontine, the money he shall receive after fifty years, is but little more than the legal interest of the net money he has paid; the rest is made up from those whose circumstances do not require them to draw such support, and the capital in both cases defrays the expences of government."

Adam Smith in *The Wealth of Nations*[2] discusses the nature of tontine investments, although he seems a little naïve given the recent failures of the 1757 and 1765 British government tontine proposals. He is sensitive

[1] Paine, Thomas, *Rights of man. Part the second. Combining principle and practice*, [London]: Jordan, 1792.

[2] Smith, Adam, *An inquiry into the nature and causes of the wealth of nations*, Volume 2, [London]: Strahan and Cadell, 1776.

K. McKeever, *The Role of Tontines, 1750–1800*, Palgrave Studies in the History of Finance, https://doi.org/10.1007/978-3-032-12849-2_14

to the issue of "the liberation of the public revenue does not commence till the death of all the annuitants comprehended in one lot." However, he goes on to say, "An annuity, with a right of survivorship, is really worth more than an equal annuity for a separate life, and from the confidence which every man naturally has in his own good fortune, the principle upon which is founded the success of all lotteries, such an annuity generally sells for something more than it is worth." This was a common argument made in favor of tontines at the time. His evidence seems to be the popularity of the French tontines.

These are examples of the concept of the tontine taken seriously by serious thinkers. Not as a gamble, but as a way to meet the economic needs of the average man. Paine's proposal anticipates the development of Social Security systems by roughly one hundred years. Given that they were particularly effective in funding local infrastructure projects, it is odd that tontines still provoked debate as to whether or not they were legitimate investments or simply reckless gambles.

The Niche for Tontines

While tontines were never a large part of the market, they did serve to provide both financing at a relatively low level for numerous projects and as a form of savings for the middle classes in an economic environment which had yet to develop broader institutions to fill that need. The market for the Consols could be quite volatile, while shares in tontines were comparatively steady.

The Economy of Britain in the Eighteenth Century

Eighteenth-century England was a confusing matrix of trends involving population growth, entrepreneurial innovation, early industrialization, urbanization, and war.

The population grew roughly two-thirds from Gregory King's estimate of 5.5 million in 1695 to the first census, in 1801, showing a population of 8.8 million. The number of accounts listed as owning shares in securities in 1750 was estimated by Peter Dickson at slightly under 60,000.

He then estimates the figure to have grown to around 500,000 in 1815.[3] The first part of this period is when tontines entered the system.

Slowly increasing industrialization and major transportation projects were constant during this period. These both caused and allowed large population shifts to occur. In the latter part of the century, the United Kingdom fought three major wars: the Seven Years' War, the American Revolution, and the French Wars at the end of the century. T. S. Ashton, in *An Economic History of England: the Eighteenth Century*,[4] stated: "In a century of costly wars, the chief borrower was the government. When its need for resources was urgent it offered a high rate for money, and the prices of stocks bearing a fixed rate of interest accordingly fell. The yield on government stocks gave the ply to the whole system of interest rates." The French Wars, in the 1790s, caused a significant drop in the prices of the Funds, so that Government Securities were trading at half their face value, this doubling the effective interest rate.

The everyday use of credit also exploded during this period. As expressed by historian John Smail in *The Culture of Credit in Eighteenth-Century Commerce*,[5] he points out that "the system of credit became more complex, more sophisticated and more comprehensive during the course of the century." He goes on to state: "one significant element of this story is the financial revolution of the late seventeenth and early eighteenth centuries, which provided Britain with a permanently funded national debt and which was instrumental in introducing new financial techniques from Europe. Important developments within commercial circles included the growing prominence of the domestic bill of exchange as the preferred way to settle debts and the complex web of commercial credit that grew up around the use of bills." Thus when the Bank of England suspended specie payment in 1797, the economic framework did not collapse.

[3] Dickson P. G. M., *The Financial Revolution in England*, London: Routledge, 1993.

[4] London: Methuen & Co., 1972.

[5] 4 Enterprise & Society 299–325, (June 2003).

Problems with Coinage

The credit culture extended right down to the lowest retail levels. One aspect of this was the retreat from the official minting of low-value coins. The government ceased minting copper coins in 1775 and silver ones in 1787 although gold guineas continued to be produced. The scarcity of coins resulted in local, low-value, private tokens being minted and accepted throughout the country. They tended to be used only in the vicinity of their initial distribution and no version was ever accepted on a nationwide basis. The situation was described by George Selgin in *The Institutional roots of Great Britain's 'big problem of small change:'*[6]

> Having faced an especially severe small-change problem, Great Britain was also the first nation to solve the problem. It first did so unofficially, using privately minted 'tradesmen's tokens' or 'commercial coins', starting with 'Druids' issued by the Parys *[copper]* Mining Company in 1787. By 1797, 20 private mints, including Matthew Boulton's Soho mint, had struck 600 tons of commercial copper coins — an amount half again as great as the Royal Mint's copper output for the previous half century.

This coinage trends, combined with a fear of hoarding and a flow of bullion out of the country, culminating in the Bank of England's halt of specie payments in 1797. The investors and merchants in Great Britain had to accept paper payments for roughly the next twenty years.

The fairly sophisticated credit market allowed for the economy to thrive even with a dearth of official coinage. The oversized 'cartwheel' pennies and tuppences of 1797 were the first sign of a return to official coinage, but it was not until 1816 that full range of silver coinage returned.

In the first part of the eighteenth century, the retail price index stayed substantially stable until around 1760, when it slowly and irregularly increased roughly 100% through 1800. The price of gold was essentially unchanged from 1720 to 1800 at around £4.25 an ounce.

[6] 14 *European Review of Economic History* 305–334 (August 2010).

Projects Requiring Investor Capital

Within this context, group investments were typically achieved via partnership, but for projects needing significant capital and managerial flexibility, such as canals, turnpikes, and bridges, some form of corporate structure became necessary even without the classic corporate form. The tontine became a relatively standard means of entrepreneurial investment and development. There were three main strands in the evolution of the tontine: government borrowing and revenue, construction projects, both government and private, and long-term or intergenerational financial instruments.

During the latter part of the eighteenth century, tontines were simply another variation in the many ways the upper middle class could invest. The mortality risk which seems so off-putting today was simply another factor in a financial economy in which risk was a large part of the picture. The reliability of the Consols and other national debt-related securities came with a relatively low interest rate. Tontines teased a slightly higher initial interest rate bolstered by the potential increase over time and the possibility of being one of the 'winners' of the final distribution.

The Perpetual Quest for Dependable Savings

Schemes for individuals to generate sufficient savings to provide support for themselves and their families in times of illness or old age have been an object of economic planning since the invention of money. For the upper classes, land served this function. By the eighteenth century, a significant portion of the upper-middle class was essentially unlanded, having made their fortunes as merchants and other forms of entrepreneurship. The purchase of a country estate was often the final step in middle-class aggrandizement.

While holding and passing on land was an option for the very rich, annuities could serve a similar purpose for the others. In eighteenth-century Britain, annuities of the income variety, as opposed to the government loan funds called annuities, existed in various forms. There were annuities from the government, similar to pensions; annuities purchased through private transactions; and annuities provided by companies designed for that purpose.

David R. Bellhouse's *Leases for lives: life contingent contracts and the emergence of actuarial science in eighteenth-century England*[7] devotes a chapter to 'The Annuity Bubble of the 1760s and 1770s.' In it he describes the emergence of a number of annuity companies in that period and the ultimate failure of virtually all of them. He describes the analyses and debates relating to the accuracy of the math underlying annuity schemes among the more sophisticated mathematicians of the time. There were a number of critics, but the polymath Richard Price's *Observations on reversionary payments*...[8] was the most influential text due to his particularly clear presentation in something of a catechism format, that avoided drowning the reader in too much math. The first of the financial tontines, Jacob Siprut's Society for Annuities Encreasing to Survivors, was started amid this annuity scheme bubble, in 1768–1769.

The Evolution of Tontines

The initial appearance of tontines was for what we would now consider local infrastructure projects. They were created to support the construction of assembly rooms, workhouses, inns, bridges, and similar relatively small-scale or local endeavors. The tontine aspect, promising increased returns over time, lifted them beyond the comparably-sized, bond-based investments such as turnpike trusts. Canal companies tended to be a quantum leap higher in budget and corporate complexity and their returns could be more significant once they became operational. It also became clear that the interest tontines initially had to pay was a little more than the government annuities paid. In that sense they competed with turnpike trusts.

The relatively few large-scale financial tontines, and the tontines based on landed estates met a different market demand and competed successfully with the fragile annuity companies, the Irish Tontines, and the National Tontine of 1789.

If legitimate, the small-sum, short-term tontines, provided some level of savings for the less affluent investors, but both corruption and the introduction of the idea into a long-term falling stock market meant most of them disappointed their subscribers.

[7] Cambridge: Cambridge University Press, 2017.

[8] London: Cadell, 1771.

Tontine Issues: A Gamble?

Many discussions of tontines swirled around whether it was a legitimate investment or a simple gamble. The question was debated at the time. The eighteenth-century risk environment needs to be understood in order to come close to resolving the issue adequately. The financial environment included a roughly annual government lottery which was sold via the everyday stock exchange and by people who were also stockbrokers. The stock exchange itself was perceived by a portion of the population as little more than a gambling den. The National Tontine of 1789 was in part driven by Pitt's desire for the government to receive a full amount for the subscriptions to the 1789 Loan rather than continuing the tradition of pricing new government debt at the current market rate. That market rate meant the state had to take an immediate discount on par value every year.

When the National Tontine of 1789 showed signs of failing, the Government drafted an amendment that allowed purchasers to substitute a Long Annuity valued at 4.25% or keep the tontine subscription. The choice was, in effect, a vote on a tontine versus a traditional annuity. Grellier[9] reported in 1799 that 'a greater part were in the following year exchanged....'

On the other hand, this 1799 proposal exemplifies the opposite notion, that a tontine could be yet another adventure in the Georgian world of betting and gambling:

> SCHEME OF THE
> ANDOVER LOTTERY TONTINE SOCIETY
>
> A TONTINE for SEVEN YEARS, each member to pay £10 the capital arising from which to be invested in the public funds, and the interest annually laid out in the purchase of LOTTERY TICKETS, the produce to be added to the capital, and at the end of seven years the whole to be divided amongst the survivors.
>
> A committee of five members resident in Andover will transact the business, and no agents are to be employed,
>
> Persons desirous of further particulars and who wish to become members, will please signify the same to Mr J H TODD as early as possible.

[9] Grellier, J. J., *The terms of all the loans which have been raised for the public service during the last fifty years....*, London: Galabin, et al., 1799.

While clubbing together to buy lottery tickets was common, this addition of a tontine element represents chance piled on chance piled on chance. The single reliable factor was that the British Government did pay the dividends on its 'public funds,' i.e., the Consols, year after year.

With the Three Percent Consols selling around £62, at £10 a share, one hundred subscribers could spend a £1,000, which would purchase about £1,600 worth of Consols in December 1799. This would generate roughly £48 a year in interest. At the same time, the price of lottery tickets was around £15, so the investors had a share in just three or four tickets, unless they bought sub-shares to spread the risk, although that would also cut the return. No matter how they were purchased, the price of lottery tickets would vary throughout the year, depending on how close the drawing was.

Note that John Henry Todd was not a charlatan. He was an attorney in Andover who, among other things, served as a Coroner for the County of Southampton, and Clerk to the Commissioners of Pavement, as well as Secretary to a couple of charitable organizations. He served as an Ensign in the Andover Volunteer Infantry. In the 1820s and 1830s, he was elected a Bailiff and then Justice in Andover.

This proposed scheme is extreme. However, one of the primary points of this text is how unremarkable tontines were during this period. The broadest class of tontines was a simple solution for funding local civic improvement. The investors got a slightly higher interest rate than the government securities and contributed to an institution that was recognized as serving a useful local purpose, such as a bridge, an inn, or a theatre. At the same time, they bought into a framework that provided for a trickle of income for a child or grandchild after the subscriber's death, with an element of a possible large payout years in the future.

Tontine Issues: Misconceptions of Mortality

In the debate surrounding the implementation of the National Tontine of 1789, a classic overstatement can be found in the *Public Advertiser* of May 11th, 1790. It … "is clear that one hundred pounds laid-out in 3 or 4 per cents. can never give more than 3 or 4 per cent. whereas one hundred pounds laid out in Tontine, must in a few years give double that sum, and may give one thousand pounds per annum."

An equally misbegotten attitude toward actual mortality is expressed in an advertisement[10] in 1791 for the City of London, Westminster, and Borough of Southwark Universal Tontine, one of the small-sum, short-term tontines popular at the time. It stated that:

> [W]hen the most able and experienced calculators declare, there is no stage in human life, whether male or female, is entitled to more than thirteen years purchase, while in plans of this kind, the Benefit of Survivorship gives more than
> 8 per Cent, the second year.
> 16 per Cent, the third year.
> 25 per Cent, the fourth year.
> 33 per Cent, the fifth year.
> 41 per Cent, the sixth year.
> 50 per Cent, the seventh year.

The only way to make sense of this is to think the death rate among the fellow tontineers will result in a fifty percent return on investment at the end of seven years. This is staggeringly unrealistic. However, it is a good illustration of the problems with understanding the rates of mortality that prevailed with the general public at the time. The increase in probable returns was constantly overstated, and, in the long run, disappointing, when it did not pan out.

An attempt to counter that kind of thinking appeared in the *Gazetteer and New Daily Advertiser* of October 15th, 1790:

> Suppose the society (*ie., the tontine*) to be composed of 1000 members and their mean age to be between 30 and 40 years, 880 persons will live to the end of seven years -- so that if the whole 1000 lived to make their last payment, and none of them died till just before the final distribution of the stock, the share of the survivors would be only £24/1/0 for each person. But if it be supposed (which is really the case) that they will be continually dying from the time of the first subscription to the conclusion of the tontine, the share of each survivor will not amount to £23. Nay, when the necessary expences of management are deducted, I am convinced that the shares will even fall greatly below this sum, and the surviving members will have the satisfaction to find, at the end of seven years, that they have barely

[10] *Diary or Woodfall's Register*, December 14th, 1791, and elsewhere.

received their principal and interest, after having endangered the loss of the greatest part of it by dying in the meantime.

This was part of the text of a letter attacking the small-sum, short-term tontine generally. It is far more realistic about the reality of mortality rates. However, tontines thrived on the misunderstanding that author was trying to counter.

In the *Monthly Magazine* of 1812, this letter encapsulated the archetypical complaint:

> I am holder of a share in the *Third,* or *Youngest, Class* of the Irish - government Tontine, established in 1775, which began with paying an annuity of six per cent. in Ireland, or five percent. if receivable in England. This annuity receivable in England has only encreased to seven per cent, after a lapse of thirty seven years. It is impossible to suspect any improper management in a public fund of this description; at the same time so small an encrease after so long a period is not easily reconcilable with our general notions of the uncertainty of human life.

A responding letter explained that the experience of a contemporary insurance company showed the figure given by the complaining letter was realistic.

An 1897 Dutch text,[11] essentially a compilation of descriptions of schemes that evolved into life insurance in the Netherlands, took this attitude toward the Dutch tontines (*contracten van overleving*) of the mid-eighteenth century:

> In this way our forefathers tried their luck. The attractiveness of this method of saving for them lay in the lottery-like nature that formed the basis of these "Contracts of Survival". Born merchants that they were, they did not let any "opportunity" pass unused and thus they took the often capricious death of a certain number of people in pursuit of financial gain. For a bet of 10.- you could get 1000.- back! How delightful! It is now well known that *all these tontines have aroused disappointment and nothing*

[11] Algemeene Maatschappij van Levensverzekering en Lijfrente, *Bouwstoffen voor de geschiedenis van de levensverzekeringen en lijfrenten in Nederland,* Amsterdam: De Maatschappij, 1897.

but disappointment. The representation of the likely outcomes later turned out to have been far too high.[12]

Attempting to Make Tontines more Appealing

Avoiding the 'disappointment' induced a number of variations in the terms of later tontines.

An early instance was finding ways of reducing the number of classes of subscribers. The French system of classes of ten years for each pool was imitated by the National Tontine of 1789. The Covent Garden Tontine had two classes, under or over thirty years old. The Ipswich Tontine eliminated classes by establishing price discounts based on the age of the nominees in fifteen groups of varying ages, but putting all the shareholders into one pool. The Richmond Bridge Tontine made no age distinctions.

While virtually all tontines did not allow changing of nominees, one, the St. John's Street Tontine in Swansea, did allow a switch upon transfer, but the new nominee had to be with five year of age of the original.

Limits were introduced either of the life of the tontine itself or requiring a minimum age, sixty or above, for the nominees. The short-term, small-sum tontines tended to be for only five or, more commonly, seven years. By the early nineteenth century many project tontine proposals were limited to roughly a twenty-year existence. The proposals that included a minimum age for the nominees were rarer and seem to have a low success rate. One version that did succeed involved the projectors creating a list of older aristocrats for subscribers to select from.

While share prices were never standardized, the earlier ones tended to reflect the £100 standard share price in the market for stocks and annuities. Many later ones were cheaper, reaching for a broader investor pool.

The ultimate 'prize' varied as well, from an individual taking over full ownership of the property involved to a small group of survivors splitting the proceeds of whatever the capital of the tontine was. This could be the sale of the property involved or simply cashing in the securities underlying the tontine.

[12] With an assist by Google Translate.

Tontine Issues: Providing for Heirs and Legatees

A common selling point for the tontines of the period was continuing income for dependents after the subscriber had died. This made the selection of children as nominees to be particularly appropriate. A 1792 copy of the will of Richard Wordsworth, uncle and guardian of the more famous Dorothy Wordsworth, reads in part:

> And whereas I have advanced in the Second class of the British Tontine the Sum of one hundred pounds and thereupon nominated my second daughter Dorothy Now I do hereby will and direct that notwithstanding the said nomination of my daughter Dorothy the interest of the said sum of one hundred pounds shall be paid to my said Wife during her life and after the death of my said wife the Interest thereof shall be paid to my said Daughters Dorothy and my daughter Ann in case they shall both be unmarried and in case of the marriage of either of them before then, the whole Interest thereof shall be paid to the unmarried Daughter during the life of the said Dorothy and so long only as such unmarried daughter shall remain unmarried...

This clause neatly summarizes the use of tontine income as provision for surviving spouse and for surviving children, as long as the nominee stayed alive.

Tontine Issues: Administrative Complexity

The standard investment in England at this time was the Bank Annuity in its various forms paying three to five percent annual interest. The administration of the income provided by these annuities was fairly simple at the retail level. Twice a year, dividends were issued and could be picked up by going to the Bank of England or other issuing institution, identifying yourself to the relevant clerk, who would confirm your entitlement and issue a pay warrant for the amount. Another clerk would cash that warrant and you would leave the bank with cash in hand. A system based on power of attorney forms enabled this to be done by others on your behalf.

On the other hand, the continuing life of the nominee in a tontine had to be proved before payment of the dividend could be issued. While individual tontine rules varied, the general practice was to require the presence of the nominee at the payment point, or presentation of a current document confirming the life signed by the nominee's local minister and churchwardens or local judge, along with the original participant's certificate or debenture in order to obtain payment. The minister could charge a small fee for the life certificates.

The failure to present this confirmation could result in forfeiture, as indicated by the 1817 nudging letter to Messrs Farrer, Atkinson & Johnson, Lincolns Inn Fields as shown in Fig. 14.1.

The list of nominees published in 1792 shows the nominee for share number 1087 was Elizabeth Susanna Touchet, aged eight, and 1088 was her brother, George John Thicknesse, aged seven. They were the children of the nineteenth Baron Audley.

The diary of John Longe,[13] a vicar in Suffolk, records sending two tontine life confirming certificates to his London bankers, Childs, in 1826 and 1831. Presumably, they held his power of attorney. Longe and his younger brother were nominees and legatees within the Third Class of the Irish Tontine of 1773.

The added burden faced by parish priests is illustrated by this excerpt from *The Diary of a Country Parson, the Rev James Woodforde* from 1791. It shows him being paid for an earlier certification, and then executing another batch shortly thereafter:

> April 29 Friday... Rec'd of Mr Baker the Official who lives in the Close for signing my Name to a Paper sometime back brought me by Mr Custance of his Children's Age concerning the Tontine Act at 1 shilling 0 pence each Child [total] £0/7/0 ....
>
> July 5, Tuesday.... Had a printed Letter this Evening from G. Atwood Esq. Treasury Chambers, Whitehall, London, brought by Mr. Custance's Servant from Norwich. It was a Letter respecting Mr. Custance's Children they being put into the Tontine Act, late passed. For a Certificate from me of their being Alive. [mildly tweaked for clarity]

George Atwood was the 'Inspector of Tontine Certificates' for the National Tontine of 1789.

Another example is provided in a 1792 letter from a Mr. W. Bray to Daniel Beaumont, Esq., held in the Bedfordshire Archives on loan

[13] Longe, John, *The Diary of John Longe, Vicar of Coddenham, 1765–1834*, edited by Michael Stone, Woodbridge: Boydell Press/Suffolk Records Society, 2008.

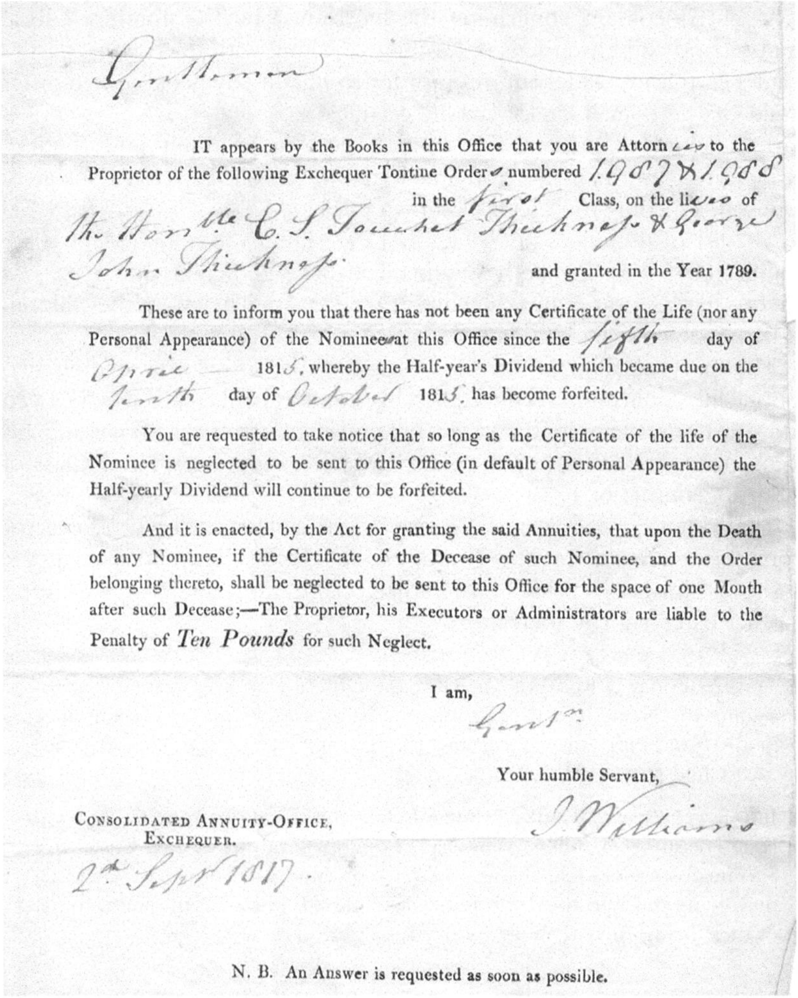

Gentlemen

IT appears by the Books in this Office that you are Attornies to the Proprietor of the following Exchequer Tontine Orders numbered 1.987 & 1.988 in the first Class, on the lives of the Honble C. S. Touchet Thicknesse & George John Thicknesse and granted in the Year 1789.

These are to inform you that there has not been any Certificate of the Life (nor any Personal Appearance) of the Nominees at this Office since the fifth day of April 1815, whereby the Half-year's Dividend which became due on the Tenth day of October 1815, has become forfeited.

You are requested to take notice that so long as the Certificate of the life of the Nominee is neglected to be sent to this Office (in default of Personal Appearance) the Half-yearly Dividend will continue to be forfeited.

And it is enacted, by the Act for granting the said Annuities, that upon the Death of any Nominee, if the Certificate of the Decease of such Nominee, and the Order belonging thereto, shall be neglected to be sent to this Office for the space of one Month after such Decease;—The Proprietor, his Executors or Administrators are liable to the Penalty of *Ten Pounds* for such Neglect.

I am,
Gentn
Your humble Servant,
J. Williams

Consolidated Annuity-Office,
Exchequer.
2d Sepr 1817.

N. B. An Answer is requested as soon as possible.

Fig. 14.1 The 1817 letter from Consolidated Annuity Office to attorneys for a tontineer requiring proof of life for two nominees, Elizabeth Susanna Touchet and her brother George John Thicknesse. Collection of the author

from Duke of Bedford's archives at Woburn Abbey.[14] The gist is that Mr. Bray's son and Tontine nominee was at school in Scotland and Bray needed the Headmaster to complete the form attesting to the continued life of the son in order to receive the dividends due Bray. He was asking Beaumont to send the cover letter and tontine form to the Headmaster, David Malcolm, and to receive the response and forward it to 'Mess. Cox, Cox, & Greenwood—Craigs Court' who were primarily army agents but also served as bankers.

There are no mail markings on the letter. Beaumont was associated with the 'Bedford Office' and served as an agent for the Duke of Bedford. Bray was a nearby attorney who seems to have represented the Duke. Contemporary directories show their offices were within walking distance of each other. Cox, Cox, & Greenwood were bankers, but were primarily army agents for a number of regiments within the military. David Malcolm, a sometime poet, was the headmaster of a school in Madderty, Perthshire.

The nominee life certification process also meant that the secondary sale of a tontine share saddled the buyer with this documentation requirement for nominees they likely did not know. This was illustrated by the letter from Kinloch to Buchan mentioned in Chapter 7.

The awkwardness could also include distance. Volume three of *The Correspondence of Jeremy Bentham*[15] includes a reference to obtaining a certificate of life of his brother Samuel then resident in Russia. A footnote transcribes the text of the certification from Bentham's letter copybook.

> I, the Revd. Euthemius Swarsk Minister of the Parish of St. Parascivia in the Town of Crechoff in White Russia Do hereby Certify that Samuel Bentham Youngest Surviving Son of Jeremiah Bentham and his first wife Alicia was living at the said Parish the twentieth of April last present and is still living as I believe though not now here. Witness my hand this 17th of August 1787, Euthemius Suwarski.

Samuel Bentham was a nominee in the Third Class of the Irish Tontine of 1773. The middle part of his career as a naval architect and soldier was spent in the service of Catherine the Great.

[14] Bedfordshire Archives: R3/1190: *Correspondence from Bray, William, Tavistock to Daniel Beaumont.*

[15] London: UCL Press, 2017.

Other Administrative Issues

This level of regular documentation meant there had to be staff assigned to maintaining tontine records. Tontines with a relatively small number of shareholders could be handled by a small office. The Richmond Bridge and Covent Garden tontines fit this model. The Ipswich Tontine, administered via a local bank, was a well-run medium to large scheme.

If the issuer already had an administrative unit that could absorb the process, the administrative burden was acceptable. The Covent Garden Tontine interest payments were initially executed via the office of the attorney who had drafted the tontine. That task then shifted to a bank owned by one of the trustees, and ultimately the payments were made at the box office. The box office already handled the administration of the theatre's Renter's Shares, so the addition of the Tontine was not a great disruption. Similarly, the Clerk of the Richmond Bridge Tontine was also the Parish Clerk in Richmond and related advertisements directed readers to the 'Clerk's House.'

Government Tontine Bureaucracy

But scaling up could be difficult. For the Irish Tontines and the National Tontine of 1789, the national governments had to create special offices to administer them.

As per a 1797 report, the British Tontine was administered through an office that executed both the Tontine paperwork and the lingering 'American Claims.' The American Claims involved petitions and payments made to British loyalists from the debenture system established after the Revolutionary War. The office, structurally reporting via the War Office, had four employees whose salaries amounted to £670.

The first clerk was an overall supervisor as well as being the person in charge of 'Assignments, Powers of Attorney, Wills, &c' and 'transacts all Matters relating to Transfers.' The second clerk posted all orders passed for payments '...and makes a Half Yearly Account of Defaulters and Deaths...and calculates the Dividends.' The third and fourth clerks recorded all the details necessary in the books and filed the 'Certificates of Lives' and assisted in 'any other Part of the Office Business.'

The tontine payment procedures also caused the addition of six clerks to the office of the Clerk of the Pells.[16] This office executed tasks that today would be roughly equivalent to tasks executed by bookkeepers and accountants. According to the *Parliamentary Register* of 1797, the clerical salaries amounted to £880 a year.

> The clerks in the office of the Clerk of the Pells, for their service in the execution of the Acts 29th and 30 Geo. III for granting annuities on lives, with benefit of survivorship, for six months, due 10th October 1796…….£440.

In another report from the House of Commons Select Committee on Finance, there was an annual payment of £700 to 'defray expenses' made to George Atwood, Esq., as 'Inspector of Tontine Certificates.' No attempt is made to link the entries to provide a complete picture of the underlying administrative costs.

In comparison, the buying and selling of standard funds, such as the Consols, and the dividend distribution procedure for the interest paid by the annuities, had been refined over the years to a fairly simple process administered primarily by the Bank of England.

Tontines Issues: A Local Product

The tontines also provided a means for investment at the local level. The securities market was awkward for non-London-based investors. Dividends were expected to be picked up personally at the London offices, or else a power-of-attorney form had to be filled out (for a fee). A locally-based tontine meant a nearby payment source for the subscriber. For the financial tontines, the Trustees or Directors handled the receipt of dividends in London and the local holders simply picked up their share at the local office, upon presentation of the evidence that the nominee was still living.

The extant records of the scattered tontines supporting inns, for example, show mainly, if not exclusively, local subscribers. Unless a project temporarily parked its accumulated subscription payments in the Consols during the construction project, the money taken in and spent was essentially a local process.

[16] Pells is an archaic term for parchment.

Tontine Issues: Who Really Benefited?

Since financial projects tend to involve someone making a profit, it is worth contemplating how tontines fit into the spectrum. At a basic level, the construction tontines benefited the community. In fact, that record is pretty strong, with tontine-financed edifices scattered throughout the British Isles.

However, every tontine had a cluster of individuals involved in its creation and execution. Many proposals were initially presented with a list of leading citizens at the head of the advertisement. Some of them were destined to be the trustees of the project, but many were never associated with the project in the long run. Many were local officeholders, including Members of Parliament. It is unclear if any people in these groups were paid, although some tontines advertised the fact they were not paid.

Each tontine tended to have what, in the period, was known as a 'Projector.' That role tended to evolve into being the primary administrator of the tontine in the long run. In 1769, Jacob Siprut wrote himself in for a £20 annual fee for running each Century of the Society for Annuities Encreasing by Survivorship. The Ipswich Tontine included a fee to its Secretary on a per subscriber basis. This had the effect of reducing the fee as tontineers died off.

At the other end of the spectrum, it is clear that some of the small-sum, short-term tontines were structured to give an exploitative, disproportionate payout to their administrators.

All the tontines had to have a banker. The impression is given by some of the advertising that some bankers were effectively the projectors. The Ipswich Universal Tontine's long-time secretary was Emerson Cornwell, who was also a partner in the bank that held the Annuities that formed the corpus of the Tontine. The bankers also could include the annuities held as assets, to help their balance sheet. They were also the recipients and distributors of the income of the tontine.

Because most tontines did not have a corporate existence, but were effectively trust institutions, the administration incurred fees as trustees retired and were replaced. All of the underlying property, usually annuities, had to be formally transferred from the departing trustee(s) to the new one(s) which incurred brokers' fees. These could be quite substantial. Brokers often also had a role in the initial sales of shares in the tontines.

In one of the rare instances of a voice for the shareholders, some tontines would hold a meeting in order to select or elect new trustees.

From the *The Times* of July 1st, 1815, forty years after the founding of the tontine:

> FREEMASONS' TONTINE -- Notice is hereby given, That a MEETING of the SUBSCRIBERS or PROPRIETORS of the FREEMASONS' TONTINE: will be held at Freemasons'-hall, Great Queen-street, Lincoln's-inn-fields, on Tuesday July 11, at two o'clock in the afternoon, to nominate and appoint FIVE new TRUSTEES, in the room or place of those who are deceased or have resigned. WM. H. WHITE, Registrar.

The advertising for the Covent Garden Tontine directed readers to a solicitor. Lawyers drafted and vetted the proposals, deeds, and other documents involved in creating tontines. Participants in some tontines received full formal indentures as their share documents, although these evolved into simpler share certificates as the tontines became more commonplace.

The Richmond Bridge Tontine was a creature of Parliament, with an underlying commission structure. This was very similar to the Turnpike Trust operations of the same period. There was no major exploitative role in the process.

Eventual Disappearance of Tontines

Classic tontines gradually disappeared in the nineteenth century. The word survived as a common name for mutual aid societies providing sickness and funeral benefits and regular surplus dividends. This was the result of an accumulation of causes. Factors included an improved understanding of mortality rates, the complexity of administration of large tontines, the creation of friendly societies and savings banks, the simplification of the rules and the process for creating corporations, and the taint of unreliability induced by both the small-sum, short-term 'tontines' and the number of failed tontine proposals during the middle of the nineteenth century.

The gradual creation of a modern company law through a sequence of Acts providing for the creation, registering, and winding-up of companies meant the tontine became less attractive. The repeal of the *Bubble Act of 1720* in 1825 was the first step in the creation of the modern corporate form. The *Joint Stock Companies Act* of 1844 clarified the process for forming a Company. *The Limited Liability Act* of 1855 further increased the attractiveness of the corporate form. Reasons to reject the tontine form included its complicated trustee-based structure, the legal limbo in which the subscribers had few rights, and the complicated process of confirming the lives of the nominees.

The various company-related statutes seem to have made an orphan of the tontine: A letter from 'J.M.D.' published in the *Law Times* in 1854 gave his explanation of how tontines fell into regulatory cracks.

The writer was responding to an earlier query as to why tontines, once popular, are no longer being proposed. He stated he had recently investigated that very issue and contended that the registrar acting under the new Joint-Stock Companies Registration Act declared that tontines were trading companies and fell within the aims of that statute. Per that statute a license from the Board of Trade had to be obtained for the tontine to hold land, and tontines, as a rule, were based on holding land.

After the statute came into effect, the registrar changed the policy and asserted it was illegal for tontines to hold land. He requested the Board of Trade consult with the Attorney and Solicitor General for an opinion. The registrar then refused to list tontines under the Act. The writer goes on to state: "It has, however, been recently discovered that tontine companies are not trading companies, and are, therefore, not within the provisions of the Joint-Stock Companies Act."

By the time of the writing of the letter, 1854, tontines could still be established by deed of settlement. Even though their actions closely resemble those of large commercial enterprises, they were not corporations. Technically, they were large-scale partnerships and are not required to have a license from the Board of Trade to hold land.

Arguably, the investing population understood the nature of a corporation but may have been mystified or confused by their rights under a deed of settlement structure.

Is This a Tontine or a Raffle?

To come full circle from the 'investment or gamble' question asked in the first chapter, is the proposal described below an investment or a gamble? The scheme was created by the landowner/contractor who built the two buildings comprising the tontine. They were both already let at a rent of £120 a year. From the *Caledonian Mercury* of September 12th, 1850:

> Bridge of Allan Tontine -- The scheme for disposing property by a tontine, as adapted at Bridge of Allan. in one instance has certain new features that entitle it to notice. The nominees must be persons of 75 years old or upwards.

The capital of the Tontine was a pair of newly built houses. Their rents would be accumulated for the five-year term of the tontine, expiring January 1st, 1856. At that point, the shareholders with the two eldest nominees would take ownership of the houses for a fee of £100 each, and that money and the accumulated rents would be distributed among the twenty-four shareholders whose nominees were the next older ones still alive. The target was four hundred and sixty shares at £5 each. The projector would take the entire £2300 subscriber investment. The proceeds to be divided at the end were the two houses for the two primary winners with the next twenty-four in line to divide the winners' fees of £200 and accumulated rents of £1,200. They would take just short of £60 each.

The project played out to its planned end. From the *Stirling Observer*, January 10th, 1856:

> Bridge of Allan Tontine.—The closing of the year 1855 was of peculiar interest to those holding shares in this scheme. To the many it brought disappointment, but to a few success; and we are happy to state that Dr Syme, of Alloa will have the first choice of the two properties in Bridge of Allan, his nominee being 103 years old, and the oldest of the nominees now alive.

Fading from Sight

Below is the text of a letter of Anthony Trollope, to T. Todd Walton, Postmaster of Bristol, in 1860:

> Do you know what is a tontine? I do not. But I have an interest in a tontine — whatever that is — established in Bristol heaven knows how many years ago — I know nothing more about it than that this interest is derived from a share in such undertaking originally the property of the Rev W Milton who then lived at, or in the neighborhood of, Bristol — and that the life (still living) which he put into the concern was that of his daughter, then Mary Milton, now Mrs Clyde. Have you, without giving

> yourself any trouble, the means of learning whereabouts in Bristol, or from whom, I could learn anything as to this tontine?[17]

It is possible Trollope, who worked within the Post Office until 1867, may have been having a bit of fun with his Post Office colleague. Trollope's knowledge of trade and finance is clear in his depictions of parliamentary maneuvering within some of his novels, especially the Palliser series, of which the first was published in 1865. And the details of the letter, involving the ideas of a purchaser and a nominee on whose life the income depended, are accurate.

Reverend William Milton was Trollope's maternal grandfather who died at the age of 81 in 1824. The nominee would have been an aunt. Martin was noted in Bristol for having made the original proposal that led to the creation of the floating harbor, allowing better river traffic control and for an increase in the cargo capacity of the city. He was honored in 1804 with a 'handsome piece of [silver] plate' inscribed: "The Board of Directors of the Bristol Dock Company, to the Rev. W. Milton, A.M. (Vicar of Heckfield, Hants, and formerly Fellow of New College, Oxford), in testimony of the high sense they entertain of his Original Suggestion for the Improvement of the Harbour of Bristol, communicated to the Society of Merchants in the year 1791."

The possible tontines owned by Rev. Milton include the St. Stephen's Warehouses in Bristol which were built in 1783 via a tontine, although it was reported as wound up in 1850–1851. Another possibility is the 1784 Brunswick Square Tontine, which was wound up in 1860. A third is the Lewinsmead or Lewin's Mead Tontine Society of which no details have been found except a property insurance record in 1793 and an oblique reference in a bankruptcy notice in 1828.

A more important aspect of the letter is Trollope's profession of ignorance—real or feigned—of tontines in 1860. Even if the intent is primarily humorous, it is a strong indication of the disappearance of the idea from general public consciousness by that time.

In the latter half of the nineteenth century, newspaper references to tontines were of two types. Some were references to meetings and other activities of the funeral insurance style tontine societies. The others were nostalgic historical pieces explaining what a tontine was, articles on

[17] Trollope, Anthony, Ed. B. A. Booth, *The Letters of Anthony Trollope*, London, etc.: Oxford UP, 1951.

the origin of the word, and tales of extraordinary longevity related to historical tontines.

A simple and clear illustration of the abandonment of the tontine can be found in the much acclaimed eleventh edition of the *Encyclopedia Britannica,* volume 27, published in 1911. It dismisses the tontine in a couple of paragraphs, one focused on Tonti and the French experience, and the second a summary of English government tontines with a glancing mention of the tontine elements in American life insurance schemes. The entry concludes with "…newer and more ingenious forms of contract have now made the tontine principle practically a thing of the past."

Tontine Financed Projects that Still Exist

The survivors list includes the Richmond Bridge, London; the Forehoe Poorhouse (now residences), Norfolk; the Clerkenwell Session House, London; the Tontine Inn, Ironbridge; the Tontine Inn, Peebles; the Tontine Hotel, Greenock; the Tontine Inn, Cleveland (Northallerton); St. Peter's Parish Church, Wallsend; Norfolk Crescent, Bath; Royal York Crescent, Bristol, and the Tontine Buildings (residences), Cirencester, and the façade of the Truro Assembly Rooms.

The old Tontine Inn in Melverley is now a private home, bed-and-breakfast combination. It is unlikely this was actually financed by a tontine.

Revival?

The revival of the tontine has recently been proposed as a relatively simple and attractive tool to deal with sustaining income during the latter portion of the increased lifespans of our time. Moshe A. Milevsky, who has been the main proponent of the revival, recently published *How to build a Modern Tontine,* Cham: Springer International Publishing, 2022, which is both a proposal and a survey of the current work.[18]

[18] See Winter, P., and F. Planchet, Modern Tontines as a Pension Solution: A Practical Overview, 12 *European Actuarial Journal* 3–32 (2022), Fullmer, Richard K., and John A. Turner, Robo Tontines, 10 *The Journal of Retirement* 63–73 (2022), https://doi.org/10.3905/jor.2022.1.115, Dhaene, Jan & Moshe A. Milevsky Egalitarian pooling and sharing of longevity risk aka can an administrator help skin the tontine cat? 119 *Insurance,*

Our current environment, with longer lives and the subsequent longer periods of retirement, has placed some stress on the standard systems, such as pensions and annuities, used to provide an income after retirement. Our prolonged lives tend to involve longer periods of a relatively flat income accompanied by rising health and care costs for which the increasing dividends of a tontine would be a good match. Modern computer-based record keeping would make the day-to-day administration much easier than the Georgian models. A late starting tontine, based on the life of the subscriber, could be the means to provide a gently increasing income stream as the living participants age and others slowly die off. However, any proposals along these lines would need sophisticated analysis as well as being integrated into modern regulatory frameworks and are beyond the scope of this text.

Mathematics & Economics, 238–250 (2024), Muis, J. *An Individualized Tontine Pension on the Blockchain: A Blockchain Enabled Way of Sharing Longevity Risk*, Master's thesis, University of Twente, and Chen, A., and M. Rach, Actuarial Fairness and Social Welfare in Mixed-Cohort Tontines, 111 *Insurance, Mathematics & Economics,* 214–229 (2023).

Glossary

Annuities on survivorship The earliest English phrase meaning a tontine. An annual payment would be paid for as long as a named party survived.

Annuity A financial instrument which paid a set sum annually either for a term of years, the life of the beneficiary, or indefinitely. The payment could come from the government, or from an individual, a bank, or company. The government annuities of the period were roughly the equivalent of the modern treasury note.

Bills A generic term for government payment orders. Exchequer bills were used to pay basic everyday government debts. Navy, Victualling, Ordnance, and Transport bills paid for those services as needed by the Navy and Army.

Bill of exchange Used roughly the way we would use a check, although the merchant or bank agreeing to give cash on such a bill would usually take a fee, known as a discount. For long distance transactions, an issuer might send two or three bills of exchange to cover the same debt. They would be sent by different means—mail, coach, boat, etc.,—to cover the possibility of one being lost in transit. The text would say first, second, third, etc. Once one was presented for payment, the others became null.

The Calendar Change of 1752 In accordance with a 1750 act of Parliament, England and its colonies changed calendars in 1752. By that time, the discrepancy between a solar year and the Julian Calendar had

K. McKeever, *The Role of Tontines, 1750–1800*, Palgrave Studies in the History of Finance, https://doi.org/10.1007/978-3-032-12849-2

grown by an additional day, so that the calendar used in England and its colonies was 11 days out-of-sync with the Gregorian Calendar in use in the other parts of Europe.

England's calendar change included three major components. The Julian Calendar was replaced by the Gregorian Calendar, changing the formula for calculating leap years. The beginning of the legal new year was moved from March 25 to January 1. Finally, 11 days were dropped from the month of September 1752.

The changeover involved a series of steps:

December 31, 1750 was followed by January 1, 1750 (under the 'Old Style' calendar, December was the 10th month and January the 11th)

March 24, 1750 was followed by March 25, 1751 (March 25 was the first day of the 'Old Style' year)

December 31, 1751 was followed by January 1, 1752 (the switch from March 25 to January 1 as the first day of the year)

September 2, 1752 was followed by September 14, 1752 (drop of 11 days to conform to the Gregorian calendar.)[1]

Consols Colloquial term for the core Government Annuities, a shortening of the word 'consolidated.' From 1751 onward, the regular nation loans were issued through these instruments, with the primary one paying three percent annual interest. Variations of up to five percent were issued from time to time. They were 'consolidated' because each new issue was consolidated into the accounts of the previous ones. Financial tontines tended to invest in these.

Country Bank A private bank based in a provincial city providing local services paralleling the services offered by the private banks in the city. Country banks tended to have a named corresponding private bank in London as a means of asserting their stability.

Freeman A person entitled to vote in City elections, qualified through owning property and being a member of a Livery Company.

Funds A generic term encompassing all the different forms of securities: Stock, Annuities, Bills, Bonds, Shares, etc., that one could invest in. In this sense, it usually took the definite article: 'the funds.'

Livery Companies A trade association connected to a particular industry, membership of which was a prerequisite to becoming a Freeman of

[1] Source: https://libguides.ctstatelibrary.org/hg/colonialresearch/calendar.

the City and thus a vote in elections. While the original core of a Livery Company would be the craftsmen or tradesmen focused on the subject of the company, such as needlemakers, membership could be purchased, so bankers and brokers were often members by purchase in totally unrelated Livery Companies.

Merchant A catch-all term that originated in commercial trading businesses but came to have a secondary meaning when the businessman shifted his activities away from his original trade into becoming middleman in financial transactions, without becoming a formal bank.

Terms for Money *Cash* can mean coin or Bank of England Bills; *Specie* means metallic money, copper, silver, or gold; the *pound* was divided into 20 *shillings*. The *shilling* was divided into 12 *pence*; there were also sub-penny units—the *ha'penny* (½penny) and the *farthing* (¼penny.) A *Guinea* was a gold coin valued at one pound plus one shilling. Financial transactions were calculated down to the farthing.

Nominee The person named by a subscriber whose life was to be the term of their investment. In most cases, a child of the subscriber, although not always.

Omnium A wholly paid for, and transferable, but as yet unregistered share of a new issuance of a stock or annuity.

Contracten van overleving Early Dutch form of a tontine which translates as 'contract for survival.' Note that virtually all of the modern Western European languages use some close variation on the word 'tontine' for the financial instrument.

Private Bank These retail level institutions evolved in the latter part of the seventeenth century from the deposit and exchange services provided by goldsmiths in London. A parallel evolution occurred within the Merchant community as the richer ones became involved in negotiation of bills of exchange independently of their core business. In the Georgian era private banks were limited by statute to no more than six partners although they usually had substantial clerical staff. They tended to serve either merchants or society clients.

Projector The main entrepreneur of a tontine.

Ready Money An actual payment, with money and title to stock changing hands, as opposed to simply a promise to pay.

Scrip The paid portion of a new government annuity or stock share. The stock was paid for in scheduled installments with the value increasing as each installment was paid. Scrip was transferable and trade in them was a major portion of speculative stock market activity. The term was short for 'subscription.'

Shut The ready money transfer operations in the various funds were closed for two periods during the year in order for the managing institutions to confirm their records and calculate and allocate the appropriate dividend for each fund and each shareholder. These tended to be for six week periods. The market for Three Percent Consols closed in June and December to allow for dividends to be issued in early July and January. The shut periods varied according to the dividend schedules for each fund.

Stock Confusingly, a share in a company, but also used as a synonym for 'the funds' in a much broader sense of a financial instrument paying interest. The Government Tontines were included in the reports of stock prices.

Stock Jobber A stockbroker who trades primarily for his own benefit. Usually, but not always, used in a pejorative sense.

Subscriber In regard to tontines, an initial shareholder. The subscriber received the dividends and named the person whose life was to his or her representative in the tontine process, i.e., the 'nominee.' The term was also used for the 'monied men' who bought the annual government loan in large amounts as it was issued. When a subscriber died, he or she usually, but not always, left the rights to the nominee.

Sworn Broker An elite broker of anything, not just stock, originally limited by law in the late seventeenth century to 118 people of whom only 12 could be Jewish. In fact, many hundreds more acted as brokers every day. The number of brokers admitted grew over decades by 1794 the published list shows roughly 600.

Turnpike Trusts The administrative entity for the many, many turnpike roads developed in Georgian England, rarely worth more than £5000 in capital. Their bonds usually paid a fraction more than the government funds. Over time, many merged to form regional networks. These were the main competitors for tontine projects because the share prices were similar and they often had similar civic purposes.

Bibliography

Archival Sources

Bath Record Office. *Articles of Agreement entered into and agreed upon between all and every the Subscribers of the New Assembly Rooms;* 1 May 1769 signed on the 4th of May. Reference number 0028A/1

Bath Record Office. *A Journal of the Proceedings of the Subscribers to a New Set of Assembly Rooms….*, seemingly mis-described as Item 0028A/3, *List of Subscribers to the New Assembly Rooms, 1769–1814.*

Bayly v Harris, Court of the Exchequer, Transcript, Trinity Term 1837, Anglo-American Legal Tradition Website, http://aalt.law.uh.edu/AALT6/E126/E126no55/IMG_0063.htm, et seq

Bedfordshire Archives. Woburn Abbey; Miscellaneous correspondence, Bray to Beaumont, Ref R3/1190

Bedfordshire Archives. *Fulneck (Moravian) Tontine Draft Documents,* A-22-5-076

Berkshire Record Office. *Deed of privilege of free admission to Covent Garden Theatre; Granted to Robert Palmer during the lifetime of his son Richard, aged 20, 1785, with memorandum relating to its reassignment, 1799.* Ref GB 005

Bodleian Library, Oxford University. Jack Johnson Collection of Ephemera. *1808 Covent Garden share valuation*, digitized at: https://www.bodleian.ox.ac.uk/collections-and-resources/special-collections/catalogues/johnson/finding-aids/digitised

Bristol Archives. *Account book for a slaving voyage of the Jason gally and later household accounts for the Becher family, 1743–1818,* Ref number 45167/1

K. McKeever, *The Role of Tontines, 1750–1800*, Palgrave Studies in the History of Finance, https://doi.org/10.1007/978-3-032-12849-2

Bristol Archives. *Circular Stables: Declaration of Interest of Edward Harford the Younger, etc.* Ref 19835 (8)K

Bristol Archives. *Estates Title Deeds 45: Indenture of articles of agreement: 1) Becher Heylym, Smith Barnes and Curtis; 2) Subscribers of the Assembly Rooms, 1754 Jun 24–1754 Sep 30,* Ref 01287

Contract van overleving No 1, Groningen: 31st August, 1763, Projectors: "Messrs W WICHERS Rentmeefter of this Province, E IPPIUS Lawyer Fiscal of this Province, S GOCKINGA Sworn of this City and Dr FRED SIBINGA ....*[Google Books*—https://www.google.com/books/edition/Contract_van_overleving/WyJcx40b1r0C?hl=en&gbpv=1&dq=contract+van+overleving+1763&pg=PA1&printsec=frontcover*]*

Dorset History Center. *Deeds: Weymouth. Declaration and assignment of Robert Cooper's share in Weymouth Assembly Rooms and Hotel, 1773 and 1793, with list of proprietors of the Weymouth Hotel Tontine (formed 1773) living in 1842.. 1773–1842,* Ref: D-49/5

Gloucestershire Archives. *Brunswick Square Tontine documents,* Ref. D361/F4

Hertfordshire Archives. *A list of the surviving members of the Third Class of the Society for Annuities increasing to the Survivors, established in the year 1769, who are intitled to the Benefit arising therefrom.... in February, 1804,* Ref 14994

Kreson Kernow, ie. Cornwall Centre, Old Assembly Rooms: *Deed of Limitation,* Ref DCT, 200, (1810), and *Abstract of Title, Old Assembly Rooms,* DCT 202, (1892).

Lincolnshire Archives. Ipswich Universal Tontine, *List and particulars of the names, and miscellaneous other documents,* Ref E43340-K and E43340-KJ

London Metropolitan Archives. Kew Bridge Tontine. *Life Annuities certificate no. 41,for Samuel Castell*...in the name of Catherine Louisa Castell, daughter, aged seven....June 24th, 1785. Ref ACC/2103/001 (The word tontine is not used.)

London Metropolitan Archives. *Robert Burton Esq and others and Thomas Harris esq. Copy of the deed of trust regarding tontines on accounts increasing by survivorship in two places on the Theatre Royal,* Ref E/BER/CG/E/08/10/002

National Library of Ireland. *O'Hara Papers*, Collection List 66, page 56 et seq.

North East Wales Archive. (Chester Tontine) Richardson: Bond in £100, Finding/Object Number: D/KK/595

North Yorkshire County Record Office. *Tontine Annuity for Rev. William Roundell,* Ref Z.726

Northamptonshire Archives. Correspondence: *Rye_x_7244_035 Letter Robert D Rye to Peter Rye; Rye_x_7244_173 Letter H Woodhead to Peter Rye*

Richmond Local Studies. *A List of subscribers and their nominees in Richmond Bridge Tontine for raising the sum of twenty thousand pounds in shares of one hundred pounds each at interest after the rate of four pounds per cent, per annum, commencing with benefit of survivorship the 29th of September, 1776, so that the longest survivor will receive eight hundred pounds per annum.*

Shropshire Archives, Ipswich Universal Tontine. *Abstract of deed of trust for establishing universal tontine on lives of all ages at Ipswich, co. Suffolk at various subscription rates,* Ref 484/506

Shropshire Archives. Ironbridge Tontine Inn. *Books of Acts of the Tontine subscribers,* 16 April 1784–1791, System Ref X245/6, Document Ref 245/6

Somerset Archives: DD/GC/1.*"Farell and Jones families. 1742–1804",...* includes Joseph Farell's share certificate in the Assembly Room to be built in Prince Street in St Stephen Parish in Bristol, 1754.

Suffolk Archives, Ipswich Universal Tontine. *Triennial Statement*]HD1656/1] *Deed of trust* [HD 827/1/1/3/3/1].

Surrey Heritage. *Annuity certificates nos 79 and 80 for two shares of 100 in the second class of the tontine known as 'The Earl of Cork's Tontine' (payable out of the estates in Ireland of Edmund, Earl of Cork and Orrery and his son) originally issued in August 1789 to Catherine Savery of Richmond, spinster, on the life of Dorothea Juliana Savery, then aged 25 (and now the wife of Thomas Newbery of Fleet Street, City of London, linendraper) and reissued upon report of loss of originals. Annotated with notes of payment, 1821–1844.* Ref SHC Ref No. 3116/1–2.

University of Reading, The Museum of English Rural Life & Special Collections. *Agreement: Thomas Harris Thomas Longman and others to Josiah Barnard of Cornhill London. Privilege of free admission into Covent Garden Theatre,* Ref MS 1393 2/129/12.

West Glamorgan Archives, Swansea, St John's Street Tontine Association. *Articles of agreement,* Ref Numbers. GB 216 RISW T, GB 216 RISW/SFS 5a-b.

West Sussex Records Office. Chichester Theatre Tontine Documents: *Papers of William Brooks,* ref RAPER/256–262.

Sources Focused on Tontines

Anonymous. *Tontines calculated, and their Principles and Consequences explained, and exemplified, in the Yorkshire Tontine....* [London]: Published by Clarke and Son, 1791.

[Boston, Lincolnshire]. *Abstract of an Indenture for securing the payment of Annuities increasing by Survivorship.* Boston: Printed by Kelsey, February 1815.

Bridges, Gladys and Sandra Thomas. A Tontine, a theatre, and its thespians: the Swansea Theatre 1805–1899. 45 *Gower: The Journal of the Gower Society.* Bridgend, 1994.

City of London, Westminster, and Borough of Southwark Tontine. *State of the City of London, Westminster, and borough of Southwark tontine at the end of the seven years.* [London]: 1798 (Gale ECCO).

Clements, Diane. *Invested in identity: the Freemasons' Tontine of 1775.* Masters thesis, University of London, School of Advanced Study. (2018) https://sas-space.sas.ac.uk/9207/

Cleveland Tontine Inn. *Rules and Subscriber List, printed with a list of the subscribers to the new turnpike Road from Thirsk to Yarm....* Stockton: Christopher & Jennett, 1804.

Cooper, Robert W. *An Historical Analysis of the Tontine Principle.* Philadelphia: Heubner Foundation, 1972.

Cork Tontine Association. *Copy of the deed or charter, entered into by the Associated society to raise a fund for erecting a coffee-house and other buildings in the city of Cork;....* Cork, Edwards, 1794.

[Forehoe Tontine]. *A correct list of the Subscribers and Nominees to the Hundred of Forehoe House of Industry....* Norwich: Crouse, 1777.

Gautier, Charles. Un Investissement Genevois, Le Tontine d'Irlande, 1777. 10 *Bulletin, Société d'Histoire d'Archeologie de Genève (1951):* 53–68.

Glynn, Gale. Some tontines commemorated on English plate. 8 *Silver Society Journal* (1996): 445–461.

Great Britain, Office of the Exchequer. *A list of the nominees appointed by the Lords Commissioners of His Majesty's treasury, To hold shares on the part of the public in the tontine of the year 1789: in pursuance of an act of Parliament, made and passed in the thirtieth year of the reign of Our Most Gracious Sovereign King George the Third,....* [London]: The Office, 1792.

Great Britain, Office of the Exchequer. *A list of the nominees appointed by the contributors to the tontine of the year 1789: in pursuance of an act of Parliament, Made and passed in Twenty-Ninth Year of the Reign of our Most Gracious Sovereign King George the third.....* [London]: The Office, 1792.

Great Britain, Parliament. House of Commons, *Second Report from the Committee on Irish Tontine Annuities,* ordered printed May 4th, 1812.

Green, David R. Tontines, Annuities, and Civic Improvements in Georgian Britain. *Urban History,* Volume 46, Issue 4, November 2019: 649–694.

Hellwege, Phillip. *A History of Tontines in Germany.* Berlin: Duncker & Humblot, 2018.

Hellwege, Phillip, Ed. *The Past, Present, and Future of Tontines.* Berlin: Duncker & Humblot, 2018.

Hesse, H. Een lijfrentebreif in 1671 uitgegeven door Midwolda en Nieuwolda. *Groningse Volksalmanak (1931):* 105–117.

Jennings R. M. and M. P. Trout. The Irish Tontine (1777) and Fifty Genevans: An Essay on Comparative Mortality. 12 *Journal of European Economic History* 611 (Winter 1983).

Leeson, Francis. *A Guide to the Records of the British State Tontines*, Shalfleet Manor: Pinhorns, 1968.

Li, Yilang and Casey Rothschild. Selection and Redistribution in the Irish Tontines of 1773, 1775, and 1777, 87 *Journal of Risk and Insurance* 19 (2020).

[Liddell (A.)] A Birmingham Tontine, the Royal Hotel. [Signed: A. L.] In *Central Literary Magazine*, Vol. 12 (1895): 14–22.

A List of the persons on whose lives the sum of 265000l. was subscribed...., Dublin: Ireland Exchequer, 1775.

McDiarmid, Andrew. The Development of Mutual Aid Tontines in Nineteenth Century Ireland, *Irish Economic and Social History (2024):* 1–16.

McDiarmid, Andrew. *The Tontine, a history*, London: Routledge, 2025.

McMahon, James. *The Pery Square Tontine*, Limerick: Limerick City Trust, etc., 1999.

Milevsky, Moshe A. *How to build a modern tontine.* Cham: Springer International Publishing, 2022.

Milevsky, Moshe A. *King William's Tontine: Why the Retirement Annuity of the Future Should Resemble its Past.* Cambridge Univ. Press, 2017.

Milevsky, Moshe A, and Thomas S. Salisbury. *The Riccati Tontine: How to Satisfy Regulators on Average.* Arxiv, q-fin, arXiv:2402.14555, 2024.

Moulin, Jacques. *Des Tontines.* Paris: Rousseau, 1903.

Parish, Charles. *History of the Birmingham Library.* London: Library Association, 1966. (Appendix F, Copy of the Tontine Deed.)

A Proposal for a yearly increase of wealth, by subscriptions to advance money upon lives.... [London]: Hill, [1682].

Proposals for Raising by Tontine the sum of 20,000... [Mr Drew's Tontine, Jamaica], NP: np, [1803 per annotation in digitized form, but actually 1805.]

Proposals for the grant of ten annuities of £600 each.... [Morland & Ransom Co.] London: printed by Luke Hansard & Sons, 1818.

Queen's Tontine, for Building Sixty Houses, On an Eminence beautifully situated near Ashley, In the Parish of St. Paul, Bristol. Bristol: Bulgin and Rosser, 1792.

Quinn, Kevin. The Armagh Tontine Assembly Rooms, 1794–1907, 4 *History Armagh* No. 1 (2017): 5–9.

The Regality Club. Vol. 2, entry on the Glasgow Tontine Coffee House by C D Donald (1889).

Rietsch, Christian and Georges Gallot Hamonno. *Lorenzo Tonti,* chapter 2 in Hellwege Phillip, *The Past, Present, and Future of Tontines.* Berlin: Duncker & Humblot, 2018.

[St. Andrews, Scotland] Conditions of Subscriptions for the Bath Tontine Hotel of St. Andrews, (glued within a letter wrapper addressed to Earl of Bredalbane, London, marked 1811).

[Sayre, Stephen]. *The new impression of the English tontine, or, life annuity plan.* [London]: [1774]. (digitized in Gale ECCO)

Tyldesley, Bruce, *The Prince Street Assembly Rooms 1755–1956,* (Bristol), The Spas Research Fellowship at https://osborne.house/profilego.asp?ref=284 1383A

Wagenvoort, Hermann. *Tontines, een onderzoek naar de geschiedenis van de lijfrenten....* Diss. Utrecht: 1961.

Wagenvoort, Hermann. Contracten van Overleving en Andere Tontines. *Tijdschrift voor Rechtsgeschiedenis,* Vol. 35, Issue 3 (1967): 584–594

Whitnell, Sandy. *The Public Rooms of the County: the History of the Tontine Hotel, Peebles 1803–1890.* Self/Amazon, 2012.

Miscellaneous Other Sources

Adcock, A. Notes on the George Hotel, Northampton. 20 *Journal of the Northants Natural History Society and Field Club* (1919-1920): 81–88.

Algemeene Maatschappij van Levensverzekering en Lijfrente. *Bouwstoffen voor de geschiedenis van de levensverzekeringen en lijfrenten in Nederland.* Amsterdam: De Maatschappij, 1897. (Hathitrust)

Anderson, Adam. *An historical and chronological deduction of the origin of commerce.* London: J. White, 1801, Volume 3.

Anonymous. *Mirth and wisdom, in a miscellany of different characters....* London: B. Bragg, 1703.

Appendix to the First Report of the Commissioners: Report on the City of Dublin, Part two. London: Clowes and Sons for His Majesties stationery Office, 1836.

Ashmore, Thomas. *An analysis of the several bank annuities from the first year of their creation down to the present time.....* London: Richardson & Urquhart, 1774.

Ashton, John. *A history of English lotteries.* London: Leadenhall Press, 1893.

Ashton, T.S. *An Economic History of England: The 18th Century.* London: Methuen & Co., 1972.

Atwood, George. *Review of the statutes and ordinances of assize, which have been established in England from the fourth year of King John, 1202, to the thirty-seventh of his present Majesty.* [London]: Egerton, 1801.

Bagshaw, Samuel. *History, gazetteer, and directory of the County Palatine of Chester...* Sheffield: Ridge, 1850.

Barratt, William. *The history and antiquities of the City of Bristol...* Bristol: Pine, etc., [1789].

Bartlett, Thomas. The O'Haras of Annaghmore c. 1600—c. 1800: Survival and Revival. 9 *Irish Economic and Social History* (1982): 34–53.

Beawes, Wyndham and Thomas Mortimer. *Lex mercatoria rediviva: or, the merchant's directory....* [London]: Rivington, et al., 1783.

Bellhouse, David. *Leases for lives: life contingent contracts and the emergence of actuarial science in eighteenth-century England.* Cambridge: Cambridge University Press, 2017.

Bellamy, Daniel. *The present state of the Church of Petersham….* [London]: 1777, reprinted 1824.

Bentham, Jeremy. ed. Ian R. Christie. *The Correspondence of Jeremy Bentham,* Vol. 3, London: UCL press, 2017.

Bogart, Dan *The Turnpike Roads of England and Wales.* https://www.campop.geog.cam.ac.uk/research/projects/transport/onlineatlas/britishturnpiketrusts.pdf

Bogart, Dan. Turnpike trusts and the transportation revolution in 18th century England, 42 *Explorations in Economic History (2005):* 479–508.

Bolton, John. *An Account of the loss of the American Clipper Ship Tontine.* Pittsburgh: Callow, 1861.

Bradley, Tom. *The old coaching days in Yorkshire.* York: Yorkshire Conservative Newspaper Co., 1859.

Brown, Alison and Jonathan Harlow, Eds. *Atlantic Venture Accounts of Eighteenth Century Bristol.* Bristol Record Society, Vol. 74, 2021.

Campbell, Sybil. Usury and the annuities of the Eighteenth Century 44 *Law Quarterly Review* (1928): 473–491.

Clark, Geoffrey. *Betting on Lives, The Culture of Life Insurance in England, 1695–1775.* Manchester: Manchester University Press, 1999.

Clarke, L. A. *Minehead United Turnpike Trust.* Somerset Industrial Archaeological Society, 2002. (Good introduction to Turnpike environment and processes.)

Clay, Christopher. The Price of Freehold Land in the Later Seventeenth and Eighteenth Centuries. 27 (2nd Series) *Economic History Review* (1974): 173–189.

Cleary, E.J. *The Building Society Movement,* London: Elek, 1965.

Cleland, James. *The rise and progress of the City of Glasgow….* Glasgow: Young, Gallie & co. for J. Brash and co: 1820.

Clements, Diane. *Annuity loans and private credit in Britain, 1750–1813.* Doctoral thesis, School of Advanced Study (2022). https://sas-space.sas.ac.uk/9748/

Clews, Stephen. Banking in Bath in the reign of George III. 5 *Bath History* (1994): 104–124.

Cookson, Brian. *Crossing the River.* Transworld Books, 2015, unpaginated.

Cordery, Simon. *British Friendly Societies 1750–1914.* Palgrave Macmillan, 2003.

Cowan, William. The buildings at the east end of Princes Street…. in *The Book of the Old Edinburgh Club for the year 1908,* Edinburgh: Printed by T & A Constable, 1908.

Crisp, Richard. *Richmond and its inhabitants from the olden times.* London: Sampson, 1866.

Cummins, Daniel. Exclusive oratories and magnificent pagodas: the Anglican proprietary chapels of eighteenth-century Bath. 85 *Historical Research* (2012): 254–264.

Denholm, James. *The history of the city of Glasgow and suburbs.* 2nd Ed. Glasgow: printed by and for R. Chapman, and Stewart and Meikle, 1798.

Dickson P. G. M. *The Financial Revolution in England.* London: Routledge, 1993.

DuBois. *The English Business Company after the Bubble Act, 1720–1899.* NY: Commonwealth Fund, 1938.

Evans, D. M. *The City; or, The Physiology of London Business.* London: Groombridge & Sons, 1852.

Fairman, William. *The Stocks examined and compared....* London: Galabin et al., 1795.

Farren, Edwin J. *Historical essay on the rise and early progress of the doctrine of life-contingencies in England, leading to the establishment of the first life-assurance society in which ages were distinguished.* London: Smith, Elder & Co., 1844.

[Finlaison]. *Tontines and life annuities: copy of the report and observations of Mr. Alexander Finlaison, actuary of the commissioners for the reduction of the national debt, relating to tontines and life annuities, and to the duration of life among the nominees.* London: ordered by the House of Commons, to be printed, 25 August, 1860.

Fiske, Willard. *Chess tales & chess miscellanies.* London: Longmans, Green, 1912. (George Atwood biography pp. 233–245)

Fortune, Thomas. *An epitome of the stocks and publick funds....* London: Boosey, 1796.

Freeman, Pearson and Taylor. Law, politics and the governance of English and Scottish joint-stock companies, 1600–1850. 55 *Business History* (2013): 636–652.

Fry, Thomas. *A New System of Finance.* London: Sold by J. S. Jordan and C. Chappel, 1797.

Gilbert, Lady, ed. *Calendar of Ancient Records of Dublin* (CARD) Volume XVIII (Dublin: Dollard, Ltd., 1922): 434-452.

Graunt, John. *Natural and Political Observations Made upon the Bills of Mortality.* London: Thomas Roycroft, 1662.

Great Britain. *Laws relating to the turnpike roads. I. The General Turnpike Road Act. II. Acts relating to Colnbrook Turnpike. With a Plan of the Road from Cranford-Bridge, in Middlesex, to Maidenhead-Bridge, in Bucks.* Eton: Pote, 1772.

Great Britain, Parliament. *An act for better regulating the poor; maintaining a nightly watch; lighting, paving, and cleansing the streets, rows, and passages;*

providing fire engines and firemen, and regulating the hackney-coachmen, chairmen, carmen, and porters, within the city of Chester. 1762, 2 Geo III, c. 45.

Great Britain, Parliament. *An Act for better securing certain Powers and Privileges intended to be granted by His Majesty by Two Charters for Assurance of Ships and Merchandizes at Sea, and for lending Money on Bottomry; and for restraining several extravagant and unwarrantable Practices therein mentioned.* 1720, 6 Geo 1. c. 18, ('Bubble Act').

Great Britain, Parliament. *An Act to repeal so much of an Act passed in the Sixth Year of His late Majesty King George the First, as relates to the restraining several extravagant and unwarrantable Practices in the said Act mentioned; and for conferring additional Powers upon His Majesty, with respect to the granting of Charters of Incorporation to trading and other Companies.* 1825 6 Geo. 4. c. 91 ('Bubble Repeal Act').

Great Britain, Parliament, House of Commons. *Appendix to the First Report of the Commissioners: Report on the City of Dublin, Part two.* London: Clowes and Sons for His Majesties Stationery Office, 1836.

Great Britain, Parliament, House of Commons. *A collection of rules and standing orders of the House of Commons; relative to the applying for and passing Bills, for inclosing and draining of lands, making turnpike roads, navigations, and other purposes.* London: Hingeston, 1774.

Great Britain, Parliament, House of Commons. *First (twenty-second) report from the Select Committee on Finance.* 1797, Appendix D1.

Great Britain, Parliament, House of Commons. *Public income and expenditure. Return to an order of the honourable the House of Commons, dated 24 July 1866... Treasury chambers, 9 March 1867.*

Great Britain, Parliament, House of Commons. *Twenty-third (thirty-sixth) report from the Select Committee on Finance* 1798, appendix D.

Great Britain, Parliament, National Debt. *Report by the Secretary and Comptroller General of the proceedings of the Commissioners for the Reduction of the National Debt, from 1786 to 31st March 1890.* Command Paper Number: C.6539 (P 178 +, Lottery Loans).

Great Britain, Royal Commission on Historical Manuscripts. *Eighth Report, Appendix, Corporation of Chester.* (HMSO 1883/1908): 401-402.

Grellier, J.J. *The terms of all the loans which have been raised for the public service during the last fifty years....* London: printed by H. L. Galabin, 1799.

Hales, Charles. *The Bank Mirror or a guide to the funds ....* Cheapside: Adlard, et al., 1796.

Harris, Ellen. Handel the Investor. 85 *Music & Letters* (2004): 521.

Harris, Ian. What was Parliamentary Reporting....1780–1796. 39 *Parliamentary History* (2020): 255–275.

Heath, George. *The new Bristol guide: containing its antiquities, deduced from the best authorities: historic annals from William the Conqueror 1066 to 1799....* Bristol: Edwards, etc., 1799.

Home, H. Oliver. *A History of Savings Banks.* London: Oxford University Press, 1947.

Hoppit, Julian. Myths of the South Sea Bubble. 12 *Transactions of the Royal Historical Society* (2002): 141–165.

Howard, Thomas. An *essay on the nature of a loan: being an introduction to the knowledge of the public accounts.* York: A Ward; London: Debrett, 1782.

Huggins, Mike. *Horse Racing and British Society in the Long Eighteenth Century.* Woodbridge, Suffolk: Boydell, 2018.

Hume, Robert D. The Value of Money in Eighteenth Century England: Incomes, Prices, Buying Power–and Some Problems in Cultural Economics. 77 *Huntington Library Quarterly* (2015): 373.

Hutton, William. *A brief history of Birmingham.* Grafton & Reddell, 1797.

Ismay, Penelope. *Trust among Strangers: Friendly Societies in Modern Britain* Cambridge University Press: 2018.

Ison, Walter. *The Georgian Buildings of Bristol.* London: Faber & Faber, 1952.

'J.D.D.' *Miscellaneous information on matters connected with the transaction of business in the public funds.* London: Blaine, 1832.

Keltie, John S., ed. *History of the Scottish Highlands, Highland clans and Highland regiments,....* Edinburgh: Jack, 1887.

Lewis C. P. and A.T. Thacker, Ed. *History of the County of Chester:* Volume 5 Part 1, the City of Chester: General History and Topography. London: 2003. British History Online http://www.british-history.ac.uk/vch/ches/vol5/pt1 [accessed 26 November 2022]

Lewis, Chris. Building Chester's First Workhouse. 38 *Cheshire History* (1998-1999): 50–54.

Ley, Charles. *The nobleman, gentleman, land steward, and surveyor's compleat guide.* printed by Robinson, 1787.

Longe, John. *The Diary of John Longe, Vicar of Coddenham, 1765–1834.* Ed. Michael Stone. Woodbridge: Boydell Press/Suffolk Records Society, 2008.

Martin, John Biddulph "*The Grasshopper" in Lombard Street.* London: The Leadenhall Press, Ltd., 1892.

[Matthews, William]. *The New History, Survey, and Description of the City and Suburbs of Bristol....* Bristol: W. Matthews, 1794.

Michie, Ronald. *The London Stock Exchange, A History.* Oxford University Press, 2001.

Minchinton, W. E., Ed. *The Trade of Bristol in the Eighteenth Century.* Bristol: Bristol Record Society, 1957 Reprinted 1966.

Molleson, William. *The reports of the Commissioners appointed to examine, take, and state the Public Accounts of the Kingdom, presented to his majesty, and to both houses of Parliament: with the appendixes complete.*

Mortimer, Thomas. *Every Man His Own Broker.* Multiple editions, especially 1761 and 1785 (13th = 1801) (TM 1730–1810).

Mortimer, Thomas. *A grammar illustrating the principles and practice of trade and commerce.* London: Philips, 1810.

Murphy, Anne L. *Making the market: trading debt at the Eighteenth-Century Bank of England.* EABH Papers, number 15–05, April 2014.

Nicholls, J.F. *Bristol Past and Present.* Bristol: Arrowsmith 1881–1882.

Nicoll, S. W. *An account of the York Saving Bank.* York: Alexander, 1817.

Ottaway, Susannah. *The Decline of Life: Old Age in Eighteenth-Century England.* Cambridge: Cambridge University Press, 2004. (one reference, to the Yorkshire Tontine, p.74)

Paine, T. *Rights of man. Part the Second.* 3rd ed., Dublin: P. Byrne, No. 108, Grafton-Street, 1792.

Paul, Helen. *The South Sea Bubble: An Economic History of its Origins and Consequences.* Routledge, 2010.

Penley, Belville S. *The Bath stage; a history of dramatic representations in Bath.* London: William Lewis & Son, 1892.

Poitras, Geoffrey. *Equity Capital, From Ancient Partnerships to Modern Exchange Traded Funds.* New York: Routledge, 2016.

Powell, J.W.D. *Bristol Privateers.....* Bristol: Arrowsmith, 1930.

Price, Richard. *The Supplement to the Doctrine on Annuities.*

Price, Richard. *Observations on Reversionary Payments....* London: Cadell, 1771.

Priestley, Joseph. *Historical account of the navigable rivers, canals, and railways....* London: Longman, 1831.

Rayment, Robert. *The income and expenditure of Great-Britain of the last seven years.* London: Debrett, 1791.

Redford and Riches. *The history of the ancient town and borough of Uxbridge,....* published in 1818.

Report from the Select Committee on Metropolitan Bridges. July 14th, 1854.

Reynolds, E. Wesley. *Coffeehouse Culture in the Atlantic World, 1650–1789.* London: Bloomsbury, 2022.

Richardson, William. *History of the parish of Wallsend,* Newcastle-upon-Tyne. Northumberland Press, 1923.

Robinson, Margaret Fothergill. *The spirit of association: being some account of the gilds, friendly societies, co-operative movement, and trade unions of Great Britain.* London: Murray, 1913.

Rouwenhorst, K. Geerts. *The Origins of Mutual Funds.* Yale School of Management - International Center for Finance, working paper 04–48.

The Royal kalendar; or Complete and correct annual register for England, Scotland, Ireland, and America, for the year 1785. [London]: Debrett et al., 1785.

Schmidt, Albert J. The Country Attorney in Late Eighteenth Century England, Benjamin Smith of Horbling. 8 *Law and History Review* (1990): 237–271.

Scoresby, William. *The Northern Whale Fishery.* London[?]: The Religious Tract Society, 1849.

Scott, William Robert. *The constitution and finance of English, Scottish and Irish joint-stock companies to 1720.* Volume 3. Cambridge: University Press, 1911. (Section IV, page 275, on the Million Bank)

Selgin, George. The Institutional roots of Great Britain's 'big problem of small change. 14 *European Review of Economic History* (August 2010): 305–334.

Smail, John. The Culture of Credit in Eighteenth-Century Commerce. 4 *Enterprise & Society* (June 2003): 299–325.

Smiles, Sam. Turner and the slave trade: speculation and representation, 1805–1840. *British Art Journal,* Vol. 8, 2007.

Smith, Adam.*An inquiry into the nature and causes of the wealth of nations..* Volume two. London: Strahan and Cadell, 1776.

Stainton, J. H. *The Making of Sheffield 1865–1914.* Sheffield: E. Weston, 1924 (pp. 66–84).

Steer, Francis W. *The Chichester Theatre.* Chichester: City Council, 1957.

Thornton, Henry. *An Enquiry into the Nature and Effects of the Paper Credit of Great Britain.* 1811.

Trollope, Anthony. *The Letters of Anthony Trollope.* Ed. B.A.Booth. London, etc.: Oxford University Press, 1951.

[Trusler, John]. *The Economist. Shewing, in a variety of estimates, from fourscore pounds a year to upwards of 800l. how comfortably and genteely a family may live, with frugality, for a little money. Together with the cheapest method of keeping horses and carriages.* [London]: Bell, 1774.

Turner, John D. *The Development of English Company Law Before 1900*, Queen's University Centre for Economic History. Working Paper 2017–01 (2017). (This text is also a chapter in: *Research Handbook on the History of Corporate and Company Law:* Edward Elgar, 2018.)

Walford, Cornelius. *The Insurance Cyclopedia.* London: C. and E. Layton, 1871–1880. (Six remarkable volumes, but it was never finished, only reaching 'H' in the alphabet.)

Ward, J.R. *The Finance of Canal Building in Eighteenth Century England.* Oxford University Press, 1974.

Ward, J.R. Speculative Building at Bristol and Clifton, 1783–1793. 20 *Business History* (1978): 3–18.

Winston, James. *The theatric tourist....* London: Woodfall, 1805.

Wood, John. *A description of the Exchange of Bristol.* Bath: Leake, 1743.

Woodfall, William.*An impartial report of the debates that occur in the two houses of Parliament, In the Course of the Sixth Session of the Seventeenth Parliament of Great Britain, called to meet at Westminster, Thursday the 29th of October, 1795*. London: published by T. Chapman, No. 151, Fleet-Street, 1795.
Wright, G.N. *The Historic Guide to Bath*. Bath: R.E. Peach, 1864.
York Assembly Rooms: https://www.yorkconservationtrust.org/our-buildings/assembly-rooms

Database Sources

Gale Digitization Projects

Burney Newspapers Collection, (Primarily London, 17th & 18th Centuries)
British Library Newspapers
The Times Digital Archive
The Sunday Times Digital Archive
Eighteenth Century Collections Online
Making of the Modern World
Etc.

ProQuest

Access to ProQuest extensive holding is through a research library database.
Early English Books Online https://www.proquest.com/eebo/advanced
U. K. Parliamentary Papers https://parlipapers.proquest.com/profiles/hcpp/search/basic/hcppbasicsearch
British Periodicals https://www.proquest.com/britishperiodicals/advanced?

Other Sources

Hathitrust Digital Library https://www.hathitrust.org/
London Lives1690–1800 https://www.londonlives.org/
Anglo-American Legal Tradition http://aalt.law.uh.edu/
National Library of the Netherlands: Delpher, (digitized newspapers, etc.), https://www.delpher.nl/

Index

K. McKeever, *The Role of Tontines, 1750–1800*, Palgrave Studies in the History of Finance, https://doi.org/10.1007/978-3-032-12849-2

O

P

R